T0357314

In his erudite manner, Lee Strobel once again puts his Yale-trained legal mind to work investigating claims of the supernatural. From near-death experiences and miracles to angels and demons, Lee tackles the tough questions, revealing substantial evidence for a world beyond the visible. This book will greatly increase your faith with the hope and confidence that there is more than we visibly see, and that God is at work all around us.

John Burke, *New York Times* bestselling author of *Imagine Heaven* and *Imagine the God of Heaven*

There's more to reality than meets the eye. Here Lee Strobel brings together many of the best of his research interviews that support Christian faith and address contemporary challenges. Like an exciting adventure, this book is too engaging to easily put down. It reminds us that God is real and active, as is the living hope he has placed before us.

Craig S. Keener, F. M. and Ada Thompson Professor of Biblical Studies, Asbury Theological Seminary

Seeing the Supernatural covers a wide range of topics that build a strong, cumulative case for the existence of a realm beyond the natural—more specifically, to the Christian faith. The inescapable reality of the soul, documented miraculous healings and near-death experiences, dramatic and life-changing visions of Jesus in Islamic contexts, demonic activity, and the historicity of Jesus' bodily resurrection— all of these experiences and phenomena are most adequately explained by the truth, goodness, beauty, and power of the gospel of Jesus Christ.

Paul Copan, Pledger Family Chair of Philosophy and Ethics, Palm Beach Atlantic University (Florida); author of *Loving Wisdom*

The Bible talks about a supernatural world beyond our own, but is there any evidence to back that up? From evidence for the soul to documented miracles to deathbed visions, Lee Strobel investigates the existence of a supernatural realm beyond what we can see and touch. What he finds confirms the biblical account— and has eternal implications for every person. Open this book to find compelling answers to satisfy your heart and mind.

Kirk Cameron

When Lee Strobel publishes a new book, I know it will matter, and I read it for several reasons. He is a dear friend, an expert and brilliant journalist, and a committed student of God's Word and follower of Christ.

Sheila Walsh, author and television host

I believe there are two main essentials of an intellectually responsible case for supernaturalism: (1) a competent rebuttal to the common claim that a scientific view of the world necessarily excludes immaterial entities and miracles, and (2) well-documented accounts of phenomena that powerfully suggest such realities. *Seeing the Supernatural* provides both in spades. With his classic attention to detail, accessible language, and captivating journalistic style, Lee Strobel builds a compelling case for a spiritual dimension inhabited by agents that transcend and influence the material world. In addition, he offers an invigorating reminder of the blessed eternity that awaits those who trust in Christ.

Melissa Cain Travis, Fellow, Discovery Institute's Center for Science and Culture; author of *Science and the Mind of the Maker*

Born in 1948, I became a Jesus follower in 1968 and was privileged to have been a part of the Jesus movement of the '60s and '70s. But the most exciting revolution in my lifetime was the explosion of many intellectually gifted, well-trained, and winsome apologists and philosophers who collectively put Christian truth claims back on the table for serious consideration. In my opinion, alongside William Lane Craig, Lee Strobel is the main figure with the greatest impact for promoting a rationally defensible form of Christianity. And this book is among Strobel's top offerings. Quite simply, it is a must-read. Honestly, I could not put it down. You will love and profit from it.

J. P. Moreland, Distinguished Professor of Philosophy, Biola University; author of *A Simple Guide to Experience Miracles*

A masterpiece of authoritative, cogent, evidence-based, rock-solid proof of the supernatural rooted in the truth of God's Word.

Jeremiah J. Johnston, PhD, Prestonwood Baptist Church; Christian Thinkers Society

Lee Strobel has personally encouraged my faith for more than twenty years. In *Seeing the Supernatural*, he will encourage your faith as well. Buy several copies and read it with people who have questions about the Christian faith.

Derwin L. Gray, cofounder and lead pastor, Transformation Church; author of *Lit Up with Love*

Despite the skeptical attitudes of our increasingly post-Christian culture, there seems to be a renewed interest in the supernatural. In fact, claims of the miraculous have never gone away. In this superbly researched and written book, veteran journalist Lee Strobel reveals why tales of the supernatural are more than mere legend. Exploring the historical, scientific, and philosophical case for healings, miracles, and spiritual encounters, this is essential reading for seekers, skeptics, and believers. Read this book and find out why God is closer than you think.

Justin Brierley, author of the book and documentary
podcast *The Surprising Rebirth of Belief in God*

Christianity makes a startling claim: There's more to the world than we can see with our eyes. If this isn't true, biblical claims about angels, demons, the soulish nature of our identity, and life after the grave are worse than mere wishful thinking; they're *lies*. In *Seeing the Supernatural*, Lee Strobel turns his award-winning skills as an investigative reporter on the mysterious supernatural realm. If you want to understand the truth about the unseen forces in the universe, the nature of our existence, and our eternal destination, this book is a *must-read*.

J. Warner Wallace, *Dateline*-featured cold-case detective; senior
fellow at the Colson Center for Christian Worldview; author
of *Cold-Case Christianity* and *Person of Interest*

The Christian faith at its core is both spiritual and supernatural. The new birth we receive through Christ reveals this reality. While it's true that some go too far in emphasizing personal phenomena over proclaiming biblical truth, we shouldn't react to extremes by swinging too far the other way. I know of no one better than Lee Strobel to amplify the miraculous nature of our faith with wisdom. This book will show you how.

Ed Stetzer, dean, Talbot School of Theology

The Bible is quite clear about the existence of a spiritual realm beyond, which, though invisible, is every bit as real and perhaps even more important than the material world. And yet, too many Bible-believing Christians don't take this revealed truth seriously. *Seeing the Supernatural* is guaranteed to open their eyes and enhance their faith as a result. I predict that its wide-ranging contents on all aspects of this invisible world will also lead many unbelievers to Christ, as is true with all of Lee's inspiring books. I've read a great deal about miracles and the supernatural world, but none are as comprehensive and readable as this book. I enthusiastically recommend it.

David Limbaugh, *New York Times* bestselling author of *Jesus on Trial*

Also by Lee Strobel

The Case for Christ
The Case for Christ curriculum (with Garry Poole)
The Case for Christ for Kids (with Rob Suggs and Robert Elmer)
The Case for Christ Student Edition (with Jane Vogel)
The Case for Christmas
The Case for a Creator
The Case for a Creator curriculum (with Garry Poole)
The Case for a Creator for Kids (with Rob Suggs and Robert Elmer)
The Case for a Creator Student Edition (with Jane Vogel)
The Case for Easter
The Case for Faith
The Case for Faith curriculum (with Garry Poole)
The Case for Faith for Kids (with Rob Suggs and Robert Elmer)
The Case for Faith Student Edition (with Jane Vogel)
The Case for Grace
The Case for Grace for Kids (with Jesse Florea)
The Case for Grace Student Edition (with Jane Vogel)
The Case for Heaven
The Case for Hope
The Case for Miracles
The Case for Miracles for Kids (with Jesse Florea)
The Case for Miracles Student Edition (with Jane Vogel)
God's Outrageous Claims
In Defense of Jesus
Is God Real?
Spiritual Mismatch (with Leslie Strobel)
Today's Moment of Truth (with Mark Mittelberg)
The Unexpected Adventure (with Mark Mittelberg)

SEEING

THE

SUPERNATURAL

INVESTIGATING ANGELS, DEMONS,

MYSTICAL DREAMS, NEAR-DEATH

ENCOUNTERS, AND OTHER

MYSTERIES OF THE UNSEEN WORLD

LEE STROBEL

ZONDERVAN
BOOKS

ZONDERVAN BOOKS

Seeing the Supernatural
Copyright © 2025 by Lee Strobel

Published in Grand Rapids, Michigan, by Zondervan. Zondervan is a registered trademark of The Zondervan Corporation, L.L.C., a wholly owned subsidiary of HarperCollins Christian Publishing, Inc.

Requests for information should be addressed to customercare@harpercollins.com.

Zondervan titles may be purchased in bulk for educational, business, fundraising, or sales promotional use. For information, please email SpecialMarkets@Zondervan.com.

ISBN 978-0-310-36988-2 (international trade paper edition)

Library of Congress Cataloging-in-Publication Data

Names: Strobel, Lee, 1952- author.
Title: Seeing the supernatural : investigating angels, demons, mystical dreams, near-death encounters, and other mysteries of the unseen world / Lee Strobel.
Description: Grand Rapids, Michigan : Zondervan Books, [2025] | Includes bibliographical references.
Identifiers: LCCN 2024042798 (print) | LCCN 2024042799 (ebook) | ISBN 9780310369066 (hardcover) | ISBN 9780310369073 (ebook) | ISBN 9780310369080 (audio)
Subjects: LCSH: Supernatural (Theology) | Spirits. | BISAC: RELIGION / Christian Theology / Apologetics | RELIGION / Christian Living / Spiritual Growth
Classification: LCC BT745 .S78 2025 (print) | LCC BT745 (ebook) | DDC 235—dc23/eng/20241122
LC record available at https://lccn.loc.gov/2024042798
LC ebook record available at https://lccn.loc.gov/2024042799

Selected interviews were edited from some of Lee Strobel's earlier books, including *The Case for a Creator, The Case for Miracles, The Case for Heaven, The Case for Faith,* and *In Defense of Jesus.*

Published in association with Don Gates of the literary agency The Gates Group, www.the-gates-group.com.

Cover design: James W. Hall IV
Cover photo: kalanustudios.com / Adobe Stock
Interior design: Denise Froehlich

Printed in the United States of America

25 26 27 28 29 LBC 6 5 4 3 2

To J. P. MORELAND—
philosopher and friend

CONTENTS

INTRODUCTION

Exploring the World Beyond

She was blind for more than a dozen years from juvenile macular degeneration, an incurable condition. She attended a school for the blind, used a white cane for mobility, and read Braille.

One night at bedtime, her husband, a Baptist pastor, got on his knees to pray. He put a hand on her shoulder as she lay on the bed. They were both crying as he said, "O God, you can restore eyesight tonight. Lord, I know you can do it! And I pray you will do it tonight."

With that, she opened her eyes—and saw her husband kneeling in front of her. "I was blind when my husband prayed for me," she said. "Then just like that—in a moment, after years of darkness—I could see perfectly. It was miraculous! . . . Within seconds, my life had drastically changed. I could see, I could see!"

Since then, the woman's eyesight has remained intact for more than forty-seven years. Four researchers published her case study—the first of its kind in scientific literature—in a peer-reviewed medical journal in 2021.[1]

Was this an example of divine intervention by a supernatural deity or merely a medical anomaly that coincidentally occurred after a prayer for healing?

It was about three in the morning, and a former US Secret Service agent was trying to get to sleep. Suddenly, he was gripped by something bizarre—the sensation of being grabbed as though someone (like a loving mother, for example) were hugging him.

"It was real. I'm telling you, it was *real*," he insisted later. "I actually jumped up. I know it sounds crazy, but I went looking for my gun. I started looking around the house."

When he realized he was alone, his emotions shifted. He felt at peace, and the experience pointed him toward the comfort of God.

Nearly two hours later, the phone rang with the stunning news that his beloved mother had died unexpectedly after a fall. In fact, she had passed from this world at about 3:00 a.m.

"I'm telling you, if I didn't believe in God and the afterlife, I would after last night," he said the following day. "I've never believed more in the power of Jesus."[2]

Could this have been some sort of a supernatural experience, or was it something with a more mundane explanation? What natural means could account for it?

Pastor John Boston was trapped in his smashed car after he plowed into a utility pole and a live transformer crashed onto his vehicle. Thousands of volts of electricity surged through the car's body, the heat causing the windshield to start melting. The driver's door was jammed shut.

"No one should've been able to touch the car," Boston said later. "I shouldn't have survived."

And yet suddenly a scruffy-looking man came out of nowhere, easily opened the crushed door, and walked Boston twenty yards away from the car—just before the vehicle exploded into flames.

"He said my name is Johnny, the police are almost here and I can't be here when they get here but you're gonna be okay," recounted Boston. "And then the man was gone."

Boston was treated for his injuries at Grant Medical Center in Columbus, Ohio—and he is convinced he had been rescued by an angel. "I don't think angels come to us with wings and white robes," he told a local television station. "I think they come as help and that's what I had that day."

Reporter Suzanne Stratford interviewed the veteran firefighters who had been dispatched that night, and they were scratching their heads over what had taken place. "It gives me goosebumps," one of them said.

Could a circuit breaker have tripped, allowing the mysterious figure to touch the car and not be electrocuted? There were no reports of electricity being out in the area, and electrical current was still coursing through the wreckage when firefighters arrived.

"I like to believe miracles happen," concluded Lt. Garey Borgan, "and it seems like one of those here."[3]

Are there supernatural beings called angels who miraculously intercede in people's lives at times of crisis? Or is there a more down-to-earth explanation for what occurred that night on Airport Road in Columbus?

⁞ ⁞

When William Peter Blatty set out to write the classic horror film *The Exorcist*, he had an agenda—and it wasn't simply to scare audiences to their core (though he did manage to do exactly that).

Reeling from the death of his beloved mother, the screenwriter best known for authoring a *Pink Panther* comedy decided there was a critically important message that needed to be shared with an increasingly skeptical populace: "The spiritual world is real."

"I wanted to write about good and evil and the unseen world all around us," he told journalist Terry Mattingly. "I wanted to make a statement that the grave is not the end, that there is more to life than death."

To Blatty, who earned an Academy Award for his script, the logic was inexorable: "If demons are real, why not angels? If angels are real, why not souls? And if souls are real, what about your own soul?"[4]

The Exorcist, which grossed nearly $430 million worldwide and was ranked as the scariest horror movie of all time,[5] succeeded in stoking fascination with the supernatural, the paranormal, and the just plain weird. A slew of other horror films followed in its wake, such as *The Omen*, which spawned five sequels, and the lighthearted *Ghostbusters* franchise.

In California, thousands flock to the annual Conscious Life Expo, which recently featured a "12th dimensional stargate meditation" and a talk by Viviane Chauvet, who says she's a member of an ancient alien race who was dispatched to share wisdom with us. "I know I look a lot like a human, but that's the idea. This was the best way to be a conduit," she said, according to the *Los Angeles Times*, which labeled the gathering "L.A.'s wackiest spiritual convention."[6]

On television, the pilot episode of *Supernatural*, which told the story of two brothers hunting ghosts and demons, scored nearly six million viewers, leading to a run of fifteen seasons on the air.[7] Among books, Sidney Dickinson's *True Tales of the Weird: A Record of Personal Experiences of the Supernatural* has been selling for more than a hundred years, despite the opinion of one British reviewer, who scoffed that the author had been "fooled by a series of practical jokes perpetrated by his second wife." (Two stars—*ouch!*)[8]

In 2024, airport newsstands around the country were festooned with copies of *Harper's Magazine*, emblazoned with the headline "The New Satanic Panic: Exorcism in the Age of TikTok"—alongside the publication *Secrets of the Supernatural*, featuring such articles as "Stars Who've Seen Ghosts" and "The Demon Whisperer." Said its breathless promotional copy, "Restless spirits of the dead, terrifying demons, and visitors from other alien worlds bewilder and frighten."[9]

Interest in the supernatural is incredibly high in our culture. And it's not just in films, in articles, or at conferences. In fact, you don't have to persuade most Americans that supernatural phenomena are authentic. They're already convinced. A 2023 Pew Research Center survey found that eight out of ten Americans believe there is something spiritual beyond the natural world. Nearly half say they have had a sudden sense of connection with something from beyond, and more than a third report that they've had a strong feeling that a deceased person was communicating with them.[10]

Yet a Gallup study that same year unveiled a weakness in some beliefs. For instance, its survey disclosed that the percentage of Americans who believe in God, angels, heaven, hell, and the devil has *fallen* by double digits since 2001, though clear majorities still believe in them (for example, 69 percent for angels and 58 percent for Satan).[11]

A literal devil, surrounded by evil sidekicks called demons—could they be real? What about guardian angels, those elusive messengers who flit between ethereal and physical worlds? How about heaven, an everlasting abode of joy and celebration? Or hell, a never-ending destination of dread and despair? Above all, what about God himself, the ultimate ruler of both the natural and supernatural realms? And are the biblical accounts of Jesus performing exorcisms and miracles really credible?

What about reports of modern-day miracles—could these in reality be nothing more than extraordinary coincidences? How about near-death experiences, where people claim to get a glimpse of another existence? Maybe these are merely the product of brain excretions under extreme duress. Are mystical dreams and visions simply subjective musings of our subconscious minds? In fact, is consciousness itself really just an illusion foisted on us by our physical brains?

In short, is it truly possible in our scientific and technological age to be a rational person and still have faith in the existence of a realm we can't see, touch, or analyze in a test tube?

Does Science Put God Out of a Job?

Without question, science and technology have made innumerable contributions to the improvement of life over the past several decades. Advancements in medicine have resulted in diseases cured and suffering eased; innovations in communications have knit the planet together; the James Webb Space Telescope has revealed breathtaking visions of the distant cosmos; and who knows what horizons will be reached through the unfolding technology of artificial intelligence?

All of this, however, has helped cement the attitude that science is the gold standard for determining what is true and real. Even more than that, many people believe it's the *only* standard. The philosophies of *scientific materialism* and its close cousin *scientism*[12] tell us that "the methods of science are the only reliable ways to secure knowledge of anything" and are "our exclusive guide to reality," wrote Duke University philosophy professor Alex Rosenberg in his book *The Atheist's Guide to Reality*.[13]

"Scientific materialism holds that any true and meaningful knowledge that we may gain about life, mind and the universe can be gotten only through the analytical methods of science," said John F. Haught, professor of theology at Georgetown University. "Everything else is sheer speculation if not wishful thinking."[14]

This worldview increasingly dominates our culture. "Since Einstein, the natural sciences have only risen in prestige and cultural influence, and the scientific community is now widely regarded as the ultimate authority on truth about the world," said science philosopher Melissa Cain Travis, author of *Science and the Mind of the Maker*. "Thus," she continued, "to be a scientifically literate person . . . is to be a materialist—to believe that the only objective reality consists of matter and energy behaving according to the laws of physics and chemistry."[15]

The spiritual implications are obvious. In the words of psychology professor Jessica Tracy of the University of British Columbia, scientific materialism "has placed a clear-cut kibosh on the possibility of a supernatural deity running the show."[16] In short, our choice seems to be science or superstition—and if we take science seriously, we can't take the idea of God seriously.

The left-wing Jesus Seminar declared that "the Christ of creed and dogma" is no longer credible. Why? Because once people saw "the heavens through Galileo's telescope, the old deities and demons were swept from the skies by that remarkable glass. Copernicus, Kepler, and Galileo have dismantled the mythological abodes of the gods and Satan, and bequeathed us secular heavens."[17]

An adherent of scientific materialism once told a Christian philosopher that "if something like religious, ethical or related claims cannot be quantified and proven in the laboratory, then the claims are nothing but hot air, mere expressions of feeling that cannot carry any authority."[18]

Fallout from the supposed clash between science and faith was apparent in a national survey I commissioned in 2023. I found that nearly half of American adults—46 percent—strongly or somewhat agree that science contradicts or disproves Christianity, with 18 percent being vehement in that conviction.[19]

This would have warmed the heart of the late evolutionary biologist and social commentator Richard Lewontin of Harvard University, an adamant atheist who wanted science to be seen as the only arbiter of what's real. In an especially candid moment, Lewontin said, "The problem is to get [the masses] to reject irrational and supernatural explanations of the world, the demons that exist only in their imaginations, and to accept a social and intellectual apparatus, *Science*, as the only begetter of truth."[20]

Why Belief in the Supernatural Persists

Ultimately, however, scientific materialism can't disprove the existence of the supernatural. A major reason is because the concept of scientism is self-refuting. Consider the sentence, "Science is the only begetter of truth." That's not a *scientific* statement that can be tested by the scientific method, but rather it's a *philosophical* assertion. It's self-contradictory, akin to saying, "All English sentences are four words in length." Consequently, the very foundation of scientism is built on scientifically unverifiable assumptions.

My friend J. P. Moreland, who has been described as "one of our greatest living philosophers,"[21] earned degrees in chemistry and theology before attaining his doctorate in philosophy at the University of Southern California and writing dozens of books, including the influential *Christianity and the Nature of Science*. His background has made him a trenchant commentator on these issues. In his book *Scientism and Secularism*, he offers a devastating critique of scientific materialism.

He said the statement "the only knowledge we can have about reality is that which has been properly tested in the hard sciences" is not itself a statement about reality that has been properly tested in the hard sciences. "So," he points out, "it cannot be a knowledge claim about reality."

In fact, he said there are things we know with greater certainty in theology or ethics than certain claims in science. For example, consider two assertions: (1) Electrons exist, and (2) It is wrong to torture babies for the fun of it.

"Which do we know with greater certainty?" he asks. The claim about the baby is the correct answer. Why? Because the history of the electron has gone through various changes since the particle was discovered. "It is not unreasonable to believe than in 50 to 100 years, scientific depictions of the electron will change so much that scientists will no longer believe that what we mean by an electron today exists," Moreland said.

In contrast, everyone knows that the statement about not torturing babies is true. "If someone denies that, she needs therapy, not an argument," Moreland quipped. "But it is hard to see what kind of rational considerations could be discovered that would render (2) an irrational belief." Thus, he concludes that we have more certainty in the statement about the baby than in the current science claim about the electron.

Besides, he said there are several things that science *can't* explain—for example, the origin and fine-tuning of the universe, the origin of the fundamental laws of nature, the origin of consciousness, and the existence of moral laws.

"The problem is not that we lack sufficient data—the problem is that these are the sorts of things that science cannot explain, even in principle," he said. "Moreover, these things are items that we know to be true. What makes all of this especially interesting is that theism can explain them."[22]

Certainly, there are plenty of things calling out for an explanation. One of the reasons belief in supernatural phenomena persists is that people, it seems, are *experiencing* things beyond the ability of science to measure or explain. While experience alone might not be enough to grant an idea full legitimacy, doesn't it make sense to take notice when the testimony of countless people begins to line up?

What We Believe to Be True

As a legal editor at the *Chicago Tribune*, I used to practically live in courtrooms as I covered high-profile criminal and civil trials around the nation. While scientifically supported evidence—such as fingerprints, ballistics, DNA, and so forth—can play a key role in a case, that's not the only sort of proof that juries find persuasive. There is also documentary evidence; eyewitness testimony, which can be subjected to various tests to make sure it's reliable; and circumstantial evidence, which doesn't mean weak evidence but simply refers to facts from which the jury can draw logical inferences.

In everyday life, we know that, apart from science, there are various other disciplines, such as history and philosophy, that can point us toward "true truths" that we can believe with confidence. We accept things as being true every day without analyzing them in a laboratory. Even our own introspection and experience can help us encounter reality on a whole different level at times.

That's what this book is about—the question of whether we can reasonably conclude from the evidence that the supernatural realm is real. In other words, if we don't rule out the possibility of the supernatural at the outset but instead call "a ball a ball and a strike a strike," as any unbiased umpire would, then where would the evidence point?

For example, what if we have persuasive historical data establishing (1) Jesus of Nazareth lived in the first century and claimed to be divine; (2) he was unquestionably dead after being crucified under Pontius Pilate; and (3) he was reliably encountered alive later by numerous eyewitnesses? From that evidence, wouldn't it be reasonable to conclude that Jesus had been supernaturally resurrected (as he predicted he would be), especially when alternative naturalistic explanations fall flat?

What about contemporary cases of medical healings where there is simply no naturalistic explanation for the instantaneous restoration of perfect health after prayers to Jesus? Wouldn't this point toward the reasonable conclusion that a supernatural miracle has taken place?

What about near-death experiences in which people see or hear things they otherwise would not have been able to see or hear if they had not had an authentic out-of-body experience? Does their encounter with the supernatural carry credibility when all other avenues of naturalistic explanation fall short?

And how about mystical dreams that are externally corroborated—for instance, people being told highly improbable things by supernatural figures in their vision that later come exactly to pass?

All of these things are interesting in their own right and worthy of careful consideration. But also at stake is what undergirds them. What kind of world do we find ourselves in? Is it limited to whatever is reducible to the material? Or does reality extend beyond what science is able to describe? Is what we call "the supernatural" simply superstition? Or is there evidence for its existence that is worth examining closer?

Extraordinary Claims, Extraordinary Evidence?

What if the evidence were to contradict the materialistic claim that the world is limited to what science can observe, quantify, or replicate? What if being human means more than being just a physical brain devoid of authentic free will? Instead, what if there's persuasive support for the existence of an immaterial soul that interacts with our brain and would have the capacity to survive death? And if it does survive death, to what realm does it go?

What about the stunning number of people who testify that they have personally had a supernatural encounter? I commissioned a national survey in which 38 percent of American adults said they have had at least one supernatural experience they can only attribute to being a miracle of God. Even if 99 percent of them were honestly mistaken, that would leave nearly a million miracles in the United States *alone!*[23]

And what do we do with a book that has uncanny credentials—for instance, prophecies being fulfilled against all odds centuries after being recorded—and that paints an exotic picture of an elaborate realm beyond our own, including a forever paradise for believers and an eternal place of torment for spiritual rebels? Because one thing is for certain: The supernatural permeates Scripture and is an integral component of Christian theology.

"The Bible asks us to believe a lot of strange things about the spiritual world," said Old Testament scholar Michael Heiser, who authored several books on the supernatural before his untimely death in 2023. "At first, we might be tempted to ignore them, but if we say we believe the Bible, we can't avoid these concepts."[24]

But all of this prompts us to ask, How strong does the evidence for the supernatural need to be? Is the existence of a realm beyond this world an extraordinary claim that requires extraordinary evidence? That might sound logical on its surface, but I think it's a flawed way of looking at the issue.

For one thing, the vast majority of people from around the globe throughout history have believed in a divine entity of some sort. Therefore, it wouldn't be extraordinary to believe that the supernatural exists; rather, it would be extraordinary to claim that it *doesn't* exist. Consequently, under this standard, it would be the atheists who would need to supply extraordinary evidence in support of their skepticism, not the other way around.

However, I don't subscribe to the idea that extraordinary claims require extraordinary proof. Rather, as in every other area of life, we simply need *sufficient* evidence.

While we won't be covering UFOs in this book, let's use one as an example here. Imagine someone were to send me a text saying that an alien spaceship has landed on the National Mall in Washington, DC. That would certainly qualify as an extraordinary claim. But if I checked it out and found confirmation from reliable sources, I could reasonably conclude that this amazing claim is true. I wouldn't need the evidence to be extraordinary; I would simply need it to be persuasive.

So what is the persuasive evidence that what we see and touch isn't the totality of our existence, but that there is actually a supernatural component to life? I hope you'll keep an open mind and heart as these pages present provocative accounts of what exists beyond our physical world.

Skeptics, I predict, will be challenged; believers, I suspect, will be encouraged. Either way, let's allow the facts to guide us through this critically important topic—and let our conclusions flow from that.

An Unexpected Visitor at Night

There I was, backstage at the taping of a national television program as I waited to be interviewed by television personality Kirk Cameron. I couldn't see the interview he was conducting before mine, but from my vantage point, I could clearly hear what was being said. As I listened, a sense of wonder swelled inside me.

The guest was Cameron's sister, Bridgette Cameron Ridenour, who was talking about her new book.[25] Kirk asked her to recount the story of her miscarriage, and I was fascinated by what she said. Could she be describing a glimpse into a world beyond our own?

Bridgette had been at home when she miscarried. She felt God gently saying, *This is your daughter. You need to say goodbye*, which she did through her tears.

Before going to the hospital, Bridgette called her mother, who gave her some odd advice: "Please do not let them do a D&C until you have an ultrasound. Refuse to go back to that operating room until they do an ultrasound *in your room*."

Bridgette didn't understand why her mother was insisting on this, but her urgent instructions were so adamant that when the nurses wanted to move her to the operating room later that day, she refused until they finally agreed to do an ultrasound.

The technician squirted jelly on her stomach. Bridgette's husband, John, held his wife's hand. "I prepared to see the womb empty," she wrote in her book.

The technician's brow furrowed. She looked at Bridgette. She looked at the monitor. She looked back at Bridgette. "You're still pregnant," she whispered, as if she didn't believe it herself.

Gazing at the monitor, they could clearly see a tiny fluttering heartbeat in the middle of the sack. By now, all three of them were crying.

The doctor came in. "I've never seen anything like this," he said.

As it turned out, Bridgette had been pregnant with identical twins. They named the deceased child Sofia. The other baby was named Reese, and Bridgette ended up carrying her to full term. Reese was born healthy and strong in March 2006.

Then one day when Reese was four, she was sitting on a rocking chair with Bridgette when she suddenly asked, "Mommy, do I have a sister?"

Bridgette's heart began pounding. "We knew someday we'd need to talk to Reese about what happened, but we thought it should be when she was much older," Bridgette wrote.

"Why do you ask?" Bridgette said to her daughter.

"Mommy," came her reply, "there is this little girl who comes to me in my dreams. She wants to talk with me and play with me."

Bridgette swallowed hard. "Do you see her a lot?"

"All the time," she said. Then Reese added emphatically, *And she looks just like me!*"

What was going on there? Was little Reese being visited by her deceased sister, who continues to live on . . . where? In another dimension? In heaven? Maybe there's a more mundane explanation. Skeptics might suggest Reese was picking up subtle clues that there had been another child and her imagination conjured up these nocturnal encounters. But if Reese truly didn't know anything about her twin sibling, how can her experiences be explained away?

Could this be a peek into an existence we know little about? How can we investigate cases like this and come to rational conclusions?

Reese's story is just one tantalizing episode among many. So go ahead and turn the page, and let's explore the cases and the corroboration, the evidence and the anecdotes, the studies and the stories, the data and the details that ultimately support an awe-inspiring conclusion: The supernatural realm is as real as the physical world you see all around you. (Maybe even more so.)

My guess is that you'll be scratching your head over some of the provocative accounts and the facts that back them up. And perhaps you'll even be prompted to seek more information about the One who rules over this world—and everything beyond it.

PART 1

THE
SUPERNATURAL
AMONG US

CHAPTER 1

THE INVISIBLE YOU: THE EXISTENCE OF YOUR SOUL

For me now, the only reality is the human soul.

Nobel Prize–winning scientist Sir
Charles Sherrington shortly before he died

Canadian psychiatrist Ralph Lewis was raised in a Jewish family in South Africa. He always considered himself a skeptic, but during his wife Karin's battle with cancer they both became atheists. After all, it seemed like a natural next step in their philosophy of materialism, which means there's no supernatural dimension beyond the physical world.

"There is simply no room for belief in a spiritual realm in a scientific view of reality," Lewis said. "Period."

Lewis believes that matter achieved immense complexity

through "spontaneous unguided processes of self-organization, further sculpted in biological organisms by powerful evolutionary forces (again, unguided)." Ultimately, human consciousness, or the mind, emerged by itself during our evolutionary history in some as-yet-unexplained way.

"The mind is the product of the brain and nothing but the brain," he said. "The mind is (only) what the brain does."[1] And when our physical brain dies, we die and decay.

This view is popular among scientists. "The prevailing wisdom . . . is there is only one sort of stuff, namely *matter*—the physical stuff of physics, chemistry, and physiology—and the mind is somehow nothing but a physical phenomenon," said atheist philosopher Daniel Dennett.[2]

Said Sir Colin Blakemore, professor of neuroscience at the University of Oxford, "The human brain is a machine, which alone accounts for all our actions, our most private thoughts, our beliefs. . . . All our actions are the products of the activity of our brains."[3]

This philosophy is broadly categorized as *physicalism*.[4] Some physicalists, such as Dennett, believe consciousness is merely an illusion. Other physicalists believe consciousness exists but is wholly a product of the physical brain, having emerged naturally as humans evolved to become more complex. Yet nobody has been able to propose any credible mechanism for how consciousness actually emerged.

"How can mere matter originate consciousness? How did evolution convert the water of biological tissue into the wine of consciousness?" asks philosopher Colin McGinn. "Consciousness seems like a radical novelty in the universe, not prefigured by the after-effects of the Big Bang. So how did it contrive to spring into being from what preceded it?"[5]

Dualism, the idea that humans are a composite of a physical body and an immaterial mind or soul, seems intuitive; in fact, it has been believed by "most people, at most times, in most places, at most ages," said philosophers Mark Baker and Stewart Goetz in *The Soul Hypothesis*.[6]

Of course, there are examples throughout history where people have held beliefs that seemed intuitive, only to have scientific advancements prove them wrong. These days, discoveries in neuroscience, including mapping the brain, are prompting physicalists to triumphantly declare that dualism is dead.

"This idea of immaterial souls, capable of defying the laws of physics, has outlived its credibility, thanks to the advance of the natural sciences," said Dennett.[7]

Not true, retort dualists. They're convinced such conclusions are—excuse the pun—wrongheaded. Declared Baker and Goetz, "Reports of the death of the soul have been exaggerated."[8]

A lot hangs on this issue. Are you only a physical brain, destined to deteriorate into oblivion when your heart stops beating, or are you also an immaterial soul capable of living on forever in a realm beyond the natural world? In short, the existence of the soul has become one of the key battlegrounds in the question of whether a spiritual or supernatural realm exists.

The Spirit Lives On

The soul is considered the seat of our consciousness, the locus of our introspection, volition, emotions, desires, memories, perceptions and beliefs—it's the ego, the "I" or the self. The soul is said to animate and interact with our body, though it is distinct from it. "When we speak of the soul, we speak of *our essential core*," said philosopher Paul Copan.[9]

The Hebrew words *nephesh* (often translated "soul") and *ruach* (frequently rendered "spirit"), as well as the Greek word *psyche* (generally translated "soul"), occur hundreds of times in the Old and New Testaments. However, they are used in a variety of contexts, leading to differing interpretations by scholars. Fueling these debates is the fact that the Bible has no direct teaching on the existence or nature of the soul.[10]

Nevertheless, both the Old and New Testaments presuppose that the soul is real. Anthropologist Arthur Custance said the Christian Scriptures indicate that human beings are "a hyphenate creature, a spirit/body dichotomy."[11] Christian philosopher J. P. Moreland describes himself this way: "I *am* a soul, and I *have* a body."[12]

Moreland argues that the Bible "implicitly affirms the reality of the soul without attempting to teach its existence explicitly." He writes, "For example, in Matthew 10:28, Jesus warns us not to fear those who can only kill the body; rather, we should fear Him who can destroy both body and soul. The primary purpose of this text is to serve as a warning and not to teach that there is a soul. But in issuing His warning, Jesus implicitly affirms the soul's reality."[13]

On other occasions the Bible simply assumes the common-sense view of dualism, he said. For example, when the disciples saw Jesus walking on the water and thought they were seeing a spirit,[14] the Bible is merely assuming we all know we are (or have) souls that can exist without the body.

Piecing together clues in Scripture, Moreland said it appears that our soul separates from our body at the point of death as we enter into a temporary intermediate state of disembodiment until the general resurrection of the body at the consummation of history.[15]

As evidence, Moreland points to Jesus telling the thief being crucified next to him that he would be with Jesus immediately after his death and before the final resurrection of his body.[16] Also, between his death and resurrection, Jesus continued to exist as a God-man independent of his body.[17] The apostle Paul says that to be absent from the body is to be present with the Lord.[18] And Jesus and Paul agreed with the teaching of the Pharisees that at death, the soul departs into a disembodied existence until the general bodily resurrection.[19]

However, Patricia Churchland, professor emerita of philosophy at the University of California at San Diego, insists that "the concept of the soul, though having a long and respectable history, now looks outmuscled and outsmarted by neuroscience."[20]

Is that true? To find out, I sought an interview with a neuroscientist who received her doctorate from Cambridge University and has conducted brain research in Britain and the United States.[21]

INTERVIEW *with*

SHARON DIRCKX, PHD

As a child, Sharon Dirckx (rhymes with *lyrics*) was watching the rain falling outside her house when she suddenly became aware of her own consciousness. Thoughts popped into her head: *Why can I think? Why do I exist? Why am I a living, breathing, conscious person who experiences life?*

These were deep reflections for a youngster of ten or eleven, and they propelled her on a lifetime quest for answers. She grew up in a religiously neutral household and always wanted to be a scientist. When Sharon was seventeen, a teacher gave her a book by evolutionary biologist and atheist Richard Dawkins, which helped form her agnostic beliefs.

"I became convinced that a person couldn't become a scientist and believe in God at the same time—they're incompatible," she recalled.

During her first week at the University of Bristol, she attended a forum featuring a panel of knowledgeable Christians, and she summoned the courage to ask a question about science and faith being at odds. The response took her aback. "They made the case that of course a person can be a Christian and a scientist at the same time," she said. "It rocked my world."

She ended up spending the next eighteen months investigating Christianity, coming to faith at twenty and going on to earn her undergraduate degree in biochemistry. Her fascination with neuroscience prompted her to get her doctorate in brain imaging at Cambridge University, and she subsequently spent another seven years conducting neuroimaging research at both the University of Oxford and the Medical College of Wisconsin in Milwaukee.

Today, she and her husband, Conrad (they met in the brain imaging lab—"very romantic," she quipped), live in Oxford with their two children. She is currently a senior tutor at The Oxford Centre for Christian Apologetics (OCCA). She lectures internationally on science, theology, mind-and-soul issues, and other topics, and she appears regularly on British radio programs, sometimes debating secular thinkers.

Her first book, the award-winning *Why? Looking at God, Evil and Personal Suffering*, came out in 2013. Then she turned her attention back to her passion for neuroscience, philosophy, and theology. The result was her book *Am I Just My Brain?*

The title piqued my interest, so I set up a face-to-face interview with her via Zoom. She was upstairs at home in Oxford, casually dressed, her brown hair in a bob, and speaking with an altogether British accent. We ended up engaging in a lengthy discussion on this first building block in the case for the existence of a spiritual realm beyond death.

Yuri Gagarin versus Buzz Aldrin

I started with a question more whimsical than probing. "When Russian cosmonaut Yuri Gagarin—an atheist—became the first person in space, he remarked, 'I looked and looked, but I didn't see God.'

You've used high-tech imaging machines to peer inside human brains. Did you see a soul?"

That evoked a grin. "Well, I wasn't looking for one," she replied. "As a neuroscientist, I was studying things like the effects of cocaine addiction on the brain. That's what scientists do—we explore the physical world. That may be partly why a lot of scientists just assume the physicalist position, because theirs is the material world of nature.

"Some people assume science can do more than it really can," she added. "For instance, it's not designed to resolve the question of whether God exists. Of course, if God is real, there will be signs pointing in his direction—as I believe there are. But science deals with the natural world.

"By the way," she said, "for every Yuri Gagarin, there's a Buzz Aldrin. He took Communion before walking on the moon and asked for silence from NASA as he read Psalm 8: 'When I consider your heavens, the work of your fingers, the moon and the stars, which you have set in place, what is mankind that you are mindful of them, human beings that you care for them?'[1] There are scientists who doubt, but others who believe."

"You mentioned, though, that many scientists are physicalists. How pervasive is that view?" I asked.

"Quite pervasive," she replied. "For example, *Scientific American* reported on studies of how brain networks are correlated to different mental states. The headline on the cover read, 'How Brain Networks Create Thought.' Now, that is *not* a scientific statement. It's not what the data tell you. That's a worldview statement, based on the belief that everything is ultimately tied to the physical and therefore it must be the brain that creates our thoughts. This happens all the time in our field."

Science, she said, could never disprove God. "That would be like scientists figuring out how all the programming works on Facebook and then declaring, 'So this disproves the existence of Mark Zuckerberg.'"

Now it was my turn to smile. "You're saying that science can tell us many things, but we still need philosophy and theology."

She nodded. "The Bible says God has made himself known in two ways—through the natural revelation of the physical world and the special revelation of Scripture. Science tells us a lot about the natural world, but we still need theology and philosophy to plumb special revelation—the Scriptures—and to give thought to questions that science cannot answer. Questions like, 'Why can we *think* at all?'"

Pen in hand to take notes, I turned to the issue raised by the title of her book: Is there any scientific evidence for—or against—the idea that we are just our physical brains?

Describe the Aroma of Coffee

I began by asking fundamental questions: "Are the mind and brain the same thing? Can everything be explained by the firing of neurons?"

"Let me explain why the answer is no," she said. "Scientists can measure activities of the brain—for instance, we see networks light up when various thoughts are taking place. But those networks aren't necessarily the thoughts themselves; they're merely correlated with our thoughts. The problem is that scientists can't access a person's *actual* inner thoughts or *qualia* without simply asking them. A person's thoughts defy traditional scientific methods."

"Qualia?"

"That's the plural of *quale,* which philosophers use to describe a quality or property that someone experiences or perceives. For example," she said, raising her cup, "you and I are both drinking coffee as we chat."

I took a sip from my mug to acknowledge that.

"If someone asked you to describe the smell of coffee, what would you say?" she asked.

I thought for a moment before realizing how vexing that really is. "I'm not sure where I'd begin," I said.

"We could give the chemical structure of caffeine, but that wouldn't get us any closer to the smell of coffee," Dirckx said. "We might talk about the physiology of what's happening in our body as we drink it, but that doesn't capture the aroma. To understand what coffee smells like, you need to *experience* it. Life is full of *qualia* like that—for example, seeing the color red or tasting a watermelon.

"It's like the difference between reading a review of a concert and experiencing the event yourself. Think about how many times someone tried to describe to you something they've experienced, like a rock concert, only to finally give up and say, 'Well, I guess you really needed to *be* there.'

"As a neuroscientist, I've measured the electrical activity of people's brains, but I can't measure their experience in the same way. I can't measure what's in their minds. I can't measure what it's actually like to be *you*. Why not? Because the brain alone is not enough to explain the mind."

To illustrate further, Dirckx described a thought experiment.[2] What if Mary were a scientist who had detailed knowledge of the physics and chemistry of vision? She knew all about the intricate structure of the eye, how it functions, and how it sends electrical signals to the brain through the optic nerve, where they are converted into images. But what if she were blind—and then one day, she was suddenly able to see?

"At the moment of receiving her sight, does Mary learn anything new about vision?" Dirckx asked.

My eyes widened. "Of course!"

"That means physical facts alone cannot explain the first-person experience of consciousness. No amount of knowledge about the physical working of the eye and brain would get Mary closer to the experience of what it's like to actually *see*."

"What's your conclusion?"

"That consciousness simply cannot be synonymous with brain activity."

"You're saying that although they work together, they're not the same thing. Consciousness—the mind, the soul—are beyond the physical workings of the brain."

"Correct. Philosophers such as Gottfried Leibniz make an important point: If two things are identical, there would be no discernible difference between them.[3] That means if consciousness were identical with brain activity, everything true of consciousness would be true of the brain as well. But consciousness and brain activity couldn't be more different. So consciousness cannot be reduced to the purely physical processes of the brain."

She pointed toward me and smiled. "You, Lee, are more than just your brain."

That did seem clear-cut—but there have been objections. "The atheist Daniel Dennett gets around this by saying that consciousness is illusory," I said.

She replied simply, "Illusion still presupposes consciousness."

"Could you explain that?"

"Illusion happens when we misinterpret an experience or perceive it wrongly, but the experience itself is still valid and real. That's a problem with what he's saying. Honestly, I think his view is absurd. By the way, it backfires. If what he claims is true, then his very argument can't be trusted."

"Why not?"

"Because it's just an illusion."

Going beyond the Physical Brain

Neuroscientist Adrian Owen spent more than two decades studying patients with brain trauma. In 2006, the prestigious journal *Science* published his groundbreaking research showing that some patients considered vegetative with severe brain injuries were actually conscious.

Said Owen, "We have discovered that 15 to 20 percent of people in the vegetative state, who are widely assumed to have no more awareness than a head of broccoli, are in fact fully conscious, even though they never respond to any form of external stimulation."[4]

"What does that tell you?" I asked Dirckx.

"It's additional evidence that human beings are highly complex, and the condition of our brains is only part of the story," she said. "Consciousness goes beyond our physical brain and nervous system. It can't just be boiled down to brain activity. We are more than our brains."

That triggered thoughts about experiments in the 1950s by Wilder Penfield, the father of modern neurosurgery, who stimulated the brains of epilepsy patients, creating all kinds of involuntary sensations and movements. But no matter how much he tried, he couldn't evoke abstract reasoning or consciousness itself.

"There is no place . . . where electrical stimulation will cause a patient to believe or decide," Penfield said.[5] For him, this evidence for a nonphysical mind distinct from the brain convinced him to abandon physicalism.[6]

But could the brain, as it evolved in complexity, have somehow generated the conscious mind? I asked Dirckx about this view, which is popular among many scientists.

"If we're dealing with a closed system of nonconscious neurons, how did these come to generate conscious minds?" she replied, letting the challenge hang in the air for a moment.

"This has been the big hurdle," she said. "Nobody can give a coherent explanation for it in a materialist world. And if all that's needed is a physical brain to create the mind, why aren't animals conscious to the same degree as we are? The discontinuity between primates and people isn't one of *degree*; it's one of *kind*. Complexity, all by itself, wouldn't be enough to get us across that chasm. Of course, there are Christians who take an emergent view, but for them, the system is not closed. If God exists, extraordinary things are possible. Then that chasm can be crossed."

She paused and then continued. "I'll add another potential line of evidence that humans are more than molecules," she said. "If consciousness and the brain were the same thing, then when a person died, their consciousness would be extinguished, right?"

"That's right," I said.

"But," she asked, "what if near-death experiences show that we can still be conscious without a functioning brain? Again, it would demonstrate that human consciousness is more than just physical brain activity."

In her book, Dirckx tells the story of Pamela Reynolds, who in 1991 suffered a severe brain hemorrhage from an aneurysm. During her surgery, called a "standstill" operation, doctors cooled her body temperature, "flatlined" her heart and brain signals, and drained the blood from her head. Clinically, she was dead—but when she was resuscitated after surgery, she astounded everyone by recalling how she had been conscious the whole time.

Thousands of patients have told stories about being clinically deceased and yet floating out of their body and watching resuscitation efforts from above. Many have described traveling through long tunnels, seeing deceased relatives, and experiencing an astoundingly beautiful realm beyond our world. In a study of 1,400 near-death experiences, cardiologist Fred Schoonmaker said fifty-five patients had their out-of-body experience during a time when they had no measurable brain waves.[7]

No measurable brain waves? Yet their consciousness continued? That would certainly put the possibility of an immaterial mind, or soul, on the table. I asked Dirckx, "Do you think these can provide good evidence for a soul and an afterlife?"

"This has certainly gone beyond mere anecdotes," she replied.

"There have been various studies conducted in the United States, the Netherlands, and elsewhere. Of course, some stories could have been fabricated, but with others, there's very intriguing evidence."

"Corroboration?"

"That's the claim. I suspect we'll see more data as research continues. But think about it this way: All we really need is *one* documented case."

"What would that do?"

"It would deal another serious blow to the idea that consciousness resides entirely in the brain," she said. "It would also suggest that even the sciences point to evidence of an afterlife."

I pondered this for a moment and then jotted on my legal pad: *Find out if NDEs are credible.*

The Illusion of Free Will

Here's another problem with the idea that we're just our brain: Many philosophers say this means we wouldn't have free will in any meaningful sense. For instance, atheist Sam Harris says that although we *think* we're acting freely, we're simply fulfilling what our genetics and environment compel us to do. Basically, our neurons fire and we obey—it's as simple as that.

"Free will *is* an illusion," declares Harris, who earned his doctorate in cognitive neuroscience from UCLA. "Our wills are simply not of our own making. Thoughts and intentions emerge from the background causes of which we are unaware and over which we exert no conscious control. We do not have the freedom we think we have."[8]

This is called "hard determinism." I wanted to know from Dirckx whether this view stands up to scrutiny.

"Let me apply three tests used to assess the legitimacy of any worldview," Dirckx said.[9] "First, is hard determinism internally consistent? Not really. If all our thoughts are driven by nonrational, mechanistic forces, then they are not really our thoughts as such.

They come from forces beyond our control, and therefore are meaningless. The person expressing a hard-deterministic view is asking you not to believe them!

"Second, does hard determinism make sense of the world around us? Again, not really. If free will is an illusion, why do we continue to imagine it's real? Why do we strive for autonomy? Why do we seek control over our finances, our health, and our careers—are we free to shape our own lives and decide our own fate or not? Hard determinism creates confusion, not clarity.

"Third, can hard determinism be authentically lived out? Not really. We don't live as though our choices are just the mechanistic firing of neurons in our brain; we live as though our decisions really do mean something. In fact, under hard determinism we wouldn't be morally responsible for our actions, since we wouldn't really have a meaningful choice in what we do. That means society couldn't legitimately punish people for their crimes or reward them for their virtue. We can't live that way."

I found the seeming absurdity of hard determinism to be another reason why it makes sense to believe we're not just our brains. We must have a distinct mind, or soul, that gives us the capacity to make *real* choices—to love or hate, to help or hinder, to engage with God or turn away from him.[10]

"I like the grid you used to test that worldview," I told Dirckx. "Could you use that criteria to assess the view that we are just our brains and nothing more?"

"Okay, sure," she said. "First, is it internally consistent? I'd say no. You see, the view that you are your brain can't even be expressed without first presupposing an inner life. It's like saying, 'My first-person perspective is that there is no first-person perspective.' To deny consciousness is itself a conscious act.

"Second, does it make sense of the world? Well, it doesn't explain what it means to be a person. Brains don't write books. Brains don't have longing and desires. Brains don't make plans.

Brains don't experience disappointment. *People* do these things *using* their brain. There's a huge explanatory gap between the experience we have of this world and the view that you're just a bunch of cell voltages and neurotransmitters.

"And third, can it be lived? Truly, we don't live as though we're a walking pack of neurons. We live as though we each have a unique and valid perspective of the world. Besides, we want to treat others as though they're conscious beings. For example, we're outraged at human trafficking precisely because we believe that the people involved are not packs of neurons, but rather are conscious human beings who experience suffering.

"The idea that we're just our brains fails all three of these tests," she concluded. "We're not machines. Our brain and our mind are fundamentally distinct, though they work together. The brain offers a third-person perspective; it's the mind that provides a first-person experience."[11]

The Ultimate Purpose of Consciousness

All of which brought back us to dualism and the issue of the soul. In ancient Greece, shortly before he drank hemlock in 399 BC, Socrates expressed a kind of dualism when he said, "When I am dead, I shall not stay, but depart and be gone . . . to a state of heavenly happiness."[12]

It was Socrates's student Plato who became renowned for philosophizing about the soul, which was a concept, by the way, that had already been a commonsense belief among ordinary people, write philosophers Stewart Goetz and Charles Taliaferro. They credit Plato and his pupil Aristotle as being "the most important ones in shaping the history of the soul."[13]

Nevertheless, the Hebrew concept of the soul goes back even further, Dirckx said. "The Christian faith also has a lot to say about the soul. The soul is that which makes us more than matter, more than advanced primates, more than simply our brains. The soul is the impenetrable core of a person, given by God."[14]

"Here's a key question," I said. "Are the findings of modern neuroscience compatible with the idea that God exists?"

"Yes, absolutely," she replied. "It's important to point out that the recent discoveries of neuroscience are *entirely* compatible with the existence of God. In no way does *any* discovery in brain research rule out God. That would be a complete misunderstanding of the data."

"What happens," I asked, "if you start out with the worldview that God does exist?"

"Well, then everything begins to make more sense."

"But," I asked, "is it rational to adopt that worldview? Do you believe there are solid, independent reasons to believe that the God of Christianity is real?"[15]

"I do. That helped bring me to faith and has helped me grow deeper ever since."

"Some philosophers say because God is conscious, it explains why we are conscious. Is that persuasive to you?"

"Yes, it is," she replied. "Genesis 1:1 says, 'In the beginning, God . . .' Before there was anything physical, there was consciousness in the form of the Father, Son, and Holy Spirit—the Trinity. The unembodied mind of God, which has always existed, gave rise to everything else. The Bible also says that human beings were made in God's image.[16] Consequently, it makes sense to say that because God has a mind, we have a mind; because God thinks, we think; because God is conscious, so are we. That would explain a lot, wouldn't it?"

"To get there, though, a scientist would have to push beyond their materialistic worldview."

"Nobody is neutral," she said. "We can either shut off explanations or explore possibilities, but the best scientists always remain open to new ideas. I'm convinced the Christian worldview is well-founded. And if it is, then it explains where our value as human beings originates—we're made in God's likeness. It also explains why we sometimes long for more than this world. Human beings aren't temporary, but we are intended to live on for eternity.

"If the materialistic narrative is all there is, we can throw meaning, purpose, and significance out the window. We're a blip on the landscape. The cosmos is billions of years old and we appear in the last millisecond. We are utterly meaningless. People may try to achieve meaning through their accomplishments, but those ebb and flow.

"However, the existence of God provides a firm foundation for our meaning. We can't simply look to the age of the cosmos, nor is our value based on what we accomplish. It comes from God. We are created and loved by him. The reason all of us have a longing for eternity is that, indeed, we were made by God to live forever.

"God is relational, existing from eternity past as the Trinity, and so, like him, we are relational beings. This means we can interact personally with God. He is someone to be encountered. He is a first-person experience, not a third-person observation. We can go beyond facts *about* God and really *know* him."

With that, she stressed her conclusion: "Actually, that's the ultimate point of consciousness—*so that we can know God.*"

Made for Another World

For me, the case had been made. I am more than just my body. My soul is distinct from my brain. To paraphrase J. P. Moreland: I *am* a soul, and I *have* a body. It opens the door to the possibility that when my body breathes its last in this world, I can actually live on.[17]

After Dirckx and I exchanged final pleasantries, I thanked her for her time and expertise. Our transatlantic internet connection blinked off. Life goes on—as it will for a while. Hopefully, for a long, long time. But eventually, ultimately, what happens in the afterlife will be of supreme importance for each of us.

Dirckx closes her book this way: "If you are just your brain, then you were made only for this world, and the only mantra to live by is to live well and make the most out of life while you have it. Christianity says you are more than your brain—you are made for eternity. One way or another, there will be consciousness in eternity, either with Christ or apart from him. Live today with eternity in mind."[18]

The first building block in our case for the supernatural realm was in place: Death does not have to mean the end of human beings. Still, there was other evidence to consider. I lowered the screen on my laptop. Time to pursue more answers.

CHAPTER 2

ASTOUNDING
MIRACLES
TODAY

An infant was hospitalized with uncontrolled violent vomiting just days after his birth. He was diagnosed with *gastroparesis*, or stomach paralysis, an incurable condition that impairs the moving of food from the stomach into the small intestine.[1] Two feeding tubes were inserted—and they helped keep him alive for the next decade and a half.

"Living with feeding tubes was a struggle, to say the least," the patient said years later. "Growing up being an active child, it was difficult to get the hydration and nutrition necessary."

On November 6, 2011, when he was sixteen years old, the patient went with his family to a Pentecostal church. The speaker described how his own life had been spared when his intestines were severed in a serious accident. As the pastor recounted his healing, the teen reported feeling a "pulsating sensation" in his abdomen, "as if God was preparing me."

Afterward, the pastor laid hands on the teen and prayed for

Jesus to miraculously heal him. "During the prayer, I felt an electric shock that started from my right shoulder and traveling down through my stomach," the teen said. "That was the moment that I knew I had been touched by the Holy Spirit."

Indeed, doctors confirmed he had been spontaneously and totally healed. They removed the two feeding tubes, and the patient has been able to eat normally and has been completely healthy while free of any medications for more than a dozen years.

"Since I have been healed of my illness, I have had more energy than ever before, and have thoroughly enjoyed the new adventure of trying all different types of foods," he said. "I have entered into the medical field in search to help the sick and needy, and to give back the great care I received as a patient."

Three medical researchers investigated this healing and ended up publishing the case study—the first reported instantaneous healing of this otherwise hopeless condition—in a peer-reviewed medical journal.[2]

Are there miracles today that point toward a supernatural power and presence? Yes, there are. While there are cases of fraud, confirmation bias, the placebo effect, and medical mistakes, there are also authentic healings that are medically well-documented and give us confidence in the existence of a loving God.

The late philosopher Richard L. Purtill offered this definition of a genuine miracle: "A miracle is an event (1) brought about by the power of God that is (2) a temporary (3) exception (4) to the ordinary course of nature (5) for the purpose of showing that God has acted in history."[3]

Some of what we casually call miracles are probably no more than fortunate "coincidences." But when I see something that is absolutely extraordinary, has spiritual overtones, and is validated or corroborated by an independent source, that's when the "miracle bell" goes off in my mind—for example, a teen's spontaneous healing of an otherwise incurable condition as prayers for his recovery were being offered to Jesus.

In my quest to document the supernatural, I flew to Lexington, Kentucky, and then drove twenty minutes to the two-stoplight town of Wilmore—whose municipal water tower is topped with a giant white cross—to question the author of a landmark study on the miraculous.

INTERVIEW *with*

CRAIG S. KEENER, PHD

It all started as a footnote.

While working on his massive commentary on the Book of Acts (yes, *massive*—comprising nearly 4,500 pages over four volumes), Craig Keener began writing a footnote about the miracles that are found in this New Testament account of the early Christian movement.

He observed that some modern readers discount the historicity of Acts because they dismiss the possibility of miracles, believing that the uniform experience of humankind is that the miraculous simply doesn't occur. But are those claims reasonable?

Keener began researching. And writing. The footnote grew and grew. The more he discovered, the more convinced he became that miracles are more common than a lot of people think and better documented than many skeptics claim.

Two years later, his book *Miracles* was published—again, an exhaustive scholarly undertaking, so sweeping that it covers two volumes and a staggering 1,172 pages. Scholar Ben Witherington III gushed that it is "perhaps the best book ever written on miracles in this or any age." That comment prompted Professor Craig Blomberg to declare, "The 'perhaps' is unnecessarily cautious."

In the first twenty-five years after receiving his doctorate at Duke University, Keener authored twenty-one books. His award-winning, four-volume *Acts: An Exegetical Commentary* is some *three million* words in length, densely packed with scholarly insight written with a pastor's heart. "Keener is a scholar with gifts that come along once every century," said Gary Burge of Calvin Theological Seminary.

Keener's curriculum vitae is the size of a small book. His two-volume *Miracles: The Credibility of the New Testament Accounts*, which is 620,000 words in length, was followed up in 2021 with *Miracles Today: The Supernatural Work of God in the Modern World.*

Now a professor of biblical studies at Asbury Theological Seminary, Keener is married to Médine, who holds a doctorate and teaches French, and they have two adopted children from Africa. I sat with Keener in the basement office at his home, where his cluttered desk is surrounded by twenty-nine file cabinets packed with research.

He described himself as a former spiritual skeptic who "liked to make fun of Christians." But at age fifteen, after an encounter on a street corner with a few Christians who awkwardly tried to tell him about Jesus, he was alone in his bedroom and started arguing with himself. *This can't be right. But what if it is?*

"And then I sensed it," he said.

"Sensed what?" I asked.

"God's very presence—right there, right then, right in my room. I had been wanting empirical evidence, but instead God gave me something else—the evidence of his presence. So it wasn't apologetics that reached me; my brain had to catch up afterward. I was simply overwhelmed by the palpable presence of God. It was like Someone was right there in the room with me, and it wasn't something I was generating, because it wasn't what I was necessarily wanting."

At the time, Keener prayed, "God, those guys on the corner said Jesus died for me and rose again and that's what saves me. If that's what you're saying, I'll accept it. But I don't understand how that works. So if you want to save me, you're going to have to do it yourself."

"Did he?" I asked.

"All of a sudden, I felt something rushing through my body that I had never experienced before. I jumped up and said, *What was that?* I knew God had come into my life. At that moment, I was filled with wonder and worship."

Two days later, Keener sought out a minister, who led him in a formal prayer of repentance and faith. "And for the first time, I understood what my purpose was. What *the* purpose is."

"What is that?"

"Our purpose is found in God—to live for him, to serve him, to worship him." He paused, giving emphasis to one further thought: "Everything is to be built around Jesus."

A Proliferation of Miracles

A physician picked up Keener's two-volume book on miracles with one goal in mind—to further sharpen his highly skeptical worldview. "I was ready to 'see through' yet another theologian who didn't know much about psychosomatic illnesses, temporary improvements with no long-term follow up, incorrect medical diagnoses, conversion disorders, faked cures, self-deception, and the like," he said.

But he admitted, "I was blind-sided."

In Keener's book he encountered hundreds of case studies—reports of extraordinary healings and other incredible events backed up by eyewitnesses and, in many cases, clear-cut corroborating evidence.

"I read them with the critical eye of a skeptic having many years of medical practice under the belt," the doctor said. To his utter astonishment, he found many cases to be stunning. "They couldn't just be dismissed with a knowing answer and a cheery wave of the hand. *With respect to my world view, I had had the chair pulled out from underneath me.*"[1]

Another doctor agreed. In an endorsement for Keener's *Miracles Today*, Joseph Bergeron, author of *The Crucifixion of Jesus*, wrote, "As a physician, I found Keener's descriptions of physical healing credible and compelling."

Such is the persuasive power of the evidence for many miraculous claims. It's even enough to win over, well, Keener himself.

"When I was an atheist, of course I didn't believe the miraculous was possible," Keener told me. "But even after I came to faith, I still retained quite a bit of skepticism. As a Christian, I believed in miracles in principle, but I have to admit that I doubted the veracity of many claims I would hear."

Keener told me he "tried to maintain intellectual honesty" in his research and to "follow the clues wherever they led." And where did those clues take him?

"Everywhere I looked, I came across miracle claims that better fit a supernatural explanation than a naturalistic conclusion. Pretty soon, there was an avalanche of examples."

"Such as?"

"Such as . . . ," he repeated, eager to take up the challenge. Keener mentally scrolled through examples from the case studies he had encountered, and he began speaking in a tone that was at once urgent and earnest.

"Cataracts and goiters—instantly and visibly healed," he said. "Paralytics suddenly able to walk. Multiple sclerosis radically cured. Broken bones suddenly mended. Hearing for the deaf. Sight for the blind. Voices restored. Burns disappearing. Massive hemorrhaging stopped. Failing kidneys cured. Rheumatoid arthritis and osteoporosis—gone. Life given back to the dead, even after several hours.

"I have accounts from around the world—China, Mozambique, the Philippines, Nigeria, Argentina, Brazil, Cuba, Ecuador, Indonesia,

South Korea, and other countries. Multiple and independent eye-witnesses with reputations for integrity, including physicians. Names, dates, medical documentation in many cases. There's even a peer-reviewed scientific study confirming the healing of the deaf.

"And the timing is usually the most dramatic element—instantaneous results right after prayers to Jesus. Lots of cancer healings too—malignant brain tumors and reticulum-cell sarcoma, for example—but I didn't include most of those in the book, since I knew people would write them off as spontaneous remissions. Still, when the remission happens so quickly and completely after specific prayers, that's very suspicious."

"Your conclusion from all of this is—what?"

"That apart from some sort of divine intervention, many of these phenomena seem inexplicable."

"What are some of the strongest cases in terms of witnesses and corroborating evidence?" I asked.

Keener smiled and sat back in his chair. "How long do you have?" he asked.

A Deaf Child Hears

Keener started with the case of a nine-year-old British girl who was diagnosed with deafness in September 1982, apparently the result of a virus that severely damaged nerves in both of her ears.

"Her case is reported by Dr. R. F. R. Gardner, a well-credentialed physician," Keener said.[2] "What makes this case especially interesting is that there is medical confirmation before the healing and immediately afterward, which is unusual to have."

The child's medical record says she was diagnosed with "untreatable bilateral sensorineural deafness." Her attending physician told her parents there was no cure and nothing he could do to repair her damaged nerves. She was outfitted with hearing aids that did help her hear to some degree.

The girl didn't want to wear hearing aids for the rest of her life, so she started to pray that God would heal her. Her family and friends joined her. In fact, her mother said she felt a definite prompting to call out for God's help.

"I kept feeling God was telling me to pray specifically for healing," she said. "Passages kept coming out at me as I read: *If you have faith like children . . . If one among you is ill, lay hands . . . Ask and you shall receive . . . Your faith has made you whole.*"

On March 8, 1983, the girl went to the audiologist because one of her hearing aids had been damaged at school. After being examined and refitted, she was sent home.

The next evening, the child suddenly jumped out of her bed without her hearing aids and came bounding down the stairs. "Mummy, I can hear!" she exclaimed.

Her mother, astonished, tested to see if she could detect noises and words—and she could, even whispers. Her mother called the audiologist, who said, "I don't believe you. It is not possible. All right, if some miracle has happened, I am delighted. Have audiograms done."

The following day, she was tested again, and her audiogram and tympanogram came back fully normal. "I can give no explanation for this," said the audiologist. "I have never seen anything like it in my life."

The girl's doctor ruled out possible medical explanations. After repeated successful audiograms, the dumbfounded consultant's advice to her parents: "Forget she was ever deaf."

In the medical report, the child's ear, nose, and throat (ENT) surgeon used the word *inexplicable* to describe what happened. He wrote, "An audiogram did show her hearing in both ears to be totally and completely normal. I was completely unable to explain this phenomenon but naturally, like her parents, I was absolutely delighted . . . I can think of no rational explanation as to why her hearing returned to normal, there being a severe bilateral sensorineural loss."[3]

After documenting numerous case studies like this in his book, Gardner concludes, "A belief in the occurrence of cases of miraculous healing today is intellectually acceptable."[4]

He said people who are still skeptical should consider what evidence they would be prepared to accept. "If the answer proves to be, 'None,' then you had better face the fact that you have abandoned logical enquiry."[5]

"One of the Most Hopelessly Ill Patients"

Keener went on to discuss another case—one not in his book—for which there's compelling documentation. "I've personally interviewed Barbara, who was diagnosed at the Mayo Clinic with progressive multiple sclerosis," Keener said. "I've confirmed the facts with two physicians who treated her. There are numerous independent witnesses to her condition and years of medical records. In fact, two of her doctors were so astounded by her case that they have written about it in books."[6]

One of those physicians, Dr. Harold P. Adolph, a board-certified surgeon who performed twenty-five thousand operations in his career, declared: "Barbara was one of the most hopelessly ill patients I ever saw."

Another physician, Dr. Thomas Marshall, an internist for thirty years until his retirement, described Barbara as a budding gymnast in high school until symptoms began appearing. She would trip, bump into walls, and struggle to grasp the rings in gym.

Eventually, after her condition worsened, the diagnosis of progressive multiple sclerosis was confirmed through spinal taps and other diagnostic tests. Doctors at the Mayo Clinic thoroughly examined her and agreed with the dire conclusion. "The prognosis was not good," Marshall said.

Over the next sixteen years, her condition continued to deteriorate. She spent months in hospitals, often for pneumonia after being unable to breathe. One diaphragm was paralyzed, rendering a lung nonfunctional; the other lung operated at less than 50 percent. A tracheostomy tube was inserted into her neck, with oxygen pumped from canisters in her garage.

She lost control of her urination and bowels; a catheter was inserted into her bladder, and an ileostomy was performed, with a bag attached for her bodily waste. She went legally blind, becoming unable to read and only capable of seeing objects as gray shadows. A feeding tube was inserted into her stomach.

"Her abdomen was swollen grotesquely because the muscles of her intestine did not work," Adolph said.

"She now needed continuous oxygen, and her muscles and joints were becoming contracted and deformed because she could not move or exercise them," Marshall said. "Mayo [Clinic] was her last hope, but they had no recommendations to help stop this progressive wasting disease except to pray for a miracle."

By 1981, she hadn't been able to walk for seven years. She was confined to bed, her body twisted like a pretzel into a fetal position. Her hands were permanently flexed to the point that her fingers nearly touched her wrists. Her feet were locked in a downward position.

Marshall explained to her family that it was just a matter of time before she would die. They agreed not to do any heroics, including CPR or further hospitalization, to keep her alive; this would only prolong the inevitable.

Barbara entered hospice care in her home, with a life expectancy of less than six months.

"This Is Medically Impossible"

One day someone called in Barbara's story to the radio station of the Moody Bible Institute in Chicago. A request was broadcast for listeners to pray fervently for her. Some 450 Christians wrote letters to her church saying they were lifting up Barbara in prayer.

On Pentecost Sunday, 1981, her aunt came over to read her some of the letters in which people offered prayers for her healing. Two girlfriends joined them. Suddenly, during a lull in the conversation, Barbara heard a man's voice speak from behind her—even though there was nobody else in the room.

"The words were clear and articulate and spoken with great authority, but also with great compassion," Marshall wrote.

Said the voice, "My child, get up and walk!"

Seeing that Barbara had become agitated, one of her friends plugged the hole in her neck so she could speak. "I don't know what you're going to think about this," Barbara told them, "but God just told me to get up and walk. I know he really did! Run and get my family. I want them here with us!"

Her friends ran out and yelled for her family. "Come quick; come quick!"

Marshall described what happened next: "Barb felt compelled to do immediately what she was divinely instructed, so she literally jumped out of bed and removed her oxygen. She was standing on legs that had not supported her for years. Her vision was back, and she was no longer short of breath, even without her oxygen. Her contractions were gone, and she could move her feet and hands freely."

Her mother ran into the room and dropped to her knees, feeling Barbara's calves. "You have muscles again!" she exclaimed. Her father came in, hugged her, "and whisked her off for a waltz around the family room," Marshall said.

Everyone moved to the living room to offer a tearful prayer of thanksgiving—although Barbara found it hard to sit still. That evening, there was a worship service at Wheaton Wesleyan Church, where Barbara's family attended. Most of the congregation knew about Barbara's grave condition.

During the service, when the pastor asked if anyone had any announcements, Barbara stepped into the center aisle and casually strolled toward the front, her heart pounding.

"A cacophony of whispers came from all parts of the church," Marshall said. "People started clapping, and then, as if led by a divine conductor, the entire congregation began to sing, 'Amazing grace! How sweet the sound that saved a wretch like me! I once was lost, but now am found; was blind, but now I see!'"

The next day, Barbara came to Marshall's office for an examination. Seeing her in the hallway, walking toward him, "I thought I was seeing an apparition!" he recalled. "No one had ever seen anything like this before."

He told Barbara, "This is medically impossible. But you are now free to go out and live your life."

A chest X-ray that afternoon showed her lungs were already "perfectly normal," with the collapsed lung completely expanded. "The intestine that had been vented to the abdominal wall was reconnected normally," Adolph said. "She was eventually restored to complete health."

Barbara has now lived for thirty-five years with no recurrence of her illness. "She subsequently married a minister and feels her calling in life is to serve others," Marshall said.

Both physicians marvel at her extraordinary recovery. "I have never witnessed anything like this before or since and considered it a rare privilege to observe the hand of God performing a true miracle," Marshall wrote.

Said Adolph, "Both Barbara and I knew who had healed her."

I was so blown away by Barbara's story that I later traveled to Virginia, where she worked in real estate and her husband pastored a Wesleyan church, to meet with her personally. She enthusiastically recounted her story to me—and it perfectly matched Keener's description.

My mind searched fruitlessly for naturalistic explanations.

Could her recovery be written off as some sort of natural remission? If so, why would it suddenly occur after so many years right when hundreds of people were praying for her? Remissions typically take place over time instead of being instantaneous. Certainly, the placebo effect, or misdiagnosis, or fraud, or coincidence, or medical mistakes couldn't account for what happened.

Besides, what about the mysterious voice telling her to get up and walk? Or the immediate muscle tone in her atrophied legs? Or the instant and simultaneous healing of her eyesight, lungs, and so on? With so many witnesses of unquestioned integrity and expertise, plus a proliferation of corroborating documentation, her case seemed to meet even the high evidential bar typically set by skeptics.

Absent a presupposition against the miraculous, this did seem to be a clear and compelling example of divine intervention. And Keener was far from finished. He began to rattle off a series of other amazing stories he had documented in his book.

The Ankle That Was Never Broken

"In March 2006, on a trip to Missouri, Carl was checking the oil in his car when he stepped down and felt a sharp crack," Keener said. "He fainted from the pain, which was the worst he had ever endured. I have a copy of the radiology report of his X-rays, confirming the fracture. The orthopedist ordered him to stay overnight. During that night, though, Carl experienced a voice from the Lord."

"What did the voice say?" I asked.

"That the ankle was not broken."

I cocked my head. "Despite the X-rays?"

"That's right. The next day the doctor casted his leg and warned he would eventually need months of physical therapy. Back in Michigan, his family doctor ordered more X-rays, and this time the results were radically different."

"How so?"

"There were no breaks or even tissue damage where a break had been. Again, I have the radiology report that says there's no fracture. In fact, the doctor told him, 'You never had a broken ankle.'"

"But," I interjected, "what about the Missouri X-rays?"

Keener calmly continued the narrative. "The doctor looked again at those Missouri X-rays and said, 'Now, *that's* a broken ankle.' But at this point, there was no sign of a break. He removed Carl's cast and sent him home. Carl never had further problems or needed any therapy."

"What do you make of all that?" I asked.

"Personally, I don't see how this could have occurred naturally," Keener said. "Would a sixty-two-year-old man's bone heal so quickly that no sign of a fracture would remain at all? It doesn't seem likely. And, of course, that wouldn't explain how God told him in advance what would happen."

"Can Jesus Heal Me?"

Next Keener shared the story of Ed Wilkinson, whose education in neuropsychology convinced him that people who rely on faith to cure their ills are merely using religion as a neurosis to avoid dealing with reality.

"Then, in November 1984, his eight-year-old son, Brad, was diagnosed with two holes in his heart. The condition also impaired his lungs. Surgery was scheduled," Keener recounted. "As the surgery got closer, Brad started giving away his toys, not expecting he would survive. One day he asked his dad, 'Am I going to die?'"

"That's quite a question, given the circumstances," I said. "Was his father honest with him?"

"He said not everyone who has heart surgery dies, but it can happen. Then his son asked, 'Can Jesus heal me?'"

"Now, *that's* quite a question," I said.

"His father was aware of how often faith is abused, so he said, 'I'll get back to you on that.'"

"And did he?"

"Yes, a few days later, after some anguished prayers and reading Philippians 4:13,[7] Ed told him that God does heal, but whether or not he would in Brad's case, they still had hope of eternal life in Jesus. After that, a visiting pastor asked Brad, 'Do you believe that Jesus can heal you?' Brad said yes, and the minister prayed for him."[8]

Before surgery at the University of Missouri hospital in Columbia, Missouri, tests confirmed nothing had changed with Brad's condition. The following morning, Brad was taken in for his operation, which was expected to last four hours. But after an hour, the surgeon summoned Ed and showed him two films.

The first film, taken the day before, showed blood leaking from one heart chamber to another. The second film, taken just as surgery started, showed a wall of some sort where the leak had been. The surgeon said there was nothing wrong with Brad's heart, even though the holes were clearly visible the day before. The lungs were also now normal.

"I have not seen this very often," the surgeon said. He explained that a spontaneous closure rarely happens in infants, but it was not supposed to occur in an eight-year-old. "You can count this as a miracle," he said.

The hospital risk manager said firmly, "You can see from the films that this was *not* a misdiagnosis." Added the pulmonologist, "Somebody somewhere must have been praying."

Later, an insurance agent called Ed to complain about the forms he had submitted. "What's a spontaneous closure?" the agent asked.

Replied Ed, "A miracle."

Today, said Keener, Brad is in his thirties with a business and children of his own. He has never had any heart problems since his healing.

A Death, a Prayer, a New Life

Keener continued with the case of Jeff Markin, a fifty-three-year-old auto mechanic who walked into the emergency room at Palm Beach Gardens Hospital in Florida and collapsed from a heart attack on October 20, 2006. For forty minutes, emergency room personnel frantically labored to revive him, shocking him seven times with a defibrillator, but he remained flatlined.

Finally, the supervising cardiologist, Chauncey Crandall, a well-respected, Yale-educated doctor and medical school professor who specialized in complex heart cases, was brought in to examine the body. Markin's face, toes, and fingers had already turned black from the lack of oxygen. His pupils were dilated and fixed. There was no point in trying to resuscitate him. At 8:05 p.m., he was declared dead.

Crandall filled out the final report and turned to leave. But he quickly felt an extraordinary compulsion. "I sensed God was telling me to turn around and pray for the patient," he said later. This seemed foolish, so he tried to ignore it, only to receive a second—and even stronger—divine prompting.

A nurse was already disconnecting the intravenous fluids and sponging the body so it could be taken to the morgue. But Crandall began praying over the corpse: "Father God, I cry out for the soul of this man. If he does not know you as his Lord and Savior, please raise him from the dead right now in Jesus' name."

Crandall told the emergency room doctor to use the paddle to shock the corpse one more time. Seeing nothing to gain, the doctor protested. "I've shocked him again and again. He's dead." But then he complied out of respect for his colleague.

Instantly, the monitor jumped from flatline to a normal heartbeat of about seventy-five beats per minute with a healthy rhythm. "In my more than twenty years as a cardiologist, I have never seen a heartbeat restored so completely and suddenly," Crandall said.

Markin immediately began breathing without any assistance,

and the blackness receded from his face, toes, and fingers. The nurse panicked because she feared the patient would be permanently disabled from oxygen deprivation, yet he never displayed any signs of brain damage.[9]

Keener shook his head in wonder. "As you can imagine, this case got a lot of attention in the media," he said. "One medical consultant for a national news program suggested that perhaps Markin's heart had not stopped completely but had gone into a very subtle rhythm for those forty minutes."

"What was Crandall's response?" I asked.

"That he was grasping at straws. The resuscitation couldn't have happened naturally. An electrical shock administered in those circumstances would not normally accomplish anything," Keener said. "The unanimous verdict of those actually present was that Markin was deceased, and that includes Crandall, who is a nationally recognized cardiologist with many years of experience."

Indeed, in light of the circumstances, skeptical explanations seem hollow and forced—and, again, they can't account for the two mysterious urges that prompted Crandall to turn in his tracks and pray for a victim who had already been declared dead. Absent those, Jeff Markin would be in his grave today.

"The critics have to strain at the bounds of plausibility in order to keep their anti-supernatural thesis intact," Keener said.

For me, Acts 26:8 sprang to mind: "Why should any of you consider it incredible that God raises the dead?"

"I Know; It's a Miracle"

I knew Keener could go on for hours talking about the cases he unearthed in his admittedly limited survey of miraculous claims. For example, he has accumulated 350 reports just of people who have been healed of blindness. Here are several cases taken at random from his book:

- A welder named David Dominong suffered extensive third- and fourth-degree burns when he was electrocuted in October 2002. Hospitalized for more than five weeks, he was told it could be five years until he would be able to walk again. He was confined to a wheelchair and considering amputation when he received prayer and was promptly able to walk and run without assistance.

- Dr. Alex Abraham testified to the case of Kuldeep Singh, who had intractable epilepsy to the point where he would lose consciousness during frequent seizures. Ever since Pastor Jarnail Singh prayed that God would heal him fifteen years ago, he has had no more seizures or treatment. Abraham, a neurologist, said the abrupt, permanent, and complete healing of epilepsy this severe is highly unusual.

- Matthew Dawson was hospitalized in Australia with confirmed meningitis in April 2007. He was told he would have to remain under hospital care for weeks or months. But he was abruptly healed at the exact moment his father, on another continent, offered prayers for him.

- Mirtha Venero Boza, a medical doctor in Cuba, reports that her baby granddaughter's hand was severely burned by a hot iron, resulting in swelling and skin peeling off. Less than half an hour after prayer, however, the hand was completely healed without medical intervention, as if it had never been burned.

- Cambridge University professor John Polkinghorne, one of the world's foremost scholars on the intersection of science and faith, provides the account of a woman whose left leg was paralyzed in an injury. Doctors gave up trying to treat her, saying she would be an invalid for life. In 1980, she reluctantly agreed to prayer from an Anglican priest. Though she had no expectation of healing, she had a vision in which she was commanded to rise and walk. Said Polkinghorne, who has doctorates in both science and theology, "From that moment, she was able to walk, jump, and bend down, completely without pain."

- Physician John White reports that a woman with a confirmed diagnosis of tuberculosis of the cervical spine had been unable to walk, but she was instantaneously healed after prayer. He said her doctor "was bewildered to find there was no evidence of disease in her body." Said Keener, "Her illness was certain, her cure permanent, and the witness virtually incontrovertible." Not only was White the doctor who prayed for her, but he later married her.

- Joy Wahnefried, a student at Taylor University in Indiana, suffered from vertical heterophoria, where one eye viewed images at a higher level than the other. This triggered debilitating migraines that could last up to a week. A professor and students prayed for her during three consecutive prayer meetings, and Joy was suddenly healed—her eyesight now 20/20 and her incurable medical condition gone. Her eye doctor said she "can't explain it" and has never seen anything like it in four thousand patients. Keener, who has copies of her before-and-after medical reports, confirmed that she no longer even needs corrective lenses.

- A grapefruit-sized flesh-eating ulcer, with the wound going to the bone, was boring through the calf muscle of a seventy-year-old Florida man. After treatments failed, doctors declared the wound incurable and amputation was scheduled. However, one physician laid his hands on the oozing wound and prayed for healing. Recovery began immediately; within four days, the ulcer was melting away and new skin forming. By the following week, the leg was restored to normal. The doctor's opinion: "It can't happen on its own. Impossible." The patient's wife summed it up: "God's real. God healed his leg."[10]

- University professor Robert Larmer reports that Mary Ellen Fitch was hospitalized with hepatitis B. She was turning yellow; her abdomen bulged with her swollen liver. She was told she would remain in the hospital for months. After a week, though, she had a deep experience with God and committed her condition to him. The next morning, her blood tests were normal. Bewildered doctors repeatedly tested her, with the same results. Years have now passed, and she remains healed.[11]
- The director of a clinic for voice and swallowing disorders reports the case of a fifty-two-year-old man who suffered a severe brain stem stroke in the region of the medulla. Strokes in this location irreversibly damage the ability to swallow. After prayer, though, the man regained his ability to eat and swallow normally. The patient told the startled experts, "I know; it's a miracle." This was the only such recovery the clinic's director had seen in fifteen years.

God Is Still in the Miracle Business

Pretty soon, Keener and I began hearing some noises coming from upstairs. "Sounds like Médine has come home from teaching her French class," Keener said. "I'd like for you to meet her."

"Absolutely, I'd love to meet her. *Je voudrais utiliser mon français rudimentaire en parlant avec elle,*"[12] I replied, my accent awkward as usual. "But before we go, let me ask you something else. You set out to accomplish two things with your book. Did you achieve what you had hoped?"

"My first goal involved the New Testament," he replied. "I wanted to show that it's not necessary to dismiss these writings as legendary, fanciful, or inaccurate, just because they report miracles. Today's world is full of firsthand claims from people who say they have witnessed miracles, and there's no reason to suppose the ancient world was any different. If today's accounts can stem from eyewitnesses and potentially report what really happened, then the same is true of the Gospels."

Clearly, that goal had been achieved.

"And what was your second goal?" I asked.

"To show that it's rational to consider the possibility of supernatural causation for many of these miracle claims."

"Well, Professor, that's very academic sounding," I said with a grin.

"Okay, let me rephrase it," he said, clearing his throat. "It looks like God is still in the miracle business."

He stopped for a moment to let that simple declarative sentence hang in the air. Then he added, "At least, that's an entirely reasonable hypothesis from the evidence. The best explanation for what occurred is often supernatural, not natural."

"What are some of the implications of this?" I asked.

"Anti-supernaturalism has reigned as an inflexible Western academic premise for far too long. In light of the millions of people around the globe who say they've experienced the miraculous, it's time to take these claims seriously. Let's investigate them and follow the evidence wherever it leads. If even a small fraction proves to be genuine, we have to consider whether God is still divinely intervening in his creation."

Interview with Candy Gunther Brown, PhD

My conversation with Craig Keener left me wondering if scientific experiments can tell us anything about the supernatural healing impact of prayer. So from Keener's house, I drove two hundred miles north to meet with Candy Gunther Brown, who earned her doctorate at Harvard University and is a professor of religious studies at sprawling Indiana University.

Her books include *Testing Prayer: Science and Healing*, published by Harvard University Press, and *The Healing Gods: Complementary and Alternative Medicine in Christian America*, published by Oxford University Press.

I asked Brown for her opinion of a 2006 study that showed intercessory prayer having no impact—or even a slightly harmful effect—on recovering cardiac patients. She quickly discredited those results by pointing out that the only prayers offered by non-Catholics in the study came from members of a cult that doesn't believe in miracles, doesn't believe in a personal God outside of us who intervenes in people's lives, and doesn't even believe it's appropriate to ask for supernatural help.

"In the end, does this study tell us *anything* that's helpful?" I asked.

"Well," she said, "it is instructive on how *not* to conduct a study of Christian prayer."

However, she said there have been other "gold standard" studies that reached the opposite conclusion—that the group receiving prayer had *better* outcomes.

"One of the first widely publicized studies was by Dr. Randolph Byrd, published in 1988 in the peer-reviewed *Southern Medical Journal*," she said. "It was a prospective, randomized, double-blinded, controlled study of four hundred subjects."

She explained that born-again Christians, both Catholics and Protestants, were given the patient's first name, condition, and diagnosis. They were instructed to pray to the Judeo-Christian God "for a rapid recovery and for prevention of complications and death, in addition to other areas of prayer they believed to be beneficial to patients."

"What were the results?"

"Patients in the prayer group had less congestive heart failure, fewer cardiac arrests, fewer episodes of pneumonia, were less often intubated and ventilated, and needed less diuretic and antibiotic therapy," she said.

"Do you think this study was scientifically sound?"

"I believe it was. Of course, in any study like this you can't control for such things as people praying for themselves or other people praying for them outside the study," she said.

A decade or so later, a replication study by Dr. William S. Harris and colleagues was published in the *Archives of Internal Medicine*. "This was a 'gold standard' study of the effects of intercessory prayer on nearly a thousand consecutively admitted coronary patients. Half received prayer; the other half didn't. And again, the group that received prayer had better outcomes than the control group."

However, Brown cautioned that these studies don't account for the fact that often healings take place in clusters in geographic areas where the gospel is just breaking in; that some people seem to have a special gift in healing; and typically there was a physical distance between the intercessor and the prayer recipient in the studies.

"But when Pentecostals actually pray for healing, they generally get up close to someone they know, often come into physical contact with them, and empathize with their sufferings," she said. "It's what I call *proximal intercessory prayer*."

This fits the pattern of Jesus, who often touched those he was about to heal.[13] What's more, the Bible says that the ill should be anointed with oil, which also involves proximity and touching.[14]

"Have any studies looked at the effects of this kind of up-close-and-personal prayer?" I asked.

"Dale Matthews and his team did a prospective, controlled study of the effects of intercessory prayer on patients with rheumatoid arthritis, published in the *Southern Medical Journal* in 2000," she said. "They found no effects for distant intercessory prayer; however, they did find that patients experienced statistically significant improvement with direct-contact prayers, compared with patients who only received medical treatment."

"How was the study set up?" I asked.

"Over a three-day period, subjects received six hours of

in-person prayer, plus another six hours of group instruction on the theology of healing prayer," she said. "This particular study didn't clarify whether improvements resulted from the prayer itself, or from attention, touch, social support, counseling, and exchanges of forgiveness that were offered—all of which have been shown to have therapeutic effects."

"That does muddy the waters," I commented.

"Yes. Unfortunately, rheumatoid arthritis is relatively susceptible to psychosomatic improvements."

"So what's the answer?" I asked.

"I conducted a study that takes these factors into consideration," she replied.

"And the results?" I asked.

"They were fascinating."

Miracles in Mozambique

To go to a place that is reporting clusters of healing, Brown and her team flew to Mozambique, a desperately poor nation on the southeast coast of Africa. To connect with a ministry that reports a high success rate with healing, Brown's team worked with Heidi and Rolland Baker, charismatic missionaries serving in Mozambique for more than twenty years. They have described how healing miracles have accompanied the spread of the gospel there.

Brown focused on the healing of the blind and deaf (or those with severe vision or hearing problems), which aren't particularly susceptible to psychosomatic healings. Immediately before prayer, her team used standard tests and technical equipment to determine the person's level of hearing or vision. After the prayers were concluded, the patient was promptly tested again.

"The length of the prayer varied, from one minute to five or ten minutes usually, but it always involved touching," she said. "For instance, there was a woman who couldn't see a hand in front of her face at a foot away. Heidi Baker put her arms around her, she smiled at her, she hugged her, she cried, and she prayed for one minute—and afterward, the woman was able to read."

In all there were twenty-four subjects who received prayer. The results? "We saw improvement in almost every single subject we tested. Some of the results were quite dramatic," she said. "We had two subjects whose hearing thresholds were reduced by more than 50 decibels, which is quite a large reduction. The average improvement in visual acuity was more than tenfold."

Brown told me about Martine, an elderly blind and deaf woman in the Namuno village. Before prayer, she couldn't hear a jackhammer next to her. After prayer, she was able to make out conversations.

After a second prayer, Martine's eyesight improved from 20/400 to 20/80 on the vision chart. This would mean she was legally blind initially, but after prayer was able to see objects from twenty feet away in the same way a person with normal vision can see that object from eighty feet away.[15]

"What was going on during the prayers?" I asked. "What did people feel?"

"It was diverse," Brown said, "but often the recipients reported feeling heat, cold, or even tingling or itching."

To me, Brown's methodology seemed uncannily simple but intuitively valid. The only thing that changed between the pre-prayer and post-prayer tests was the fact that someone prayed to Jesus for the person to get better. And virtually everyone did improve to one degree or the other, often astoundingly so.

"Was this a scientifically sound study?" I asked.

"It was published in a peer-reviewed *Southern Medical Journal*. It was prospectively done. It was rigorous. It was a within-subjects design—a standard approach to psychophysical studies published in the flagship *Science* magazine and elsewhere. We had the proper equipment. We had a trained research team. We had statistically significant results. And the validity of the study was evaluated as being scientifically sound by the journal that published it."

I raised my pen. "However," I pointed out, "the number of tested people was pretty small."

"There's a misconception that if you've got a small sample, it's not statistically significant. Actually, that's not true," she replied. "With a smaller sample, the effects have to be larger and more consistent in order to achieve statistical significance. And our effects were."

Brown and her team then did a replication study in Brazil to check if they would get similar results—and they did. Again, sight and hearing were improved after hands-on prayer was offered in Jesus' name.

In Sao Paulo, for example, a forty-eight-year-old woman named Julia could not see details on faces or read without strong glasses. "After prayer, she could do both," Brown said. "A thirty-eight-year-old woman in Uberlândia could not count fingers from nine feet away. When she opened her eyes after prayer, she could read the name tag of the intercessor."

"What's your conclusion?" I asked.

"Our study shows that *something* is going on with Pentecostal and charismatic proximal intercessory prayer," she replied. "This is more than just wishful thinking. It's not fakery; it's not fraud. It's not some televangelist trying to get widows to send in their money. It's not a highly charged atmosphere that plays on people's emotions. *Something* is going on, and it surely warrants further investigation."

I agreed—clearly, *something* was going on with her studies, as well as with Craig Keener's own extensive research. I think it's rational to call it supernatural.

CHAPTER 3

LIFE-CHANGING
SPIRITUAL
ENCOUNTERS

*There is a sense in which Christians can
legitimately claim to know the reality of God
because of their experiences of God.*

Philosopher Harold A. Netland,

Religious Experience and the Knowledge of God

The daredevil motorcyclist Evel Knievel, a womanizer and drunk-ard who once went to prison for beating up a business partner with a baseball bat, was on the beach in Florida when he felt God "speak" to him on the inside: "Robert, I've saved you more times than you'll ever know. Now I need you to come to me through my Son Jesus."

Knievel was stunned. He sought out a book on the historical evidence for Jesus and ended up experiencing a radical conversion to

Christ. When he told his story at his baptism, seven hundred people responded by receiving Jesus as their forgiver and leader. Knievel died about a year later, and at his request his tombstone is etched with the words "Believe in Jesus Christ."[1]

Bob Passantino was a spiritual skeptic who loved to embarrass Christians by asking tough questions about faith. Then he met a seminary student who finally began to give him some good answers.

One day, Bob and his friend Bruce were in a car, discussing their concerns about the dangerous direction of the world and how they could be prepared for what might happen next. Suddenly, Bob felt the unmistakable presence of the Holy Spirit fill the vehicle. Without sound or words, he clearly heard Jesus say to him, "None of that matters. You are putting your trust in yourselves instead of in me. All that matters is that I love you. Follow me. . . . Follow me. . . . Follow me."

Shocked, Bob said to Bruce, "None of this matters! Jesus is real!" To Bob's surprise, Bruce blurted out, "Don't you feel the Holy Spirit? We have to follow Jesus! He's calling us!" Bob ended up becoming an accomplished Christian apologist who would spend the rest of his life helping others who were on the same search for truth.[2]

Nabeel Qureshi was a devout Muslim who began to investigate Christianity after getting into debates with a Christian friend. At one point, Nabeel asked God for a clear vision—and then he had a vivid and chilling dream of a banquet where he was being excluded because he had rejected the invitation.

When he asked his friend about the dream, he was told it was an uncanny depiction of what Jesus described in the gospel of Luke[3]—even though Nabeel had never opened a Bible.

"I'm a man of science. A medical doctor. I deal with flesh and bones, with evidence and facts and logic. But *this*," he said to me, searching for the right words, "this was the exact vision I needed. It was a miracle. A miracle that opened the door for me."

Ultimately, Nabeel became a renowned Christian speaker who wrote a bestselling book about his story and traveled the world to tell people about his Savior until his untimely death in 2017.[4]

For some people, as with my friends Evel, Bob, and Nabeel, it was a profound spiritual experience that dramatically opened their eyes to the reality of the supernatural realm.

For many others, it's their experience with God *after* their conversion—a profound sense of community with him and the transformation that he brought into their lives—that confirms the existence of a supernatural reality.

Religious experiences vary widely, from dramatic visions to more subtle and inexplicable encounters that change lives. For example, the wildly successful British music star Mathangi "Maya" Arulpragasam, popularly known as M. I. A., named by *Esquire* as one of the seventy-five most influential people of the twenty-first century, was "100 percent comfortable with Hinduism" and thought that Jesus was just "a silly story."

Then in 2016, she was in an unspecified "place of need" when she had a supernatural vision of Jesus. "I wasn't asleep. It wasn't a dream. It wasn't a hallucination," she said. "My first reaction was to laugh. I couldn't believe what was happening. I always thought he was made up."

The vision was brief. No words were exchanged. Yet "within a split second" she went from disbelief to belief in Christianity. "In my time of need, the God who turned up to save me was not Shiva; it was Jesus," she said. "That is the truth. . . . This experience *happened*."[5]

The prominent Welsh philosopher Henry H. Price, a professor of logic at Oxford University who was elected to the prestigious British Academy, told friends about what he called "an experience of the sense of presence" and asked them to keep it confidential until after his death, which they did. The incident occurred on a quiet Sunday in 1965 when Price was in his drawing room in England.

"In a gentle and gradual way it began to dawn on him that there was someone else in the room, located fairly precisely about two yards away to his right front," recalled his friend.[6] "There was nothing seen or heard. . . . They proceeded to have a conversation, though one conducted entirely by exchange of thoughts, about God's love for human beings, including himself. When God is said to love us this is not just some conventionally pious phrase but is to be taken literally. When we love someone we are fond of that person, or he is dear to us. In the same way, Henry was told, God was fond of him and he was dear to God."

Price's strong impression was that the invisible visitor "seemed to be very good and very wise, fully of sympathetic understanding, and most kindly disposed towards him. He did not know how long the 'conversation' lasted, guessing in retrospect about a quarter of an hour. . . . After a while he became aware that the visitor was no longer there."

The effects of the encounter "lasted for the whole of that day which, Henry said, was certainly the happiest day of his life. But it was something different from ordinary everyday happiness, more tranquil and also more profound, going down to the roots of his personality."

In the end, he concluded that *joy* was the best word for it.[7]

Contact with the Supernatural

Said influential Christian philosopher Dallas Willard, "Many might be surprised to discover what a high percentage of serious Christians—and even non-Christians—can tell of specific experiences in which they are sure God spoke to them."[8]

Cambridge-educated anthropologist Tanya Marie Luhrmann researched the practices of evangelical and charismatic Christians for her book *When God Talks Back*. "Many Americans not only believe in God in some general way but experience God directly and report repeated contact with the supernatural," she wrote. "These evangelicals have sought out and cultivated concrete experiences of God's realness."[9]

According to a study, she said, nearly one-quarter of all Americans embrace a Christian spirituality "in which congregants experience God immediately, directly, and personally."[10]

Philosopher Harold Netland, author of *Religious Experience and the Knowledge of God*, said, "Christians routinely speak of God's presence in their lives, God 'speaking' to them or guiding them, God convicting them of something sinful, God's special peace in the midst of trials, etc., and all of this involves experience."[11]

He added that "a testimony—a personal account of how one's conversion to Jesus Christ through the supernatural work of the Holy Spirit results in a dramatically changed life—gives voice to an especially important kind of experience."[12]

Christians even talk about experiencing God more deeply in the midst of their struggles. "The cancer battle has been tough," wrote Nanci Alcorn, wife of bestselling author Randy Alcorn, during a four-year fight with the disease that eventually took her life. "However, my time with [God] has been epic! He has met me in ways I never knew were possible. I have *experienced* His sovereignty, mercy, and steadfast love in tangible ways. I now trust Him at a level I never knew I could."[13]

Philosopher Douglas Groothuis is among the scholars who believe that certain religious experiences can provide "considerable evidence for the existence of a personal and relational being."[14] To check into this phenomenon further, I flew to Colorado, where Groothuis was a professor of philosophy, and drove to his office at Denver Seminary for an in-depth interview.

INTERVIEW *with*

DOUGLAS GROOTHUIS, PHD

The first time I ever interviewed Doug Groothuis (pronounced GRŌT'hice) was under difficult circumstances. His wife, Rebecca, was dying of a brain condition, and Groothuis spoke candidly with me about their emotional anguish.[1] Back then, Groothuis appeared haggard, his beard unruly and his brown hair seemingly combed with his fingers. His wife ended up dying shortly after our time together.[2]

Now, several years later, Groothuis was more animated and upbeat, leaner and clean-shaven and more dapper in attire. He had married a high school acquaintance named Kathleen, and today, in his mid-sixties, he seemed more engaged with his work than ever.

Groothuis became a serious Christian at age nineteen after forays into Eastern mysticism and atheism. He went on to earn his doctorate in philosophy at the University of Oregon. Since then he has taught at a secular college, debated atheists, written a slew of scholarly and popular articles, and authored nineteen books. My favorite is the second edition of his hefty *Christian Apologetics: A Comprehensive Case for Biblical Faith.*

Groothuis greeted me and cleared a space at a small table in his book-choked office. After updating each other on our personal lives, we began by talking about what makes experiences with God possible.

"Woe to Me! I Am Ruined!"

"Christian theology says people are rational creatures who are made in the image of God,"[3] I began as I opened my notebook. "Is that what makes experiences with God possible and natural?"

"Yes," said Groothuis. "As Francis Schaeffer pointed out, God is infinite and personal, and we are finite and personal.[4] Because of that, we have the potential of connecting on a personal, relational level. Being made in God's image opens the door to communion with him. We have affinity despite the fractures in our relationship caused by our sin. So we have the possibility of obtaining knowledge about God through general revelation, or nature; special revelation, or the Scriptures; but also through having personal experiences with the God who conceived us and created us."

"Can these experiences provide evidence that God exists?"

"Absolutely, yes, they can be part of a cumulative case for God. The key question is whether an experience is veridical."

"Veridical?" I asked. "What do you mean?"

"An experience is veridical if it conveys truth and is not deceptive. For example, a mirage of a pool of water that a thirsty person imagines in the desert isn't veridical. It's a false belief. A hallucinatory fantasy induced by drugs isn't veridical. But if an experience with God is authentic—if it's based on reality and conveys truth— then it's veridical."

I jotted the word in my notes as a reminder to ask Groothuis later about how an experience can be evaluated to make sure it's authentic.

"Let's talk about these experiences," I went on. "We tend to hear about the dramatic ones, but they really run the gamut, don't they?"

Groothuis leaned back. "Oh, there's so much," he said. "There are cases, for example, where people encounter a majestic, awe-inspiring, and compelling divine being."

"That's what the Old Testament prophet Isaiah wrote about, right?"

"Yes, he sees the Lord exalted, seated on a throne, with the train of his robe filling the temple, with angels calling out, 'Holy, holy, holy, is the LORD Almighty; the whole earth is full of his glory!' Isaiah falls on his face and declares, 'Woe to me! I am ruined! For I am a man of unclean lips and I live among a people of unclean lips, and my eyes have seen the King, the LORD Almighty.'"[5]

"Are there any theological reasons why this kind of experience couldn't continue after biblical days?"

"No, and we see contemporary accounts of amazing experiences with God all around the world. For example, there are Jesus dreams occurring among Muslims in closed cultures—this is a well-documented phenomenon. We see God breaking into the lives of people in a dramatic manner—for example, Evel Knievel feeling God speaking to him in a manner that changed his entire life. And we see more subtle experiences of God. Christians talk all the time about how God encourages, convicts, or guides them, or he gives them courage or peace, or he otherwise manifests himself in their lives. In fact, Christians undergo what's called a 'transformational experience.'"

"You mean their moment of conversion?"

"Actually, I'm thinking of the personal transformation that accompanies Christian belief, repentance, and religious commitment. The Bible promises an 'abundant' life in Christ,[6] and Christians experience significant changes in their lives and attribute these changes to the influence of God. They typically report a new moral awareness and progress, a sense of guidance or calling, and a deep sense of belonging to God. The Bible says in Galatians that, over time, Christians will experience increased love, joy, peace, patience, kindness, goodness, faithfulness, gentleness, and self-control.[7] This kind of transformational experience is to be expected if the Christian message is true."

Peace That Passes Understanding

"What about you?" I asked. "Have you had personal experiences of God?"

"I've been a Christian since 1976, and I've been through my share of difficulties and challenges. Through it all, though, I've heard God speak to me through Scripture, through sermons, through the wisdom of godly friends. And at times the experience is more profound."

"Can you give me an example?"

"I remember a prayer meeting around 1990 when several of us were fasting and praying for a friend who was quite ill. I remember going home and waking up the next day and thinking, *Something's strange.*"

"What was it?"

"I've struggled with anxiety for much of my life, and at the time I was in a very stressful period as I worked on my doctorate. And yet starting that day and continuing for two weeks, I felt absolutely no worry or anxiety. There was such an incredible sense of freedom and joy in the Lord like I'd never known before. After two weeks, it was gone, but I attribute that experience to a special presence of the Holy Spirit in that prayer meeting."

"Did you find that this experience confirmed your faith in a sense?"

"Yes, in a way. I wasn't on an antidepressant; this wasn't the result of some meditative technique; it wasn't mental discipline. It just happened. These periodic visitations of the Holy Spirit can be quite moving, though I would caution that Christians shouldn't try to live off them. If they do, they might start pursuing spiritual highs and encounter counterfeits or stray outside of biblical doctrine."

"During the time when your wife's health was deteriorating, did you find moments of peace and strength in various ways?"

"I did, but not regularly and not in exceptional ways," he replied. "For us, it was the hope that God infused into our lives—a *rational* hope. The hope of the gospel, the hope of a resurrected body, the hope of a new heaven and a new earth. Hope was the experience for us, more than joy or even peace. And that hope sustained us in remarkable ways."

The Testing of Experiences

Next, I wanted to explore how we can evaluate apparent supernatural experiences to see whether or not they are trustworthy. "The Bible says we're supposed to test the spirits to determine whether they're really from God,"[8] I said. "How can we do that?"

"There are four ways to categorize claims of religious experiences," replied Groothuis. "First, maybe someone is lying. Second, a person might have an experience that's purely subjective, like a hallucination or mirage, and incorrectly think it's an encounter with God. Third, someone might experience something extraordinary but not divine and yet incorrectly attribute it to God. And fourth, a person may experience an actual divine reality, which philosophers consider *numinous experiences*."

"Numinous experiences?"

"It's a term coined by German theologian Rudolf Otto.[9] It means experiencing a transfixing or even frightening object that is distinct from the person experiencing it. In other words, there's the subject who has the experience, there's the conscious experience of the numinous, and then there's the numinous object itself. The key is that these are encounters with something that's objectively outside of the person. It's not just conjured up by someone's overactive imagination. A numinous experience can be a conduit for knowledge because there's a relationship between a subject and an object."

"How would this apply, say, to Isaiah's encounter with God?"

"There's Isaiah, who is distinct from God. There's his conscious experience of meeting God. And then there is God, who is objectively real and separate from Isaiah."

I pondered the concept for a moment. "This would mean that religious experiences of Hindus and Buddhists wouldn't qualify," I observed.

"That's right," said Groothuis. "In Eastern mysticism, the whole notion of self disappears, as does the knowable object. The subject-object relationship is swallowed by the void. Mystics talk about pure consciousness and experiences that cannot be described. That's a million miles away from the kind of experience that Isaiah had."

The important distinction about Christian experiences, Groothuis stressed, is that "they involve an encounter with an external and personal being of transcendent significance."

"Should we be skeptical about a religious experience if we have one?" I asked.

"We can take that too far," he replied. "I like the *principle of credulity* proposed by philosopher Richard Swinburne.[10] This says that unless there's good evidence to the contrary, if a person seems to experience something, they should believe it's probably authentic. So we should generally take our experiences to be truth-conveying unless there's reason to think otherwise."

"But you might be mistaken."

"Sure. But we can't consider all truth claims and experiences to be guilty until proven innocent. We don't typically go through life treating every experience as if it's false until it's proven to be true. That's unworkable. Swinburne also proposed the 'principle of testimony,' which says, all things being equal, we don't assume that people are lying or are deceived."[11]

"But it may be that they're not telling the truth," I said.

"Maybe," he conceded, "but the burden of proof should be on establishing guilt, not assuming from the outset that a person's testimony is false. If someone says they experienced God in a particular way, we shouldn't assume they're deceived or lying unless we have indications that there's falsehood involved."

One test of whether an experience with God is authentic, added Groothuis, is to weigh it against the teachings of Scripture, because we have solid reasons for trusting the Bible's reliability. "The Bible becomes *the* guide for testing the validity of an experience," he said. "Whatever experience occurs, if it's really from God, it will not contradict the Bible."

"How can skeptics get around this?" I asked Groothuis.

"For the unbeliever, it means they have to say that precisely none of these experiences are true. They would have to explain away every single one of them as a delusion, or they have to develop some model that captures all of these experiences and shows that none of them are of God for some reason or another."

"That's a hard case to make," I said.

"Especially," Groothuis added, "when we have so much evidence for the truth of Christianity."

Of Goats and Binoculars

Because religious experiences typically happen at an unpredictable time to one individual, this means they aren't repeatable, can't be measured, and can't be scientifically tested. "Doesn't that present a significant challenge in determining their validity?" I asked.

"Well, first, it's understandable that God would be difficult to quantify or measure. After all, he's an invisible personal being who chooses when and where he wants to reveal himself. We should expect that God wouldn't be verifiable the way that a physical object can be."

Groothuis offered an analogy. "Suppose you're looking through binoculars while hiking and you see a goat. You quickly hand the binoculars to your friend, but by the time he looks through them, he doesn't see the goat. Now, what's the more reasonable response—that you lied, or that the goat moved out of view?"

"That the goat moved."

"Right, and that's analogous to experiences of God. God manifests himself as God wills. We can't force him to repeat an experience for someone else. We can't put him under a microscope or in a test tube, and we can't measure him by empirical means."

I asked, "What are some steps we can take to examine religious experiences for their authenticity?"

"First, we can compare the experience to the long tradition of religious experiences within Christianity, going all the way back to the Bible. Is the experience at least consistent with this basic tradition, even though there might be differences? Second, we can investigate to see if there are any surrounding factors that would challenge the credibility of an experience."

"Such as—what?"

"Was the person under the influence of drugs? Do they have a history of deceiving people or having mental illness? Are peripheral details—like when and where the person had the experience—shown to be inaccurate? Does the individual have something to gain from sharing the experience? Obviously, these would cast doubt on their report."

Groothuis paused to give me time to scribble notes. "And then, third," he said, "we have to keep in mind that religious experiences are only one avenue of evidence for a religious worldview. We also have to pursue other lines of argumentation and evidence."

"Can you illustrate that?"

"Let's say a Mormon missionary encourages you to read the Book of Mormon and see whether you experience a 'burning in the bosom' that supposedly confirms its authenticity. Even if you felt a warming in your heart, that experience wouldn't be confirmation that Mormonism's polytheistic teachings and revision of Christian doctrines are true. It wouldn't overcome the lack of historical and archaeological support for the Book of Mormon. So religious experience needs to be weighed against other germane sources of evidence for or against a worldview."

"What about evaluating the validity of Eastern mystical experiences?"

"The enlightenment experiences of both *nirvana* in Buddhism and *moksha* in Hinduism require the negation of individuality, personality, and language. There's no personal encounter with another being of immense holiness and power. If a mystical experience is devoid of any intellectual content, it can't possibly serve as logical evidence for any worldview."

"And Christianity?"

"If you ask me why I believe Christianity is true, religious experiences are not the first evidence I'd mention. Initially, I'd talk about the kind of evidence that Christian philosophers typically offer—evidence about the origin and fine-tuning of the universe, the existence of objective morality, the resurrection, and so forth."

"That makes religious experiences—what?"

"Corroborative," he replied. "By themselves, they don't offer conclusive proof. They're *part* of the case, but they're not *the* case. Still, they're one more persuasive category of evidence which affirms that Christianity is true."

The Psychology of Religious Experiences

Nevertheless, such figures throughout history such as Ludwig Feuerbach, Karl Marx, and Sigmund Freud have tried to undermine the legitimacy of religious experiences by saying they are the product of wish fulfillment or a projection of our psychological needs and desires. For instance, Freud said religious beliefs are an illusion, that "what is characteristic of illusions is that they are derived from human wishes."[12]

"Why can't we write off religious experiences as a psychological phenomenon in which people see what they want to see?" I asked.

A sour look spread across Groothuis's face. "That falls flat for a number of reasons," he replied.

"Such as?"

"Feuerbach, Freud, and Marx thought religious belief was based on superstition," he said. "They thought that because there's no evidential weight behind it, they could explain away faith as being purely psychological. But, Lee, you know that's not true. I've written an 846-page book on the historical, philosophical, and scientific reasons that support Christianity.

"Second," he added, "just because we have a strong wish for X doesn't mean that X isn't true. Even Hans Küng said that 'a real God may certainly correspond to the wish for God.'[13] That means it's possible for a person to come to God because of a deep psychological need, such as a quest for love or acceptance, and still hold a true belief. And finally, third, there are aspects of Christianity that are not good candidates for wish fulfillment."

I chuckled. "I'd agree with that," I said. "If I were going to make up a religion to fulfill my wishes, it would teach that we can do anything we want, whenever we want to do it, and I'd have godlike powers. No constraints!"

Groothuis nodded. "If I were creating a religion, there are a lot of features of Christianity I'd leave out. Like how strict Jesus is about our thoughts and our anger. He says that vicious thoughts are tantamount to vicious acts[14]—I'd jettison that! I certainly wouldn't invent a religion where some of my friends might end up in hell. But the Bible often goes against the grain of what we want, and numinous experiences are often a shock to the person experiencing them. You can't domesticate God."

I noted that psychologist Paul Vitz of New York University has studied the lives of well-known atheists throughout history and concluded that they may have been motivated by psychological factors to *disbelieve* in God. Their problems with their earthly fathers may have turned them off to the idea of a heavenly Father.[15]

"Yes, the charge of psychological projection against Christians can be turned against the skeptic," agreed Groothuis. "Given the fact that the vast majority of humanity has believed in God and the supernatural, it seems more likely that it's the atheists who suffer from some psychological disorder that makes belief in God difficult for them."[16]

Groothuis's foray into supernatural experiences provided a fascinating glimpse into how our Creator can intervene unexpectedly into the lives of ordinary people. I thought of the time that Evel Knievel called me out of the blue to thank me for writing *The Case for Christ* and to tell me the story of his supernatural experience on the beach in Florida.

He said God spoke to him "not through my ears, but I felt him speaking *inside* of me," he said with such sincerity. "I've never experienced anything like that. I wasn't drunk, I wasn't dreaming, I wasn't wishing for it. It just happened, and it was so deep and real and it rattled me so much that I just couldn't ignore it."

Knievel sighed, as if frustrated that he lacked the words to fully convey the impact of that moment. But I understood. If it was authentically from God, then it's understandable that the encounter would transcend our earthly ability to describe it.

For someone like me, who tends toward the rational and factual, it was fascinating to hear Doug Groothuis describe how supernatural experiences with God can count toward evidence that he is real. I knew that one of the ways God does this is through mystical dreams and visions—and that became the next topic for me to explore.

CHAPTER 4

MYSTICAL

DREAMS AND VISIONS

Rachel, a petite and soft-spoken mother with olive complexion and a kind and gentle demeanor, lives with her husband and child in an upscale suburb of Houston, Texas. I'm sure her neighbors could scarcely imagine her upbringing as a devout Muslim in a Middle Eastern country where Christianity is forbidden.[1]

When she was twenty-two years old, Rachel was hounded by personal difficulties. One night before bed, she called out to God, "Please send me one of your prophets who will release me from this miserable feeling. I badly need comfort and guidance."

That night, she had a dream of being in what looked like a movie theater, where the projector cast an intensely bright light. Suddenly, there was a face—the face of Jesus. "At first, it seemed like a portrait, but the portrait was not still," she said. "He was looking at me with very kind, concerned eyes. It was as if he could feel my pain and my sadness."

Jesus spoke to her, but the words weren't as important as the emotion they evoked—a deep and profound sense of relief, comfort, affirmation, and joy. Then his face disappeared. "My eyes opened, but I was sure I was never asleep," she said. "I was in that room with him."

By age thirty, Rachel was married and had moved with her husband to Texas, where he worked in the oil industry. One day while talking with a neighbor, she blurted out, "I would like to study the Bible." To this day, she's not sure where that comment came from, but she ended up studying the gospel of John with a friend who attended the church where I was serving as a teaching pastor.

Of course, John's gospel begins with a sweeping affirmation of Jesus not as a mere prophet of Islam but as God himself: "In the beginning was the Word, and the Word was with God, and the Word was God." And John features a revolutionary statement by Jesus that would shake the foundation of Rachel's Islamic training: "I am the way and the truth and the life. No one comes to the Father except through me."[2]

As she started studying the gospel—and before she knew anything about baptism—she had a vision. "I saw a man with a book," she said. "I was standing with him in water. I saw my friend holding my arm, and we were both looking at the man with the book open in his hands. The man was looking into the horizon with tears running down his face, and I knew that this man loves Jesus very much."

The duration of the vision, she said, "was fast—and not fast. I could see details, but it only lasted a few minutes." She had never seen the man's face before.

When Easter came, her friend brought her to our church. As they sat in the auditorium waiting for the service to begin, Rachel suddenly saw a man walking down the aisle.

"Over there—*that's* the man!" she exclaimed. It was the man from her vision—a pastor named Alan, who presides over baptisms at our church. She had never met him before, but there he was, right in front of her.

By the time she closed the last page of John's gospel in her Bible study, Rachel put her trust in Jesus as her forgiver and leader—a joyous occasion in her life, but not one she dared to share with her husband.

So one day when he was out of town, a private baptism was

arranged. "We all went into the baptismal pool," she said. There they were—the man who loves Jesus, reading from an open Bible, and her friend at her side, just as foretold.

"The vision was coming true in front of my very eyes," she said. "When the pastor spoke, tears streamed down my face. I asked him to keep me longer under the water so I could feel every moment of it."

A dream. A vision. And the words of a friend sprang to mind: "Personally, I don't think God has put the supernatural on the shelf."

Awakening the Muslim World

Rachel is just one of countless Muslims who have experienced supernatural visions or dreams—many of them corroborated by outside events—that have brought them out of Islam and into Christianity.

In fact, more Muslims have become Christians in the last couple of decades than the previous fourteen hundred years since Muhammad, and it's estimated that a quarter to a third of them experienced a dream or vision of Jesus before their salvation experience.[3] If those statistics are accurate, this phenomenon of Jesus supernaturally appearing to people is one of the most significant spiritual awakenings in the world today.

"Virtually every Muslim who has come to follow Christ has done so, first, because of the love of Christ expressed through a Christian, or second, because of a vision, dream, or some other supernatural intervention," a Christian apologist told me. "No religion has a more intricate doctrine of angels and visions than Islam, and I think it's extraordinary that God uses that sensitivity to the supernatural world in which he speaks in visions and dreams and reveals himself."

In the Bible, God frequently used dreams and visions to further his plans. From Abraham, Joseph, and Samuel in the Old Testament to the apostle John and Cornelius in the New Testament, there are about two hundred biblical examples of God employing this kind of divine intervention.

Today, reports of these miraculous manifestations seem to cluster among adherents of Islam, from Indonesia to Pakistan to the Gaza Strip. While the experiences are admittedly unique to the individual, in many cases there is authentication, such as Jesus telling the person something in the dream that he or she could not otherwise have known, or two people having an identical dream on the same night. An example is Rachel seeing Alan in her vision before she had ever met him.

In addition, the stunning consistency of these experiences across international boundaries suggests they are more than the product of overactive imaginations. A devout Muslim would have no incentive to imagine such an encounter with the Jesus of Christianity, who might lure them into Islamic apostasy and possibly even a death sentence in certain countries.

I had to admit that these divine interventions didn't fit neatly into my theological framework, which made me all the more anxious to get to the bottom of them and see what light they might shine on the existence of a supernatural realm.

Leslie and I packed the car and pulled onto the highway for a three-hour drive to Dallas, Texas, where I was scheduled to rendezvous with an author and missionary to the Middle East who is a leading expert on contemporary dreams and visions to Muslims.

INTERVIEW *with*

TOM DOYLE, MABS

After graduating from a Christian college (Biola University) and getting a graduate degree (Dallas Theological Seminary), Tom Doyle eagerly dove into his ministry as a pastor for the following twenty years. He served at churches in Dallas, Albuquerque, and Colorado

Springs, especially enjoying his role of preaching on Sunday mornings. Then in 1995, Dallas Seminary called and said they were taking some pastors to Israel. Would he be interested in joining them?

"That changed everything for me," Doyle recalls. "I was immediately drawn to the Middle East—hook, line, and sinker."

Over the next twenty years, he became a missionary to the region, eventually leading sixty tours of the Holy Land. Today, he is dedicated to challenging Christians to join the movement of God among Jews and Muslims, as well as to come alongside persecuted believers.

What drew me to Doyle was his authoritative book *Dreams and Visions: Is Jesus Awakening the Muslim World?* which he wrote in 2012. In all, Doyle has authored seven books revolving around his expertise on the Middle East.

Doyle, now in his sixties and with his brown hair graying, married his college sweetheart, JoAnn, and they have six children and several grandchildren. JoAnn ministers to women in Middle Eastern countries.

One of Doyle's friends, Christian novelist and biographer Jerry Jenkins, said Doyle's personal ministry in the Middle East gives him special authority in discussing trends there. He said Doyle has "the credibility of a man who has the smell of the front lines of the battlefield on his clothes because he was there yesterday and will be back there tomorrow."[1]

Leslie and I had dinner with Tom and JoAnn at a café the night before our interview, chatting for several hours about what grandparents usually obsess over—grandkids. Tom and JoAnn are gregarious, passionate, and empathetic—perfect qualities for missionaries.

The next morning JoAnn and Leslie went out for a while to let Tom and me have a private discussion in our hotel room.

"Did you always have an affinity for working with Muslims?" I began as we sat down, facing each other in (uncomfortable) straight-back chairs.

"No, actually I had a lot of preconceived notions," he replied.

"Prejudices?"

"You could say that."

"What changed your attitude?"

"Shortly after 9/11, I was in Gaza City. A woman in a hijab came running up, grabbed my forearm, and said, 'You're from America, aren't you?' I said, 'Yes, I am.' She said, 'When the buildings came down on 9/11, did you see the video of people in Gaza cheering and celebrating?' I said, 'Yes, I saw that on TV.' She said, 'Not me. I was crying for those people. They didn't deserve to die. That was wrong. I'm very sorry.' She tapped her heart, and then she walked away."

"How did that make you feel?"

"That was the day that God started to create space in my heart for Muslims," he said. "It comes down to this: Are we able to see through Jesus' eyes and not our own? He filters out all the news and prejudice. Once you have his eyes, you see people for who they are—daughters and sons made in his image."

"You're the One! You're the One!"

When I asked Doyle when he became aware of the phenomenon of dreams and visions among Islamic people, he recalled the first time he visited Jerusalem and met with a group of Muslims who had converted to Christianity.

"One of them, Muhammad, said he had been a fervent Muslim when he started to have dreams about Jesus. He said they were different than anything he had ever experienced. Often dreams are fuzzy or confused, but these were bright and laser focused—and they kept coming."

"What did Jesus tell him?"

"He was a man in a white robe and he told Muhammad that he loves him. They were beside a lake, and Muhammad said he saw himself walking over and embracing Jesus."

"How did you react?" I asked.

Doyle chuckled. "I didn't know if this guy was nuts or what," he replied. "But over and over, from a variety of different people, I started hearing the same basic story: Jesus in a white robe, saying he loves them, saying he died for them, telling them to follow him. It started to snowball—in Iran, Iraq, Syria, all over. There were even ads placed in Egyptian newspapers."

I looked up from my note-taking. "What kind of ads?"

"They simply said, 'Have you seen the man in a white robe in your dreams? He has a message for you. Call this number.' In other words, so many Muslims were having these dreams that Christian ministries started placing these ads to reach them."

I asked Doyle if he would give me a typical example of how these dreams play out in someone's life. He chose the story of what happened to Kamal, an underground church planter in Egypt, and a married Muslim mother named Noor.[2]

He explained that Kamal was busy with his work one day, but nevertheless he felt God was leading him to go to the Khan el-Khalili Friday market in Cairo. Frankly, it was the last place he wanted to go—this was right before Muslim prayers, and the market was crowded, noisy, and chaotic. But he went because he felt 100 percent convinced that God had a special assignment for him.

A Muslim woman named Noor, covered head to toe in traditional garb, spotted him from a distance and started yelling, "You're the one! You're the one!" She pushed through the crowd and made a beeline for him. She said, "You were in my dream last night! Those clothes—you were wearing those clothes. For sure, it was you."

Kamal quickly sensed what was motivating her. "Was I with Jesus?" he asked.

"Yes," she replied. "Jesus was with us."

Later she explained, "Jesus walked with me alongside a lake, and he told me how much he loves me. His love was different from anything I've ever experienced. I've never felt so much peace. I didn't want him to leave. I asked this Jesus, 'Why are you visiting me, a poor Muslim mother with eight children?' And all he said was, 'I love you, Noor. I have given everything for you. I died for you.'"

She said that as Jesus turned to leave, he told her, "Ask my friend tomorrow about me. He will tell you all you need in order to understand why I've visited you." She replied to Jesus, "But who is your friend?" Jesus said, "Here is my friend," and he pointed to a person who was behind him in the dream. "He has been walking with us the whole time we've been together."

Now, there in the marketplace, Noor said to Kamal, "Even though you had walked with us around the lake, I hadn't seen anyone but Jesus. I thought I was alone with him. His face was magnificent. I couldn't take my eyes off him. Jesus did not tell me your name, but you were wearing the same clothes you have on right now, and your glasses—they're the same too. I knew I would not forget your smile."

The encounter led to a deep discussion about faith that lasted some three hours. "I have never been loved like I was when Jesus walked with me in that dream," Noor told him. "I felt no fear. For the first time in my life, I felt no shame. Even though he's a man, I wasn't intimidated. I didn't feel threatened. I felt . . . perfect peace."

Kamal explained to her that religion will never bring her that kind of peace. "That's what Jesus wants to give you," Kamal told her. "Before he went to the cross, Jesus said, 'Peace I leave with you; my peace I give you.'[3] You will not—you cannot—find peace like that with anyone else. No one but Jesus even has it to offer."

I was mesmerized by Noor's story. "Did she come to faith in Christ?" I asked Doyle.

"Not on that day," he answered. "She's counting the cost, even as Jesus himself said we should. And the cost to her in Egypt could be very steep. She said she wants to find out all she can about Jesus. There are a lot of people praying for her."[4]

Stopped in His Tracks

Doyle's books are packed with stories like the one with Kamal and Noor, and similar accounts just keep coming. "I could pick up the phone right now and call Syria and ask if our people have any stories about dreams, and they would give me three or four new ones," he said. "That's how prevalent they are."

"You don't see a letup, then?" I asked.

"Not at all. Recently I met a guy in Jerusalem who grew up in a refugee camp as a Palestinian," Doyle said. "He hated Israel. He told me his goal in life was to kill as many Israelis as he could."

"That's chilling," I said. "So what happened?"

"He was on his way to meet with people who work with Hamas," he said, referring to the terrorist organization. "He didn't know anything about Jesus, but all of a sudden, a man in a white robe was standing in front of him in the street and pointing at him. The man said, 'Omar, this is not the life I have planned for you. You turn around. Go home. I have another plan for you.'"

"What did he do?"

"He turned around and went home. Later that same day, someone was moving into an apartment across the hall from him. He found out the new tenant was a Christian. Omar told him about the experience he'd had and said, 'What does it mean?' This Christian spent time with him, took him through the Scriptures, and led him to Jesus. Today, Omar is an underground church planter."

The story resonated deeply with me. "So there he was," I said, "on his way to join Hamas and perhaps embark on a life of extremism and terrorism—and yet Jesus literally stopped him in his tracks."

"Absolutely," said Doyle. "We met another guy in Jericho who was part of the Palestinian Authority. He started having dreams about Jesus. He went to his imam, who told him to read the Qur'an more. But the more he read the Qur'an, the more he had Jesus dreams. The imam told him to get more involved in the mosque, so he did—still, more Jesus dreams. The imam said to make the Hajj to Mecca."

In my mind I could picture this person among the throngs at Mecca, walking around the Kaaba, often called "the house of Allah," a black building in the center of the most sacred mosque in Islam. One of the five pillars of Islam says if a Muslim is able, they should make the Hajj pilgrimage to Mecca once in their lifetime and walk seven times around the Kaaba. More than a million people walk counterclockwise around the Kaaba during this five-day period each year.

"What happened to him?" I asked.

"You're supposed to look at the Kaaba and say your prayers. Instead, he looked over—and on top of the Kaaba he saw the Jesus from his dreams."

"That must have startled him!"

"It did," Doyle replied. "Jesus was looking at him and saying, 'Osama, leave this place. You're going in the wrong direction. Leave and go home.' So he did. Later a Christian friend shared the gospel with him and he came to faith in Christ. Today, this man has such love for Jesus that you can literally see it on his face."

"That's How Jesus Operates"

One fact seemed clear: Most of the people having these dreams were not naturally inclined to imagine a vision of the Jesus of Christianity.

"No way," Doyle said. "Many live in closed countries where they have no prior exposure to images or ideas about the Jesus of the Bible. When Jesus tells them he died for them, that's alien to everything they've learned."

"What does the Qur'an tell them about Jesus?"

"That he is a prophet, but most significantly, the Qur'an says Jesus did not die on the cross, that Allah does not have a son, and that nobody can bear the sins of another. So the very things that Christianity says are essential to faith are explicitly denied in Islamic teachings."

"And so this makes Muslims resistant when you try to initiate a conversation about faith," I said.

"Yes, exactly. A Muslim typically responds by saying the Bible has been corrupted, or Christians worship three gods, or look what happened during the Crusades," Doyle replied. "These are some of the big boulders on the path between them and the real Jesus. But in these high-definition Jesus dreams, they're gently walked around those boulders. They see Jesus for who he is, and now they're motivated to learn more.

"It's interesting," he continued, "that after a dream or vision, the typical objections that Muslims raise against Christianity disappear. I've never met someone who had a Jesus dream who is still hung up on the deity of Christ or the veracity of Scriptures. Instantly, they know this: Jesus is more than just a prophet. And they want to know more about him."

I noticed that in Doyle's description of these dreams, he doesn't say the Muslim immediately puts their trust in Jesus. I said to him, "It seems that people don't go to sleep as a Muslim, have a Jesus dream, and then wake up as a Christian."

"That's right, I've never heard of that happening," Doyle replied. "Usually, the dream points them toward someone who can teach them from the Bible and present the gospel, like Noor in the Cairo marketplace. Or like Omar, who was deterred from meeting with Hamas, went home, and 'coincidentally' found a Christian moving in across the hall," he said. "The dreams motivate them to seek the real Jesus and to find the truth in Scripture."

The Jesus they encounter in their dreams, said Doyle, is a perfect antidote to a culture based on shame and honor.

"Muslims have felt dishonor and shame ever since Muhammad, but these dreams strike a deep emotional chord because suddenly they have the opposite feeling," he explained. "They're honored that Jesus would appear to them. They feel love, grace, safety, protection, affirmation, joy, peace—all those emotions they don't receive from Islam. It rocks their world."

"Does Jesus behave in these dreams the same as the Jesus of the Gospels?"

"There's a consistency. For example, the Jesus of the New Testament reached out to the marginalized—the Samaritan woman at the well who has gone through multiple husbands, the blind and crippled, those with leprosy, the hated tax collector Zacchaeus. Today, who is more marginalized than Muslims? Jesus is showing his love for them. That's how Jesus operates."

Just how similar, I asked Doyle, are these contemporary dreams to the dreams and visions described in Scripture?

"I don't want to say that they're like what Saul experienced on the road to Damascus," came his response. "But these are earth-shattering experiences to those who have them. They're not like typical dreams—they're exceptionally vibrant. They can't shake them. They sense a love that has been missing from their life, and their response is very understandable: they inevitably want more."

"Take It Up with God"

I gestured toward Doyle. "You were educated at Biola University and Dallas Seminary, both conservative evangelical institutions," I said. "Did this dream phenomenon challenge your theology in any way?"

"Well, I was skeptical at first," he said, eliciting a nod from me, since I felt the same way. "I thought, 'Lord, why is this happening?' But as I processed it, it began to make sense."

"In what way?"

"The Western world doesn't need dreams and visions—we have easy access to God's Word. But it's estimated that 50 percent of

Muslims around the world can't read, so how are we going to get the Scriptures to them? And 86 percent of Muslims don't know a Christian, so who's going to share the gospel with them? In light of these realities, how might God reach them? I believe God is fair. The Bible says, 'Will not the Judge of all the earth do right?'⁵ I think he's going to find a way to bring Jesus to them."

"Even in such a dramatic way as this?"

"Sure. I think of Leila, who lived in Baghdad. Her husband was beating her all the time; she thought she would die. One night she said, 'God, I've been crying out to you for months and you do nothing. I keep saying, "God, where are you?" Now I'm going to change one word: "God, *who* are you?" Maybe I've been praying to the wrong God.' That night she had a dream about the Jesus who loves her."

He shrugged his shoulders. "So what should I do with that theologically?" he asked. "It's hard to deny the evidence that something supernatural is happening. Granted, it's the Word of God that leads people to faith, but these dreams plow the hard soil of Muslim hearts so they're receptive to the seed of the gospel."

Doyle let that thought linger for a few moments. Then he continued.

"Put yourself in God's position," he said, gesturing toward me. "You want your message to get around the world. Huge numbers of Muslims—who you love deeply—don't have access to Christians or the Bible. Now, what's your Plan B? How would you get their attention—especially in a culture that values dreams? I think we need to look at God's love rather than just automatically thinking we have the correct theology. It's just like our loving God to do something radical to reach them. Extreme times require extreme measures."

Still, I pressed him on this issue. "What would you tell Christians who say, yes, there were a few dreams in the Bible, but that was a different age, a different time, different circumstances—and those things just don't happen today?"

"More than two hundred times there are dreams or visions in the Bible," he replied. "We know there were dreams in the early church, and some spiritual leaders saw that as a vehicle of divine revelation. Obviously, the Word of God is our sole authority—and, interestingly, where do these dreams point people? Toward the Bible."

I said, "A theologian might point out that the canon of Scripture is closed, and this would be extrabiblical revelation that needs to be treated very suspiciously."

"Everything needs to be checked against Scripture. I haven't backed off that one bit. But how many Christians in America might say they have had an impression in a restaurant to go witness to someone sitting nearby? The Spirit leads people that way all the time. So why can't the Spirit lead them through a dream that points them to missionaries and the Bible? Frankly, our theology doesn't determine God's actions."

"And for those who remain skeptical—what would you say to them?"

"What else can I say?" Doyle replied with a sigh. "If they object on some theological grounds, I'd tell them to take it up with God."

As if an afterthought, he added, "Personally, I don't think God has put the supernatural on the shelf."

"Are You Willing to Die for Jesus?"

One way to assess the legitimacy of these dreams is to measure the kind of fruit they bear. In other words, do they lead to a superficial and short-lived faith, or do they result in thorough conversions and a deep commitment to Christ?

"No question—these dreams generally lead to radical life-change," Doyle told me. "A Muslim who comes to faith in the Middle East is exposing himself to possible rejection, beatings, imprisonment, or even death. This isn't for the faint of heart. This isn't casual Christianity."

"It's ironic," I said, "that in America, we see a proliferation of shallow commitments to Christ because of a cultural Christianity that hasn't really revolutionized the person's soul, and yet we're skeptical of how authentic these conversions are in the Middle East, where people face persecution if they pursue their faith."

Doyle agreed. "Before praying with someone to receive Christ, many leaders in the Middle East will ask two questions. First, are you willing to suffer for Jesus? And, second, are you willing to die for Jesus?" he said. "I wish we had those two questions in the New Members classes at churches in America."

"It might thin the ranks a bit," I commented.

"Probably. But even though these Muslims know that following Jesus could very well lead to rejection by their family or even death, they're coming to faith in unprecedented numbers."

"Do you see a way to explain away these dreams and visions naturalistically?"

"It's hard to see how these could be anything but supernatural, given the circumstances," he replied. "How do you explain Kamal feeling an urge from God to go to the Cairo market when he didn't want to, where he meets Noor, a woman who had a dream about him and Jesus the night before?"

"Coincidence?" I ventured.

Doyle couldn't stifle a laugh. "That would take a lot more faith to believe," he quipped.

"But why Noor?" I asked. "Why isn't Jesus appearing in everybody's dreams? He could save missionary agencies a lot of time, money, and effort if he would just appear in the dreams of every non-Christian in the world."

That question prompted a pause from Doyle. "Look, I can't speak for God. All I can do is speculate," he said. "In many parts of the world, the problem isn't a lack of access to the gospel. It's available. So in these locales, the real issue for people is, 'How are you going to respond?'

"We also know that throughout church history, God has focused on different people groups in various eras. There have been great awakenings in Asia, South America, Europe, the United States, and Africa. For whatever reason, God is reaching out today to multiple people groups that have one thing in common— a huge proportion are Muslim. I don't know what he'll do next."

As I chatted with Doyle, I had to confess that I felt a tinge of jealousy toward people who have had Jesus dreams. I've followed Christ for several decades now. I've delved deeply into the Scriptures. I've felt God's presence, guidance, and power in my life. But to have a vivid and vibrant dream of talking with a white-robed Jesus and hearing his voice offer love, grace, and acceptance—well, I have to admit that would be awesome.

"Do you envy them?" I said to Doyle as we were wrapping up our conversation. "Do you wish Jesus would appear to you in a dream?"

"Wow," he said, just thinking about the prospect. "Who wouldn't want an encounter like that? Yeah, it would be incredible. But I've got the Scriptures to tell me about Jesus; I have his Spirit to affirm and guide me; and I know I'll see him face-to-face someday."

His face looked content. "Yes," he said finally, "that's enough for me."

CHAPTER 5

THE ENCOURAGING
TRUTH ABOUT
ANGELS

My visitor had no wings, no flowing white robe, but he did seem to have a warm glow. He was affable and empathetic. Intuitively, I knew right away that he was from another realm. Deep inside, I sensed that I was interacting with a celestial being.

The encounter occurred in a dream when I was a youngster. But it wasn't an ordinary dream; it was more vibrant, more lucid, more *real*—so much so that today, it's the only dream I remember from my childhood.

I wasn't intimidated by the being. We chatted amiably. He told me something I never knew, and the revelation floored me. Essentially, he said that my efforts to be compliant and dutiful—to treat others well, obey my parents, and visit Sunday school on occasion—would never be sufficient to earn my way into heaven someday. I was stunned and flustered. I didn't know what to say. This seemed totally counterintuitive.

Then the angel made a prophecy. He said that someday I would understand. In a flash, he disappeared. Sure enough, sixteen years later, as I visited a church at my wife's behest, I learned that the angel was right. I found out that eternal life is not a reward for good behavior, but rather it is a gift from God that must be received in repentance and faith. The moment I understood the gospel, my mind flashed back to the angel—and I smiled.

Was this an authentic otherworldly encounter, or could it have been just the aftereffects of a spicy snack before bedtime? Personally, I'm convinced it was genuine because of two bits of corroboration: the angel told me something I didn't know, and he made a prediction that did, indeed, come true nearly two decades later.

I'm far from alone in reporting a possible encounter with an angelic presence. According to one survey, 75 percent of people around the world believe in angels. More than one out of three of them report having a personal experience with a celestial being—and for 15 percent of them, it happened in a vibrant dream.[1]

The Bible features about three hundred references to angels, starting just three chapters into Genesis, where God places "angelic sentries" to guard the entrance to Eden after Adam and Eve were banished from it.[2] The Bible's final mention of angels comes in its last chapter, Revelation 22:16, when Jesus says he has "sent my angel to give you this testimony for the churches."

One of the most significant scenes in Scripture occurs in Revelation 5:11–12, in which the apostle John describes a vision of Jesus in his post-resurrection glory:

> Then I looked and heard the voice of many angels, numbering thousands upon thousands, and ten thousand times ten thousand. They encircled the throne and the living creatures and the elders. In a loud voice they were saying:
>
> "Worthy is the Lamb, who was slain,
> to receive power and wealth and wisdom and strength
> and honor and glory and praise!"

Just try to picture that. "Ten thousand times ten thousand" means there were *100 million* luminous angels crowded around Christ's throne and pouring out their worship. In fact, Dr. Craig Keener points out that "ten thousand" was the highest numerical figure used in the Greek language at the time,[3] which means this phrase "may be John's way of describing an inexpressibly large company of angels—myriads upon myriads."[4]

Fascination with angels has ebbed and flowed over the past two millennia. In the early 1990s, America saw an outbreak of "angel-mania," with *Newsweek* saying that "those who see angels, talk to them, put others in touch with them are prized guests on television and radio talk shows."[5] Bestselling books about angels sometimes offered a stew of New Age and even occultic beliefs, often encouraging readers to focus on these celestial beings rather than looking to God himself.

Since then, the mania over angels has cooled off. According to Gallup, the number of Americans who believe in angels decreased from 79 percent in 2001 to 69 percent in 2023.[6] Still, curiosity about angelic beings remains strong, especially when credible people report extraordinary encounters with them.

"He Caught Me"

The story of one such encounter came while I was chatting with theologian Roger Olson from Baylor University about various attitudes that people have toward the supernatural. The Baptist professor began to get nostalgic about his upbringing in a Pentecostal home, where there had been an openhearted expectation of healings and otherworldly experiences.

"I remember one incident where a little boy in our church, probably ten years old, accidentally opened the door and fell out of the family car while it was driving down the road," he recalled. "When they rushed to pick him up, they thought he would be dead, but instead he was just standing there. They said, 'What happened?' He said, 'Well, didn't you see the man? He caught me.'"

Olson pulled a handkerchief from his pocket and wiped his eyes. "There's no doubt in my mind that an angel caught him."

Billy Graham offered the account of Scottish missionary John G. Paton, whose home in the New Hebrides Islands of the South Pacific was threatened by a hostile mob intent on burning it down killing him and his wife. Paton and his spouse prayed intently all night—and as the sun rose, they were surprised to see that the crowd had dispersed. They thanked God for sparing them.

A year later, the chief of the tribe that had been threatening them became a Christian. One day Paton asked him why they abandoned their plan to attack Paton's home that night. Replied the chief, "Who were all those men you had with you there?" Said the missionary, "There were no men, just my wife and I." The chief insisted there had been hundreds of big men in shining garments and swords drawn, encircling the home.

"Only then," wrote Graham, "did Mr. Paton realize that God had sent His angels to protect them. The chief agreed that there was no other explanation."[7]

INTERVIEW *with*

DOUGLAS E. POTTER, DMIN: PART 1

Beliefs about angels are typically an amalgam of what people pick up from popular culture, what they remember from childhood cartoons, and what they have culled from casual Bible reading. Consequently, there are a lot of misconceptions—some harmless, others theologically problematic. For instance, the idea that people become angels when they die seems to persist, despite having no biblical support. (I blame *Looney Tunes*.)

The Bible refers to angels in sixteen of the Old Testament books and seventeen of the New Testament books, and yet the primary focus of Scripture is on God and our relationship with him. This means that a lot of details about angels aren't spelled out with specificity. They aren't supposed to be. Why? Because they are a sidelight to the central plot of the Bible and unnecessary information for us to have at this point. A lot of what we can discern about angels, then, is inferred from what is revealed in the text.

Nevertheless, when we look at the totality of the Bible, we see that angels are active from beginning to end. Graham Cole, who served as a professor of biblical and systematic theology at Trinity Evangelical Divinity School, highlighted how angels were present at these key moments of redemptive history: "The exodus of God's people from Egypt (Ex. 14:19) and subsequent journey (Ex. 23:23), the giving of the law (Gal. 3:19), the incarnation of the Son of God (Luke 1:26), his ordeal in the garden (Luke 22:43), his resurrection from the dead (John 20:12), and his return in judgment (2 Thess 1:5–8)."[1]

Although Cole recognizes that angels were "minor players in the drama of redemption," their activities clearly made a difference in a lot of ways during biblical times and—if various accounts are credible—in the contemporary era as well. So when exploring the supernatural realm, it makes sense to delve into what we can know with confidence about these elusive celestial spirits.

"The greatest of Christian thinkers have consistently recognized that angels and demons are far more than a divine embellishment designed to make the Bible interesting," said theology professor Peter R. Schemm Jr. "Angels are actual beings whose existence affects human life."[2]

Ron Rhodes agrees. "Angels are real. Angels are alive. And though we rarely perceive their presence, they are very much with us here on the earth," he wrote in *The Secret Life of Angels*. "A vast world of intelligent, powerful, invisible spirit beings is all around us and warrants careful study."[3]

To investigate how these spirit beings influence our lives, I flew to Charlotte, North Carolina, to meet with a professor who had collaborated with prominent theologian and apologist Norman Geisler to write a book called *The Doctrine of Angels and Demons*.

Douglas Potter grew up in football-obsessed Ohio, where his size and strength landed him on the offensive and defensive lines in high school. When his aspirations for college football didn't materialize, he went on to earn a bachelor's and master's degree in industrial technology. But it was a college course taught by a theologically liberal professor that changed the trajectory of his life.

Potter had been raised in a conservative Baptist home and made a profession of faith at age five. He had never encountered someone who challenged the historicity of the Bible like this professor. "I was shocked at first," Potter said. "I thought it was odd that my church had sheltered me from these attacks by scholars that seemed very convincing."

He began reading popular-level books and then more advanced works on evidence for the faith, which provided a solid rebuttal to liberal theology. One day he was listening to a national apologetics radio show when he heard Geisler mention plans to start Southern Evangelical Seminary (SES). Potter called for information—and Geisler's wife answered the phone and responded to his questions.

Potter moved to Charlotte and ended up earning a master's degree in apologetics and then a Doctor of Ministry degree from SES. Along the way, he became a protégé of Geisler's and eventually authored nearly a dozen books with him before Geisler's death in 2019. Potter also wrote *Developing a Christian Apologetics*

Educational Program. In addition, he coauthored *Cross-Cultural Apologetics* and *The Teacher's Guide for the Twelve Points That Show Christianity Is True*.

Now in his mid-fifties, Potter serves as a professor of apologetics and theology and director of the Doctor of Ministry program at SES. We met in his well-organized office at the seminary, with Potter wearing a shirt and tie and bold, black-rimmed glasses. Tall and slender, he has a friendly demeanor and speaks with both precision and passion.

Contemporary Angelic Encounters

I began by mentioning that in more than forty years of following Jesus, I have never heard a sermon on the topic of angels. "Why is it important that we learn about them?" I asked. "Are we spiritually impoverished if we don't?"

"I think so," came his quick response. "They're mentioned so frequently in the Bible that clearly God wants us to be aware of their presence. And you can be in danger if you ignore them because of their role in spiritual warfare. Besides, it's easy to fall into error if you're unfamiliar with angels—for instance, the apostle Paul had to warn against worshiping them."

In his book on the doctrine of angels and demons, Graham Cole agrees that studying angelology makes the Christian worldview "all the richer. To contemplate that heaven, seen as God's abode, is a place of never ceasing praise, joy, and love reminds us that, like the psalmist, we need to lift our eyes to the hills, to the God who made *heaven* and earth."[4]

Theologian and Methodist pastor Arno Gaebelein stressed the practical side of learning about angels. "As we realize . . . that they are watching us, ready to walk with us, as we walk with Him in His ways, ready to serve us as we serve Him, ready to shield us and help us in a hundred different ways, a solemn feeling will come into our lives," he said. "Surely we shall walk softly in the presence of the Lord and His holy angels . . . Thus this truth will assist us in a holy life."[5]

I asked Potter, "How can we be sure that angels are real? What are our best sources for believing they actually exist?"

"Most importantly, there's the Bible itself, which is replete with references to angels. Of course, we have good historical and philosophical reasons to trust the contents of the Bible, as many scholars have pointed out. If the Bible is credible, then we can accept its teachings about the angelic realm."

"What if someone is skeptical about the Bible?"

"Some people might not be ready to accept the divine origin of Scripture, and yet they do respect Jesus as a good teacher. Well, Jesus taught about angels. For example, the Sadducees, who didn't believe in angels or the resurrection, challenged him about the afterlife and who would be married to whom in cases where people had multiple spouses in their life. Jesus replied in Luke 20:35–36 that the dead will neither marry nor be given in marriage, and they can no longer die; for they are like the angels. So if you're going to accept the teachings of Jesus, you have good reason to conclude angels are real too."

"What about people who say they've personally interacted with angels? You've read or heard a lot of these stories, I'm sure—people who claim an angel rescued them from danger or provided crucial guidance and so forth."

I looked at my notes for an example and read aloud this account published some time ago in a mainstream Christian publication: "The editor of a leading magazine for church leaders, *Leadership*, tells how his young daughter lay comatose one night, on the edge of death. A hospital staff worker went by the room and saw angels 'hovering' over the bed. The woman told the child's nurse that she wanted to renew her commitment to God in response. By morning, the daughter revived. The editor—who associates know as no sentimentalist—does not hesitate to believe that angels showed up."[6]

I looked at Potter. "Do these kinds of contemporary reports offer evidence that angels are real?" I asked.

Potter responded by reciting Hebrews 13:2: "Do not forget to show hospitality to strangers, for by so doing some people have shown hospitality to angels without knowing it."

"Here we have the Bible acknowledging that some people have interacted directly with angels in the past," Potter said. "And I have no reason to believe that this ended in biblical days. Consequently, if someone tells me they've had a personal experience with an angelic being, I'm open to that. Of course, we need to be discerning as well."

"How so?"

"If the report of an interaction with an angel is contrary to what is taught in Scripture, then I have good cause to doubt that it's authentic, because I have solid reasons for believing the Bible.

"And we can dig deeper," he continued. "Is the person credible or prone to exaggeration? Do they have a history of drug use or hallucinations? Do they seem to have an ulterior motive, such as promoting an unorthodox theology? Are there any other eyewitnesses to what occurred? Is there any independent corroboration? Are there any naturalistic explanations that could better account for the phenomenon? It's appropriate to ask these sorts of questions before we uncritically accept someone's story."

"But you've seen accounts that you consider to be credible, is that right?"

"Yes, for sure," he said. "I haven't personally had an experience with an angelic being, but I'm convinced there are others who have. I don't doubt that some accounts pass the kind of tests I just mentioned. Honestly, the only way to deny some of these reports is if you start off with an anti-supernatural bias and refuse to follow the evidence to where it is obviously leading."

Exploring the Nature of Angels

With so many misconceptions and caricatures about angels in popular culture, I decided to ask Potter to start at the beginning—their creation—and describe what we can know with confidence about these celestial beings.

"First of all, angels are not eternal like God is," he said. "They were created, probably at the time when God created 'the heavens and the earth'[7]—in fact, they were definitely created before the earth because they sang when its cornerstone was laid.[8] And the apostle Paul says all angels were created by God through the Son.[9] No creature exists that was not created by Jesus Christ, as John tells us."[10]

"Their number is fixed?"

"That's right. There's a finite number of them, but that number is incredibly large. The Old Testament speaks of them as being like the stars, and we can't even begin to count the number of stars.[11] They are spirit beings, and so they are immortal since they don't have bodies that decay. Because they are immaterial in nature, they have no gender and don't engage in marriage or reproduction."

I interjected: "But Scripture speaks of them with masculine pronouns."

"That's true, but I believe that's just a convention for us to understand something from a different realm. Remember, they're spirits. Now, as far as the biblical record is concerned, when they did materialize, they presented as male. Could they present themselves as female at other times? I suppose that's possible, but there's nothing in Scripture to indicate it is actual," he replied.

Concerning beliefs about angels in ancient Judaism, Mika Ahuvia, a professor of classical Judaism at the University of Washington, published a scholarly article in 2022 that concluded, "Altogether, evidence found in rabbinic literature, Yannai's liturgical poetry, liturgical practices, ritual texts, and synagogue art demonstrates that feminine angels were conceivable by ancient Jews."[12]

I asked Potter, "Can angels materialize at will?"

"At least some of them can, yes. For instance, Lot has visitors who he discovers are angels.[13] Although the nature of angels is spiritual, it doesn't mean some of them can't organize matter in such a way that they have the appearance of being a human being."

Potter continued. "Also, angels are *aeviternal*, that is, they are by nature not in time, but they can relate to time. And they are persons because they have the characteristics of personhood—intellect, will, and emotions."

"What kind of emotions?"

"Luke 15:7 says there is rejoicing in heaven whenever a sinner repents," he answered. "Job 38:7 says the angels shouted for joy when God created the world. And we see the passion of the angels when they are pouring out their worship of the Lord in Revelation 5:11–12."

"Are they omniscient? Can they read our minds and know our thoughts?"

"Only God is omniscient. First Kings 8:39 says that God alone knows every human heart, and Jeremiah 17:10 says it's the Lord who searches the heart and examines the mind. So, no, angels can't invade our thoughts directly or have intimate knowledge of what's in our hearts. Think about it this way: God can't create another eternal God; he can only create something that's finite. He can't make another of himself in any sense because he is uncreated. He can't share the metaphysical attributes of omniscience, omnipresence, or omnipotence."

"Angels might not be omnipotent, but they are powerful, aren't they?"

"Absolutely. They are called 'mighty ones who do his bidding' in Psalm 103:20 and 'powerful' in 2 Thessalonians 1:7. For example, an angel didn't have any trouble rolling away the heavy stone from Jesus' tomb."[14]

That was an impressive feat. According to estimates, the wheel of granite guarding the tomb probably weighed more than 8,000 pounds—"yet," as one scholar noted, "an angel flipped the stone out of the way as if it were a mere pebble."[15]

What about the Wings of Angels?

I was enjoying this journey through the attributes and abilities of angelic beings. I continued by asking Potter, "Are angels miracle workers?"

"Only God can do what God can do. Only he can work the supernatural, like creating life from non-life or raising the dead," he replied. "I've come to use a different term for what angels can do—*supernormal*. Maybe their ability to perform extraordinary feats is tied to the fact that they're spirits and don't have any spatiotemporal limits. Of course, God can choose to work a supernatural miracle through an angel, just as he can do it through a human being if he chooses. But that's not intrinsic to the power of the angel. It's a miracle being done through them by the power of God."

"How smart are they?"

"Angels are greater in both knowledge and power than humans," he replied. "Angels rank lower than God but higher than humans—interesting, because 1 Corinthians 6:3 tells us that we will judge angels in the end."

I couldn't resist asking one of the most common questions about angelic beings: "Do all of them have wings?"

Potter chuckled. "That's a good one," he said. "The primary reference to wings is in Isaiah 6, where Isaiah is caught up into this vision of the throne of God, and above it are angels called seraphim, who he describes as having six wings. In 1 Kings 6:23–28, we see that angels who are called cherubim also are winged. Some theologians consider this to be a metaphor, as a way of describing their power and ability to travel at great speed from place to place. I believe there are some that do have wings, at least when they're given visible manifestation, but we know from other Scriptures that it's not applicable to all of them."

Theologian Millard Erickson came to the same conclusion. "There is no explicit reference indicating that angels as a whole are winged," he wrote.[16]

"I notice that a couple of angels in the Bible have names."

"Yes, we see Michael, who's identified as an archangel.[17] According to Revelation 12:7, he is the leader of the heavenly army. Then there's Gabriel, who 'stands in the presence of God' and makes special announcements for God, such as when he announced the coming birth of Jesus to Mary.[18] Presumably, all angels have names—and if God can know all the stars by name,[19] certainly in his omniscience he would know all the names of the angels."

He added, "And there is certainly a hierarchy among the angels that Scripture alludes to—almost a military structure, although it's a bit difficult to be very precise about it based on the text. It seems that under the archangel are other 'chief princes.'[20] Cherubim are proclaimers and protectors of God's glory. Other spiritual beings, called 'living creatures,' worship God and direct his judgments.[21] Seraphim proclaim God's holiness. And Paul says there are thrones, powers, rulers, and authorities, which points to different orders of angels as well."[22]

Granted, the rankings described in Scripture can be somewhat confusing. Traditionally, nine "orders" of angels have been recognized, after the organization of Pseudo-Dionysius the Areopagite around the fifth century. These are (in descending order) Seraphim, Cherubim, Thrones, Dominions, Virtues, Powers, Principalities, Archangels, and Angels. Each has a different function, and some seem to have very different forms or appearances.

But such theologians as Graham Cole, Millard Erickson, and Karl Barth hesitate to adopt an elaborate hierarchy.[23] Anglican cleric T. C. Hammond preferred to keep it simple: "They are graded into at least three 'ranks'—Archangels, Cherubim and Seraphim, and Angels."[24]

Serving God and His People

"Why did God create angels?" I asked Potter. "What is their purpose or mission?"

"Hebrews 1:14 is a key to this," he said before reciting the passage: "Are not all angels ministering spirits sent to serve those who will inherit salvation?"

"So they minister to believers," I said.

"First and foremost, God created angels for his glory, and Colossians 1:16 says they are there to serve him," Potter replied. "And then we see throughout Scripture how God sends his angels to minister to God's people as well. For instance, they bring messages—in fact, the word *angel* literally means 'messenger.'[25] They communicate God's will; they meet physical needs; they provide protection, strength, and encouragement. They promote evangelism—we see this in Acts 8, where an angel guides Philip in reaching out to an important Ethiopian official with the good news about Jesus."

"What else?" I asked.

"They can rescue believers from danger. For example, in Acts 12 we see Peter imprisoned by King Herod, but an angel comes and frees him. In fact, Peter says in verse 11, 'Now I know without a doubt that the Lord has sent his angel and rescued me from Herod's clutches.' We see angels escorting believers into the next world at the time of their death in Luke 16:22. And at times they can execute God's judgment in the world."

My mind flashed to an example. In Acts 12, the Bible describes how God authorized judgment against King Herod, who had withheld praise from him, and the result was that "an angel of the Lord struck him down."[26]

"Should Christians pray to angels?" I asked. "I know this is permissible in Roman Catholic theology, primarily because of a passage in the apocryphal book of Tobit."[27]

"The book of Tobit is included in the Catholic and Eastern Orthodox canons, but Protestants don't recognize it as being holy Scripture," Potter said. "Frankly, I don't see an example in Scripture of anyone praying directly to angels. We're instructed to pray to our heavenly Father in the name of Jesus, but we have no instructions to directly access the angelic realm."

"Do you see a risk in doing it?"

Potter nodded. "I'd be concerned about a slippery slope where prayer could turn into worship. We see in Revelation how John encounters an angel and instinctively falls down to worship him. But the angel rebukes him by saying, 'Don't do that! I am a fellow servant with you. . . . Worship God!'"[28]

"But," I said, "we could pray to the Father and ask for angelic help, couldn't we?"

I thought about the incident in Gethsemane when Jesus was confronted by a mob, including Judas, and arrested. "Do you think I cannot call on my Father," Jesus asked, "and he will at once put at my disposal more than twelve legions of angels?"[29] At the time a legion was about five thousand soldiers, which means Jesus was saying God could have immediately dispatched sixty thousand powerful angels in his defense.

"Yes, for us to ask God for angelic assistance is certainly fine," said Potter. "We can trust that God will respond to all of our prayers in the best possible way. I mentioned how an angel rescued Peter from prison—well, the Bible says this was in response to prayers to God by Christians. When I was growing up, my grandmother would always pray to God for a hedge of angelic protection around us, and those are certainly appropriate prayers."

Martin Luther would concur. His evening prayer to the Father in his *Small Catechism* concludes with this sentence: "Let Your holy angel be with me, that the evil foe may have no power over me. Amen."[30]

Do We Have a Guardian Angel?

Next I broached a controversial topic that Australian theologian Michael Bird has conceded is "complex"[31]—Does each individual have a "guardian angel" assigned to them by God to watch over and protect them?

"The issue is not whether angels guard," Graham Cole observed. "They clearly do. The issue is whether a specific angel is assigned guardianship of a specific human person. The great early church Bible translator Jerome (347–419) certainly thought so. . . . In the medieval period, Aquinas, following Jerome, whom he quotes, certainly thought so."[32]

Catholic philosopher Peter Kreeft put it this way: "There are twice as many persons as we see in every place, every kitchen or classroom, every hospital or nursery. Only half are *human* persons. There is an angel standing next to each bag lady."[33]

Moreover, the Orthodox tradition teaches that at baptism God assigns every individual a guardian angel.[34]

Theologian Herman Bavinck is among the scholars who disagree. "There is not even a hint that every elect person is assigned his or her own angel," he wrote. "The idea is found only in the apocryphal book of Tobit."[35]

I said to Potter, "One scholar says the idea of individually assigned guardian angels is a text-less doctrine.[36] What's your opinion?"

"I wouldn't characterize it as a text-less doctrine," he said. "How many biblical texts do you need to establish a doctrine if there's a fairly clear reference? And there is a reference to guardian angels in Matthew 18:10, where Jesus himself says, 'See that you do not despise one of these little ones. For I tell you that their angels in heaven always see the face of my Father in heaven.'"

Potter cleared his throat. "Notice that Jesus is referring to *their* angels. T-H-E-I-R. Jesus doesn't elaborate, but that doesn't diminish the reference here. This is Scripture, and it's not denied anywhere else in the Bible."

I interrupted to point out that according to Graham Cole and Michael Green, the emphasis of that text is not on guardianship but on representation of these "little ones" before God.[37]

"Still," said Potter, "it's a reasonable inference that guardian angels exist based on the specific language of the verse. There's another interesting passage too."

"Which one?"

"In Acts 12, Peter, fresh from escaping prison, showed up at the house of Mary, the mother of Mark, where some Christians had gathered. He knocked on the door and the servant Rhoda recognized his voice and announced it was Peter, but the others doubted it because they thought he was still imprisoned. So in verse 15, they say, 'It must be *his angel.*'"[38]

I pointed out that some scholars believe this reflects a popular Jewish belief in the first century that every Jew had a guardian angel and that the author of Acts is *reporting* this rather than *endorsing* this view.[39]

Potter shook his head. "Given Jesus' teaching, I don't think the author of Acts would intentionally mislead readers if the belief about Peter's angel was a falsehood. Why would he do that?" said Potter. "All in all, it's a reasonable inference that guardian angels are real. The texts are sufficiently clear, and they aren't negated elsewhere. Besides, we know there are certainly a sufficient number of angels to carry out this task."

"How does it affect you personally to believe there's an angelic being who is overseeing your life?" I asked.

"It's encouraging. It's comforting. It's such an expression of God's love," he replied. "You know, we can protect ourselves from physical harm by learning martial arts or getting a permit to carry a gun. But what protection do we have in the spiritual realm? There are battles going on there that affect us personally. And knowing I've got some protection immediate to me is reassuring."

He paused. "I'll add this," he said. "The overall study of angels has highlighted to me that what I see and touch—this physical world in which we live—is only part of reality. There's an enormous but hidden supernatural arena populated by angelic spirits that are as real and active as you and me. And when I think that God created them to minister to us—well, that's a blessing that deserves our gratitude."

I reached over to click off my tape recorder. Potter had done an admirable job of describing this fascinating world of angelic beings, but so far we had only discussed part of the story. We hadn't talked about how angels were created by God to be good and holy, and yet an angelic being named Lucifer ended up rebelling and luring many of his compatriots into sin and debauchery. This has initiated an era of spiritual warfare that threatens every person on the planet.

Exactly who is this fallen angel now known as Satan? What influence can his band of demons have on you and me today? And how will this drama eventually play out?

We stood up to take a break before delving into the sinister side of this supernatural realm.

CHAPTER 6

THE SOBERING REALITY OF

SATAN AND DEMONS

Something bizarre occurred in the home of Ivy League–educated psychiatrist Richard Gallagher. Typically, his two cats got along well with each other. "But one night around 3:00 a.m., loud screeching sounds startled me and my wife out of our sleep," he said. "Our two normally docile cats were going at it like champion prizefighters, smacking and clawing at each other, intent on inflicting some serious harm." Even after they were separated, "they continued to growl and bristle." Gallagher and his wife were mystified.

The next morning, as previously planned, a Catholic priest arrived on Gallagher's doorstep, accompanied by Julia, the self-described "high priestess" of a satanic cult. The plan was for Gallagher to examine her to determine if she really was possessed by a demonic spirit.

Julia gazed at him with a smirk. "How'd you like those cats last night?" she asked.[1]

This was just one of the bone-chilling encounters that Gallagher has experienced in twenty-five-plus years of investigating demonic possessions and attacks. Calling himself "a man of science," he started out skeptical about the satanic realm. Then his firsthand work led him to conclude that there are some individuals who aren't mentally compromised but rather are under the influence—or even the temporary control—of malevolent spirits.

What gives his conclusion particular weight is his professional standing as a physician trained in psychiatry at Yale University and psychoanalysis at Columbia University. He has been a professor of clinical psychiatry at New York Medical College and a faculty member of the Psychoanalytic Institute at Columbia University. No less an authority than Joseph T. English, past president of the American Psychiatric Association, called him "highly respected" and "superbly credentialed," with "unimpeachable integrity."[2]

As encouraging as it is to learn about angels and their guarding and guiding of people, as discussed in the previous chapter, it's daunting and disturbing to explore the world of "fallen angels," the pack of rebellious spirits that Christian theology says is led by Satan himself. These evil beings have turned the supernatural realm into a tumultuous battleground for the souls of people like you and me, an otherworldly dimension where malicious creatures scheme to snatch us before we can enter God's eternal embrace.

"To the untrained eye, many possessions may be thought to fall into the psychiatric categories of various psychoses and severe personality and dissociative disorders," said Gallagher. "However, for well-trained psychiatrists and other health professionals, [demonic] possessions differ from such disorders in significant ways."[3]

Gallagher's book *Demonic Foes* documents his role as—in the words of a CNN correspondent—"the go-to guy for a sprawling network of exorcists in the United States."[4] Among the numerous supernatural encounters described are these:[5]

- Exorcisms where demon-possessed people spontaneously speak in Latin or other languages they don't know, growl threats and hurl blasphemous insults at clergy, recoil at holy water but ignore tap water, disclose "hidden knowledge" about people, and even—in one case with eight eyewitnesses—levitate for half an hour.

- Demon-harassed people who experience spiritual "beatings" that leave bruises and scratches that can't otherwise be explained.
- A petite woman, in the throes of deliverance, showing superhuman strength by hurling a two-hundred-pound Lutheran deacon across a room. "That's not psychiatry. That's beyond psychiatry," said Gallagher.
- When Gallagher and a Catholic priest were on the phone discussing the case of the satanic priestess Julia, they were suddenly interrupted by the same guttural threats they had heard during her exorcism: "We said LEAVE HER ALONE, YOU ******* PRIEST. She belongs to us, not you. You'll be SORRY."[6]

Some skeptics have sought to discredit Gallagher's conclusion that demonic possessions are very real, although rare.[7] However, naturalistic explanations seem facile and unconvincing in the face of eyewitness accounts. Clearly, a bias against the supernatural prevents some people from following the evidence wherever it leads, even if it points toward a supernatural reality. And of course, remarkably consistent beliefs about these malevolent spiritual beings can be found in cultures around the world and throughout history.

"We live in a world that is both seen and unseen, and these two realms can influence each other in unimaginable ways," Gallagher said. "A segment of that invisible world seems to be mysteriously but remarkably hostile to human beings and seeks their physical and spiritual destruction. On rare occasions, like some kind of cosmic terrorist, that segment shows its true colors."[8]

The apostle Paul put it this way in Ephesians 6:12: "Our struggle is not against flesh and blood, but against the rulers, against the authorities, against the powers of this dark world and against the spiritual forces of evil in the heavenly realms."

"I Now Know Satan Is Real"

Gallagher isn't the only well-credentialed psychiatrist to abandon skepticism and come to believe in a literal Satan and demons. Harvard-educated M. Scott Peck, best known for his 1978 bestseller *The Road Less Traveled*, also didn't believe in the devil—at least, initially.

"I was a scientist, and it didn't seem to me I should conclude there was no devil until I examined the evidence," he said in an interview. "It occurred to me if I could see one good old-fashioned case of possession, that might change my mind."[9]

Then he came upon cases that were "unexplainable by any kind of traditional psychiatric terms."[10] The result? "I now know Satan is real," he said. "I have met it."[11] Peck, who was baptized as a Christian at age forty-three, described his personal involvement with two exorcisms in his book *Glimpses of the Devil*.[12]

Globally and throughout history, interest in evil spirits has persisted. Some sort of belief in a devil and demons has had a "near-universal appearance in almost every culture since the dawn of time," said journalist Billy Hallowell in his book *Playing with Fire*, which investigated demons and exorcisms.[13]

Craig S. Keener, professor of biblical studies at Asbury Theological Seminary, wrote that "anthropologists have documented spirit possession or analogous experiences in a majority of cultures, although interpretations of the experiences vary." He cited Erika Bourguignon, who sampled 488 societies and found that 74 percent of them believed in some sort of demonic possession.[14]

In the United States, belief in the devil has dropped ten percentage points since 2001, although a majority—58 percent—still affirm his existence. In contrast, nearly one in three Americans is convinced that hell and Satan aren't real. Eight out of ten Protestants believe in a literal devil, while six out of ten Catholics agree. For Republicans, 78 percent say the devil exists, compared to 44 percent of Democrats.[15]

"Some people throughout church history have claimed that Satan is not a real person—an idea no doubt inspired by Satan himself," said prominent apologist Ron Rhodes. "After all, without a real enemy, no one will prepare for defense. And with no preparation for defense, the enemy can attack at will and work his evil while remaining incognito."[16]

Contemporary Christian music pioneer Keith Green gave voice to this idea in his classic song "No One Believes in Me Anymore (Satan's Boast)": "I used to have to sneak around, but now they just open their doors. You know, no one's watching for my tricks because no one believes in me anymore."[17]

Fighting an Enigmatic Enemy

How much can we know with confidence about Satan and his sinister underworld? The Bible contains numerous references to this deceiver and his malevolent crew, using a variety of names and descriptions, including accuser of our brothers and sisters (Revelation 12:10); Beelzebul, or "lord of the flies" (Matthew 12:24); murderer and father of lies (John 8:44); prince of this world (John 12:31; 14:30; 16:11); devil (Matthew 4:11); tempter (Matthew 4:3); serpent (Genesis 3:1–2; Revelation 12:9); roaring lion (1 Peter 5:8–9), and evil one (1 John 5:19).[18]

"Scripture makes it clear . . . that Jesus and his followers took demons seriously," said cultural anthropologist Charles Kraft of Fuller Theological Seminary. "They acknowledged their existence and used the power of the Holy Spirit to fight them. . . . In the gospel of Mark, for example, over half of Jesus' ministry is devoted to delivering the demonized."[19]

Still, many details about Satan's domain remain obscure because Scripture doesn't fill in a lot of specifics, said T. Desmond Alexander, a senior lecturer in biblical studies at Union Theological College in Belfast, Northern Ireland.

"We catch but occasional glimpses of this shadowy opponent. This should not surprise us," he said. "As divine revelation, the Bible . . . is not designed to promote knowledge of the enemy, beyond what is necessary for comprehending the world in which we live. Consequently, many questions remain unanswered when we collate what the Bible says about the devil or Satan."[20]

Noted biblical scholar Walter C. Kaiser Jr. agrees. "Of all the major personalities in the Bible," he said, "Satan is perhaps the most enigmatic."[21]

I wanted to pin down what we can know for sure about this fallen angel who leads a dangerous dimension of the supernatural realm. After our discussion on angelology in the preceding chapter, I prepared to continue my conversation with Douglas Potter, who collaborated with the late theologian Norman L. Geisler to write the book *The Doctrine of Angels and Demons*.

I intended to avoid falling into one of the extremes mentioned by C. S. Lewis. "There are two equal and opposite errors into which our race can fall about the devils," he wrote in *The Screwtape Letters*. "One is to disbelieve in their existence. The other is to believe, and to feel an excessive and unhealthy interest in them."[22]

INTERVIEW *with*

DOUGLAS E. POTTER, DMIN: PART 2

Seated back in Potter's austere seminary office, I resumed our interview by quoting historian W. Scott Poole, author of *Satan in America*: "In the United States over the last forty to fifty years, a composite image of Satan has emerged that borrows from both popular culture and theological sources."[1]

I looked up from my notes. "Poole said the opinions of most

American Christians about Satan are a blend of what they learn from movies with what theological traditions teach," I said. "He's right, isn't he?"

"Unfortunately, most people have learned more about the demonic world from watching *The Exorcist* or *The Omen* than from reading the Gospels," came Potter's reply. "Often, people are more attracted to lurid claims in the media and entertainment industry rather than doing a sober-minded study of the Scriptures."

Indeed, a "satanic panic" swept America in the 1980s, which Poole attributed to "a rash of false claims, media sensationalism, and religious entrepreneurs who either claimed to be reformed and redeemed ex-Satanists or to have knowledge of vast networks of conspiracy."[2] Scholar Bill Ellis said the result of this satanism scare was a "needless ruin of reputations and livelihoods."[3]

And perhaps we're entering another phase of national fixation on Satan. The cover of *Harper's Magazine* in August 2024 called attention to what it called "the new satanic panic" and "the new age of American exorcisms."[4]

"How can we know that Satan is an actual being and not just a metaphorical personification of evil, as many liberal Christians believe?" I asked Potter. "What is the evidence that he really exists?"

"Most importantly, we have the biblical confirmation," he replied. "Every writer of the New Testament recognized the reality of Satan as an authentic spiritual being. He is depicted as having all the traits of personhood—intellect, for instance; he's described as 'cunning' in 2 Corinthians 11:3. He has emotions, such as desire, jealousy, hate, and anger.[5] He has a will—for example, he gives commands.[6]

"And," he added, "if you're unsure of the Bible's divine credentials but respect Jesus as a teacher, look at how he refers to Satan some twenty-five times in the Gospels. These are four ancient biographies that bear the earmarks of historical credibility.[7] Here we find Jesus personally encountering Satan and being tempted by him.[8] He talks directly to Satan and demons.[9] Jesus never taught that Satan was just an idea or personification of evil; to him, he was a personal being who was very real—and dangerous. So when people deny the existence of a personal Satan, they're really impugning the integrity of Jesus."

I interrupted. "Is there any other corroboration of Satan's existence?"

Potter weighed the question for a moment. "Consider Israel as a people," he said, looking at me intently.

"What do you mean?"

"Statistically, they're just a tiny fraction of the number of people on the planet. And yet look at history—they have consistently, throughout the centuries, been the victims of attempted genocide, all the way through medieval pogroms to Hitler to modern Islamic terrorism. The Jews are the people through whom Jesus entered our world on his journey of redemption. Is this rabid hatred of Jews merely a coincidence? I think the historical antipathy toward them is best explained as emanating from one sinister evil mind.

"Then, we have convincing reports of demonic possessions in contemporary times that can't be explained in traditional psychological terms," he continued. "In fact, we're seeing an increase in demonic influence in the world—a seemingly unified conspiracy against God and his people. Again, this is consistent with a leader of a demonic force."

"Anything else?" I asked.

"I'd add this," he said. "We're seeing an extraordinary proliferation of false religions and cults that are pointing people away from salvation through the one true God. In my view, this also suggests the existence of a great deceiver."[10]

Persuasive points, I mused. Taken together, they seemed to bolster the likelihood that belief in a satanic reality is credibly rooted rather than simply being a superstitious supposition. Still, I needed to delve deeper to further my understanding of the topic.

Where Did Satan Come From?

I wanted to go back to the beginning and explore when and how Satan and his army of demons came into existence. While I knew that the biblical accounts of this momentous event are stingy on details, there is nevertheless sufficient information to reconstruct an outline of what took place—the good angel Lucifer, whose name means "morning star," transformed into the evil Satan, whose name means "adversary."

"Most people presume that sin entered the world with Adam and Eve, but there was a prior spiritual rebellion," I said to Potter. "Tell me about it."

"Lucifer was created by God as an angel[11]—in fact, many scholars interpret Ezekiel 28:14 as saying that he was the highest of all created beings and a cherub."

"So he was created good."

"That's right. God cannot create evil. But God did endow the angels with free will, which Lucifer used to turn away from his creator. The nature of his sin was pride. Interpretations of this passage vary, but Isaiah seems to say that Lucifer bragged, 'I will raise my throne above the stars of God' and 'I will make myself like the Most High.'[12] The bottom line is that Lucifer wanted to be the ultimate being and have dominion over everything."

"He wanted to be worshiped," I observed.

"Yes," said Potter. "In fact, isn't it interesting that when Satan tempted Jesus in the wilderness, he promised he would give him all the kingdoms of this world 'if you will bow down and worship me.' He craved Jesus' worship. And Jesus rebuffed him by declaring, 'Away from me, Satan!' and saying that only God should be worshiped and served."[13]

"When did the fall of Lucifer occur?"

"Definitely prior to Adam and Eve's sin in Genesis. We know this because Satan appeared as the serpent in the Garden of Eden and tempted Eve. Some believe Lucifer's fall came on the second day of creation, since that's the only day that was not called 'good' in Genesis."

"The result of Lucifer's rebellion was—what, specifically?"

"He was expelled from heaven,[14] his character was corrupted,[15] his power was perverted,[16] and he led some other angels—we're not sure precisely how many[17]—into following in his defection, all of which will lead to their final destruction in the end, according to Revelation 20:10."

I pointed out that Swiss theologian Karl Barth contended Satan was never a good angel in the first place.[18] He cited John 8:44, which says that Satan was a murderer from the beginning.[19]

Potter shook his head. "It's clear from the context that John was referring to the beginning of human history," he explained. "Otherwise, you run into theological problems. God would have been responsible for creating evil, which he cannot do."

"Some people make the incorrect assumption that Satan is the polar opposite of God, and that they're somehow equal in power," I said. "But since Satan is an angelic being, though a powerful one, he's limited to what angels can do."

"Exactly. He *is* powerful, but he's not omniscient. His knowledge is limited. He can't read our minds. He's a spirit being, but he's not present everywhere as God is. He can't work supernatural miracles, though he can achieve supernormal feats. For instance, the book of Job tells us he can cause fire from the sky and a mighty wind."[20]

A look of disgust came over his face. "Typically, Satan tries to imitate what God can do," he said. "In a sense, he's a master magician. He likes to fool people into thinking he's more powerful than he really is."

"The Prince of This World"

Although the term *fallen angels* is never specifically used in the Bible, the term *demon* is found numerous times, as early as Deuteronomy 32:17, which says, "They sacrificed to demons that were not gods" (ESV). Every book in the New Testament, except Hebrews, mentions demons, and Jesus not only affirmed their existence but cast them out and authorized his disciples to do the same.[21]

"There's a popular belief that demons are the spirits of deceased evil people," I said to Potter.

"That's ancient folklore," he replied. "As I mentioned, demons are spirit beings—angels—that fell with Satan, who they regard as their prince.[22] Many have already been confined, which may be only temporary for some of them. Again, they have the same powers that are common to angelic beings, though their agenda is to follow Satan in opposing the plan and goodness of God."

"How do they do that?"

"They promote immorality. They can afflict people through physical disease. Paul said the so-called thorn in his flesh was instigated by a demon.[23] They can stoke mental disorders. They help corrupt the culture. As for Christians, they can tempt them, cause division, promote jealous and selfish ambition. They pervert the gospel. Revelation 2:8–10 says Satan and demons can also be the cause of persecution."[24]

"Clearly," I said, "demons believe in the existence of God."

"Yes, and James 2:19 says they shudder as a result. That's a good reminder that believing *that* God exists isn't enough to save a person; this requires a belief *in* God—that is, repenting and putting our trust in him through his Son Jesus."

"Could demons ever be redeemed by God?" I asked. "After all, humans are sinners, and Jesus died to make our redemption possible."

"No," came Potter's quick reply. "Christ assumed *human* nature—not angelic nature—when he came to redeem the world. The Bible portrays the lost state of demons as final and eternal. In other words, once they made up their mind, it was fixed forever, just as ours would be fixed at death if we reject the gospel."

Potter searched his memory. "Besides," he added, "I can't recall a single instance in the Bible where demons are called on to repent, as people are."

"How do demons influence people?"

"A lot of times we're led into sin by our own corrupt nature, without any tempting by Satan," he said. "Most commonly, Satan and his minions influence the world at large—after all, the apostle John called Satan the prince of this world[25]—and then in turn we're influenced by that culture."

"Give me an example."

"Satan may influence the entertainment industry to produce funny movies and television shows that subtly promote sexual immorality. People laugh at the shows, but subconsciously the content is corrupting them and prompting them to sin. Satan doesn't always have to individually tempt people if he can poison the culture and let the culture debase the masses."

Exorcisms Yesterday and Today

There's one fact about Jesus that even highly skeptical scholars accept: He was known as a miracle worker who drove out demons. New Testament historian Gary Habermas said that due to strong historical support in the Gospels, "critical scholars virtually across the scholarly spectrum acknowledge that Jesus was a healer and an exorcist."[26] Even the highly skeptical historian Marcus Borg conceded that "on historical grounds it is virtually indisputable" that Jesus healed the sick and expelled the demonic."[27]

I pivoted in my conversation with Potter to discuss this provocative topic of demon possession and exorcisms. "Isn't it likely that Jesus and others in his era mistook mental illness as demon possession?" I asked.

"Actually, we see a delineation between those who were physically sick and those who were under demonic attack," said Potter.

"For example, Matthew 8:16 reads, 'When evening came, many who were demon-possessed were brought to [Jesus], and he drove out the spirits with a word and healed all the sick.' This recognizes the difference between those needing physical healing and those requiring an exorcism. Plus, in some cases, demons can cause disease and affliction."

"How do you define demonic possession?" I asked.

"This is when one or more demons exercise their will or power in control of a human being," he said. "Because demons are spirits that can't materialize on their own, they seek embodiment in physical beings. Consequently, possession is something that occurs on the inside, whereas demonic oppression is an attack from without."

"How do you react when you see a contemporary media report that someone is demon-possessed or undergoing an exorcism?"

"I'm careful with this," came his response. "Frankly, I find that there's a lot of fakery, a lot of exaggeration, and even a lot of outright lies in this area, so I start out with a degree of skepticism. Still, there are rare cases that do have the characteristics of being authentic. I don't see anything in Scripture to suggest this phenomenon ended in biblical days, and there are possession accounts today that do come from credible sources."

"When we say that demons can possess a person, what does that entail?"

"We see in the Gospels how demons can produce physical afflictions, such as muteness," he replied. "Matthew 9:32 described a man who was demon-possessed and could not talk. Matthew 12:22 says another demon-possessed man was both mute and blind. Luke 9:37–43 describes how demons possessed a boy and threw him into convulsions."

Potter continued. "Sometimes people who are demon-possessed show supernormal strength, like the man who lived in the tombs and was so wild that no one was strong enough to subdue him. He broke his chains and the irons on his feet before Jesus cast out the demons.[28] The apostle John said another demon-possessed man became 'raving mad.'[29] In another instance, demons seemed to bring occultic power to a person."[30]

"Are there activities that people engage in that make them vulnerable to demonic attack?" I asked.

"A pattern of unconfessed sin can make a person susceptible," he said. "And dabbling in the occult can open that door. It's like inviting a grown tiger into your house, thinking he'll be a docile pet, when he ends up tearing the place apart and terrorizing you. You want to get the tiger out, but guess what? He wants to stay. You need to have a stronger power to remove him, just as the power of the gospel is needed to chase out the demonic."

"So your advice is . . ."

"Don't get mired in sin. Steer clear of the occult. Don't dabble in Ouija boards. Don't consult psychics. Don't tinker with the dark arts. Don't open the door to the tiger."

"And if someone does become possessed by an evil spirit, how can they be rescued?"

"Different traditions stress different approaches," he replied. "For example, Roman Catholics have an elaborate rite of exorcism."

I knew there are more than 250 trained Catholic exorcists in Italy alone. There's even an International Association of Exorcists that was founded in the early 1990s. The Catholic rite of exorcism, revised in 1999, has 6,295 words "and involves numerous prayers and appeals to God, Mary, and the saints," said theologian Graham Cole in his book *Against the Darkness*.[31]

Churches in the Orthodox tradition have exorcism prayers drawn from the early church fathers.[32] Modern charismatic churches offer prayers of deliverance for those who are spiritually afflicted.

To Potter, the most effective antidote to the demonic remains the gospel message. "Paul said in Ephesians 1:19–20 that the gospel carries the same power that raised Jesus from the dead," Potter said.

"And if the individual comes to an authentic faith in Christ, they can no longer be occupied by the demonic at the same time."

Can Demons Possess a Christian?

The Bible describes a variety of ways in which Satan and his demons seek to harm people who are Christians. Satan tempts believers to sin and engage in sexual immorality; he accuses and slanders them; he incites persecution; he stokes spiritual doubts; he instigates jealousy and friction between believers; and he can foster spiritual pride in their hearts.[33] In light of the ability of demons to tempt, attack, and oppress Christians, it's no wonder that James 4:7 offers this stern admonition: "Resist the devil."

That brings up an obvious question. "Can demons actually possess a Christian?" I asked Potter.

"I don't see any passage in Scripture where a believer is possessed by an evil spirit," said Potter. "I don't think it's possible, because believers are indwelt by the Holy Spirit and therefore can't be indwelt by an evil spirit at the same time. When a person comes to faith in Christ, he becomes the possession of God through sealing and the permanent indwelling of the third person of the Trinity. No demon can coexist with God in our life."

A possible exception came to mind. "What about Peter?" I asked.

I was referring to the incident in which Jesus foretold the sufferings and death awaiting him in Jerusalem and Peter rebuked him by saying, "This shall never happen to you!" Jesus' response was to say: "Get behind me, Satan!"[34]

"Was Jesus suggesting that Peter was possessed by Satan at that point?" I asked Potter.

"No, nothing in the text mentions possession," he said. "Satan may have been *influencing* Peter, and Jesus' response seems to have been prompted because Peter's words were reminiscent of Satan's previous temptation to circumvent the cross."

"What about Ananias, who was a believer?" I asked. "When he and his wife sold some property and he withheld part of the money for himself, Peter said Satan had filled his heart.[35] Doesn't that indicate he was possessed by demons?"

Potter wasn't buying it. "We see elsewhere that the term *filled* can mean 'influenced,' and I think that's what was going on there" he said.[36]

"How about Judas?" I asked. "John 13:27 clearly says Satan entered into him."

"No question that Judas was influenced or possibly possessed by Satan," he replied. "But keep in mind that we have good reasons to conclude he was not an authentic believer."[37]

"What if a Christian comes under demonic influence or oppression, short of being demonically possessed?" I asked. "What's the best course of action for them to take?"

"They should confess their sin, renounce Satan, disengage from any occultic involvement, flee from temptation, meditate on the Word of God and apply it in their life, live consistently with biblical truth, and, of course, bring it to the Lord in prayer and seek the prayers of others," he said. "Remember that God's power exceeds Satan's on all levels."

What Is Spiritual Warfare?

In 2012, theologians James K. Beilby and Paul Rhodes Eddy published a book that explored four different perspectives related to "spiritual warfare."[38] Another theologian responded by offering four more models.[39] While there are differing viewpoints on the issue, it's clear that Christians today are in dire need of a strategy to fight back against the malignant influences of Satan and his minions. That's because even though Jesus paid the price of redemption two thousand years ago, supernatural evil continues to flourish, since history has not yet culminated with the demise of Satan.

French Lutheran scholar Oscar Cullmann offered this analogy: D-Day occurred in 1944 when the Allies stormed the beaches at Normandy, which was the decisive victory in the European theater of World War II. However, final victory in the war didn't come until the following year with Germany's surrender at V-E Day. Cullmann said that, eschatologically speaking, Christians are living between D-Day and V-E Day.[40]

"The cross was decisive, but much remains to happen before evil is finally extinguished," Graham Cole wrote. "The contest between good and evil continues."[41] He cited the apostle Paul in Galatians 1:4, where our time frame is called "the present evil age."

The term *spiritual warfare* can't be found in the Bible, though it's definitely described. The apostle Paul said in 2 Corinthians 10:3–4, "For though we live in the world, we do not wage war as the world does. The weapons we fight with are not the weapons of the world. On the contrary, they have divine power to demolish strongholds."

Cole defines spiritual warfare as "our common struggle as Christians against the machinations of malevolent spiritual creatures that are intent on thwarting God's redemptive plan for his human creatures."[42]

Billy Graham's global evangelism ministry certainly stirred opposition from cosmic forces of evil. He described our circumstances by saying, "This invisible spiritual conflict is waged around us incessantly and unremittingly. Where the Lord works, Satan's forces hinder; where angel beings carry out their divine directives, the devils rage. All this comes about because the powers of darkness press their counterattack to recapture the ground held for the glory of God."[43]

"What's your perspective on spiritual warfare?" I asked Potter. "How can Christians protect themselves against what the apostle Paul called the flaming arrows of the evil one?"[44]

"I can't do any better than Paul in Ephesians 6," came his reply.

"He reminds us that our real struggle is against the spiritual forces of evil in the heavenly realms. He not only urges us to stand firm, but then he gives a strategy through the imagery of the armor worn by Roman soldiers at the time. This is defensive warfare—how we can endure in the face of Satan's attacks."

With that, Potter walked through what Paul described as putting on "the full armor of God, so that you can take your stand against the devil's schemes."[45]

"There's the breastplate of righteousness," began Potter. "This means living in light of our righteous standing or position in Christ, which comes to us because of the substitutionary work of Christ on the cross.

"Then there's the belt of truth, which gives us the ability to answer the lies of Satan. We need to be conversant with the truth of Scripture so we can discern when the evil one is trying to deceive us. Next is the sandals, which clad the soldier's feet and represent our willingness to share the peace of God through the gospel.

"The shield of faith is a defensive weapon that enables us—through our faith and trust in God—to make spiritual advances while under attack. The helmet of salvation protects our mind. We need to have a thoughtful dependence on the salvation of God. The sword of the Spirit represents the Word of God, which we need to wield with confidence and precision to counter Satan, as Christ did when he was tempted."

I spoke up. "Paul ends this list by emphasizing the need for prayer," I said. I referred to my notes and quoted biblical scholar Clinton Arnold: "Prayer is the essence of spiritual warfare and the most important means by which believers are strengthened by God."[46]

"Absolutely," Potter replied. "We need to pray for God's protection and guidance, for his power in our lives, and for our strength, endurance, and faithfulness. Let's always remember that God and Satan are not coequals, but God's power is infinitely greater and will eventually result in Satan and his followers being thrown into the lake of fire at the consummation of history."[47]

What Everyone Should Know

The alarm on my phone buzzed. It was time to wrap up our conversation so I could catch my flight home. Still, there was one remaining question I wanted to ask Potter: "What do you wish everyone in the world knew about Satan and his demons?"

He contemplated my inquiry. I could see the weight of the topic on his face. Finally, he drew on the two errors that C. S. Lewis warned about—disbelieving in Satan or obsessing about him.[48]

"I'd want people to know that if they're not safely adopted into God's family, they face genuine danger," he said. "Satan and his demons are very real spiritual entities that are influencing our world on a macro level, while also influencing individuals on a micro scale. Not only will Satan ruin your life, but he's already in the process of destroying it, even though you don't realize it."

He paused to let the gravity of that last statement sink in. "For those people who are Christians," he continued, "I'd want them to have confidence in God's love and protection. James 4:7 says to us as followers of Christ that if we resist Satan, he will flee from us. It doesn't say he *might* flee, but that he *will* retreat. Remember Romans 8:31: 'If God is for us, who can be against us?' Then verse 34 says that Christ Jesus is 'at the right hand of God and is also interceding for us.' We are described as being 'more than conquerors through him who loved us.'[49] And finally, in the climax of this passage, Paul says this—."

Potter picked up a Bible and flipped to Romans 8. His voice took on a pastoral tone as he read, "I am convinced that neither death nor life, *neither angels nor demons*, neither the present nor the future, nor any powers, neither height nor depth, nor anything else in all creation, will be able to separate us from the love of God that is in Christ Jesus our Lord."[50]

He closed the Bible. "That's the key," he said. "Yes, Christians should be aware of the spiritual forces arrayed against them. Yes, we should stand firm and put on the full armor of God. But ultimately this encouraging biblical truth prevails: 'The one who is in you is greater than the one who is in the world.'"[51]

PART 2

THE
SUPERNATURAL
THAT AWAITS US

CHAPTER 7

DEATHBED VISIONS: GLIMPSES OF THE AFTERLIFE?

Now-retired hospice nurse Trudy Harris tells about a well-educated patient named Frederick, who was in his late seventies. As he approached his death, she found him crying "very, very hard."

"He proceeded to tell me that Jesus himself had come into his bedroom, here at the hospice center," she said. "Gesturing to a corner of the room, he explained that Jesus had stood 'right here,' near the foot of the bed. He said Jesus' presence had filled the room with the most incredible sense of compassion, beauty, and forgiveness he had ever seen. He spoke of the love and tenderness he saw clearly reflected in his eyes, and the awareness he felt of being loved deeply, just for himself."

"If I saw Jesus like you did, would I cry too?" she asked.

"Oh, yes," he replied.

"Why would I cry?"

"Because he is so beautiful," he said. "And because he loves us so much and forgives all our sins."

Harris said that despite all of Frederick's education and experience in life, he "simply did not know the depth of love God had for him. The hole in his heart was filled to capacity in the last hours of his life."[1]

Stories of supernatural deathbed encounters are much more common than people think. Actually, there are several different categories of afterlife experiences, such as people seeing angels coming to escort them to the next world, just as Jesus confirmed they do in Luke 16:22, or instances in which the dying and their relatives are both eyewitnesses to supernatural phenomena.

Billy Graham told the story about the passing of his maternal grandmother. "The room seemed to fill with a heavenly light," he said. "She sat up in bed and almost laughingly said, 'I see Jesus. He has his arms outstretched toward me. I see Ben [her husband who had died some years earlier] and I see the angels.' Then she slumped over, absent from the body but present with the Lord."[2]

Graham's former pulpit partner, Charles Templeton, became the most famous agnostic in Canada after losing his faith at a liberal seminary. However, one of his close friends believes he returned to Jesus before he died, because on his deathbed he called out to his wife, "Madeleine, do you see them? Do you *hear* them? The angels! They're calling my name! I'm going home!" Later he cried out: "Look at them, look at them! They're so beautiful. They're waiting for me. Oh, their eyes, their eyes are so beautiful." Then, with great joy, he exclaimed, "I'm coming!"[3]

Harris, president of the Hospice Foundation for Caring, had once been skeptical of such deathbed experiences, believing that the visions were the result of medication or dehydration. "Surely the visions could not be real," she wrote. "But when others who were dying and not on medication and not dehydrated were saying the same things, I started to listen, really listen."[4]

What do we hear when we really listen to the dying? Many times, say hospice workers, it takes quite a bit of prodding to get the real story, because people fear they will be considered crazy if they were to reveal what happened to them. But when they do describe their supernatural encounters, they invariably stress that these were not dreams or hazy products of their imagination but were as real as anything they had ever experienced.

For a skeptic like me, here's the key issue: Are there any circumstances that would add to the credibility of a dying patient's account? For example, what if there were scientifically conducted studies of these phenomena, where experts analyze data from thousands of cases and come to informed conclusions about their authenticity?

Deathbed visions are different from near-death experiences (NDE). In an NDE, the individual is *clinically* dead—frequently, no heartbeat or brain waves—but they describe being conscious nonetheless, sometimes seeing or hearing things that would have been impossible if they hadn't had an out-of-body experience. These people, though, return to life to tell their story. I'll explore the topic of near-death experiences in the following chapter.

In deathbed experiences, patients have a supernatural encounter of some sort toward the end of their lives and then are able to share it—usually quite briefly—before they *irreversibly* die.

"As a Christian, I'm surprised at how quickly some Christ followers dismiss stories of those near death, seemingly without careful study," said pastor and spiritual investigator John Burke.[5]

I wanted to dig beneath mere anecdotes and get to the core of these otherworldly phenomena. That prompted me to seek out a university professor who has been exploring these supernatural reports for years. In fact, they were the subject of his doctoral dissertation.

J. STEVE MILLER, PHD

Steve Miller grew up in the foothills of Dalton, Georgia, where faith was on the periphery of his life. That is, until high school when his infatuation with a girl led him to join her on a Christian ski retreat. His interactions with the speaker led Steve to ask himself, *Why am I fooling around outside God's will and missing out on his best?* Privately, he made a commitment to following Christ. No emotions, no visions—just a rational decision that made sense to him at the time.

What he lacked, though, was an intellectual foundation for his faith. And that was problematic for someone like Miller, a skeptic by nature who doggedly researches issues that trouble him.

His subsequent exploration of faith culminated in the study of comparative religions, theology, psychology of religion, and philosophy of religion at Dalton State College, the University of Georgia, Columbia International University, Trinity Evangelical Divinity School, and Southwest Baptist Theological Seminary.

Then in 2010, a relative persuaded him to read a book about someone who said they had a near-death experience. Miller's verdict was cautious. "It may have happened as they said, but I don't personally know the family, so why should I trust them?"

However, an endorsement of the book captured Miller's attention. A physician named Jeffrey Long said he had scientifically studied more than sixteen hundred NDEs. Miller was incredulous. "Scientists have been studying these things?" he asked. "I need to see if they've found anything significant."

He discovered that there is extensive and compelling research into NDEs by reputable intellectuals, including physicians, psychiatrists, and psychologists, some of whom teach in respected universities and publish in scientific journals.

Miller's own research resulted in his first book on the subject, *Near-Death Experiences as Evidence for the Existence of God and Heaven*. Along the way, he began looking into deathbed visions, which he thought would make a good topic for his doctoral dissertation if he could find a hundred or so sources. He was surprised to find no fewer than eight hundred relevant sources, including studies conducted by top-tier intellectuals at some of the most respected universities, including Harvard and Cambridge.

This led to his books *Deathbed Experiences as Evidence for the Afterlife* and *Is Christianity Compatible with Deathbed and Near-Death Experiences?* Among his other books are *Faith That's Not Blind: A Brief Introduction to Contemporary Arguments for the Existence of God*, and *Why Brilliant People Believe Nonsense*, which he coauthored with his wife.

Having received his doctorate from Columbia International University in 2018, Miller now teaches religious studies at Kennesaw State University, a large institution north of Atlanta.

I bought an airline ticket to visit him, but a sudden illness resulted in my hospitalization. Unable to travel for a while, I arranged to interview Miller via Zoom. He was wearing earphones in his home office, with a haphazard pile of books on a credenza behind him. His most distinctive feature, other than his gray hair and full beard, was his thick—and utterly charming—Southern drawl.

The Frequency of Deathbed Visions

I began by observing how common stories about deathbed visions are. When a podcast with Miller on the topic was posted on YouTube, I expected the comments would come primarily from skeptics. Instead, a flurry of people submitted story after story about deathbed experiences from their own sphere of relationships.

"Absolutely, yes, the frequency of these stories still astounds me," Miller said. "It seems that wherever I go and people find out about my area of research, so many of them spontaneously offer their own stories."

"Can you quantify how widespread they are?"

"Recent studies at an inpatient hospice facility in New York asked residents daily to report any such vivid dreams, as distinct from normal dreams, as well as visions when they were awake, such as visiting with deceased relatives or angels. One of the studies found that 88 percent of the patients reported such deathbed visions. They were so realistic that patients reported them as the most awake, alert, and present that they had ever felt."

Clearly energized, Miller leaned forward. "Let that sink in," he said. "Since the remaining 12 percent might be experiencing such visions beyond the time they're able to communicate, perhaps deathbed visions are simply intrinsic to dying. It's as if the dying aren't fading away but rather are making a transition to another conscious realm."

I asked, "Does the sheer frequency of these experiences contribute to their credibility?"

"Absolutely, in several ways. First, the cases might be more easily explained away if these were rare, anomalous experiences. Atheists would simply chalk this up to a coincidence that's bound to occur occasionally since billions of people die, and certainly out of that many, a few will hallucinate. Yet if deathbed experiences are quite common, you can't easily explain them away.

"Second, if you go to the research and collections of stories I discuss in my books, you'll find thousands of accounts that can be individually examined and studied.

"Third, their frequency allows us to investigate cases up close, among trusted friends and family who have had these experiences. It's one thing to read about the research; it's quite another to talk to a credible acquaintance about a dramatic deathbed experience they know about."

"Have you found stories about afterlife experiences among your own relatives?"

"Oh, yes," he said. "I remember when I was writing my book on near-death experiences, my mom said I should tell a relative named Bucky what I was working on. Bucky told me, 'I've had three of those.' Now, technically, these were visionary experiences. But the point is that I trust him because I know him. He's quite intelligent, holding a master's degree in history and having taught history most of his life."

"Tell me about one of his experiences."

"He woke up at three in the morning feeling an extreme weight on his chest, like people describe a heart attack. He saw a light in the distance, then left his body and observed his body from the viewpoint of the ceiling, and he saw celestial beings. He experienced the extreme peace reported by so many people. Then he found himself back in his body in a cold sweat. Immediately, the phone rang—and a nurse told him his father, who lived ninety miles away and had not been ill, had died suddenly of a heart attack."

"That's fascinating," I said. "How would you analyze his report critically?"

"On the face of it, something supernatural seemed to have occurred," he replied. "He is a credible person with no motive to invent a false story. He wasn't out sharing this with everybody. We all know the limitations of our physical senses—I don't know what's going on downstairs or next door, much less ninety miles away. His symptoms mimicked a heart attack, apparently within the hour his dad had experienced one." With that, his eyes locked on mine. "Let me ask this," he said. "What are the odds of that happening by pure chance?"

The Vision of Mark Twain

Prompted by his last statement, I asked Miller whether researchers have attempted to quantify the odds of these kind of deathbed experiences taking place by random chance.

"Two highly respected nineteenth-century academics—Henry Sidgwick of Cambridge University and William James from Harvard University—were part of a team that surveyed seventeen thousand people and found that about 10 percent of them claimed to have seen people who were not physically there. The largest subcategory was people who saw someone who had just died. The researchers narrowed the cases down to those who reported such visions within twenty-four hours of the person's death and compared this to the statistical probability that someone would die in any given twenty-four-hour period."

"What did they conclude?"

"There were 440 times more cases than the number that would be expected by sheer chance. Their conclusion was that random chance could not explain such experiences, and they published their results in a nearly four-hundred-page peer-reviewed journal article."[1]

Miller added that there would probably be even more reports of deathbed visions if people weren't reluctant to share them. "It seems to me that the pervasive assumption of materialism in our culture has made many people hesitant to share these experiences for fear of being considered a bit loony or naive," he said.

So, he added, it was no surprise that when an investigative journalist published an article about deathbed experiences in the *New York Times* magazine, more than thirteen hundred people made comments within the month, with many of them sharing stories of their relatives' deathbed visions and encounters.[2]

"Maybe they didn't feel like they had anyone in their life who would take their story seriously and as a result they kept quiet about it," Miller said. "But when they read an intelligent article that validated their encounters, they became willing to share what happened."

Adding credibility is the fact that many stories about other-worldly experiences come from spiritual doubters. "For example, skeptics claim Mark Twain as one of their own. He made fun of religion," Miller said. "But in his autobiography, he describes a vivid dream or vision he had of his brother in a metal casket, set upon two chairs, wearing Twain's suit, topped with 'a great bouquet of flowers, mainly white roses, with a red rose in the center.' It was so realistic that when he woke he believed it had really happened, and he was relieved to discover his brother was still alive."

Within a few days, though, his brother was severely injured when a boiler exploded on a riverboat, and he died within a week.

"When Twain visited the funeral and saw the casket, it was just as his vision had foreseen," Miller said. "What are the odds that all of these specifics would come true for his healthy twenty-year-old brother? The death; the metal—rather than wooden—casket; the casket being set on two chairs; Twain's coat, which he didn't even know had been borrowed; and the red flower topping a white flower arrangement."[3]

Miller paused to let me consider the scenario. Then he added, "The atheist Bertrand Russell was once asked what kind of evidence would convince him that God exists. He said if a voice from the sky predicted specific, improbable events that would happen to him in the next twenty-four hours, he would concede that there must be some sort of superhuman intelligence."

Miller leaned back in his chair. "Isn't Twain's vivid vision—and so many others like it—quite similar to the sign that Russell imagined?"

"Overwhelming Confidence in the Afterlife"

I asked Miller about the conclusions reached by researchers who have delved into various kinds of deathbed experiences. He began by referencing the study of seventeen thousand people he had mentioned earlier, concluding that mere chance can't explain away their experiences. "To me, their findings were more consistent with the afterlife hypothesis than the naturalistic hypothesis," he said.

"Then there's the study done by Karlis Osis and Erlendur Haraldsson, who had research doctorates from the University of Munich and the University of Freiburg in Germany. They interviewed more than a thousand doctors and nurses in both the United States and India regarding deathbed vision reports of their patients."

"What did they conclude?"

"That these visions could not be explained away as dreams or having been induced by drugs or dementia. They concluded that the core experience—found in two countries with vastly different expectations of death—was best explained as experiences with the afterlife.[4] And there's more," he said.

Two other researchers who focused on more than three thousand cases concluded that these experiences "are definitely not hallucinations, fantasies, or memories caused by grief. Nor are they projections of the subconscious mind or products of an overactive imagination."[5]

In addition, said Miller, "lifetime studies were conducted by such respected intellects as classical scholar Frederic Myers, physicist Sir William Barrett, and French astronomer Camille Flammarion. Over ninety years, they collected and reflected on more than thirty thousand cases and reported their research in ten volumes comprising almost six thousand pages."

"Were these religious types?" I asked.

"Actually, they were credentialed scholars who taught and researched in top-tier secular settings. Yet they all concluded that deathbed experiences, many with corroborating evidence, could not be explained away as chance events. When I read the multitudes of their cases, along with the observations and reasonings of the researchers, I came away with an overwhelming confidence in the afterlife."

Supernatural Experiences of the Dying

Miller's own research spanned several different permutations of death-related phenomenon. I decided to ask specifically about deathbed visions in which people in the throes of dying seem to get a glimpse into the afterlife.

"Can you give me an example?" I asked Miller.

"Sure," he replied. "A classic deathbed vision was reported by William Barrett, who was a professor at Ireland's prestigious Royal College of Science. His physician wife treated a patient named Doris, who was dying after giving birth."

I was familiar with the account, which Barrett describes this way in his book *Deathbed Visions*:

> Suddenly, she looked eagerly towards one part of the room, a radiant smile illuminating her whole countenance. "Oh, lovely, lovely," she said. I asked, "What is lovely?" "What I *see*," she replied in low, intense tones. "What do you see?" "Lovely, brightness—wonderful beings." It is difficult to describe the sense of reality conveyed by her intense absorption in the vision. Then—seeming to focus her attention more intently on one place for a moment—she exclaimed, almost with a kind of joyous cry, "Why, it's father! Oh, he's so glad I'm coming; he *is* so glad. It would be perfect if only W (her husband) would come too."
>
> Her baby was brought for her to see. She looked at it with interest, and then said, "Do you think I ought to stay for baby's sake?" Then turning towards the vision again, she said, "I can't—I can't stay; if you could see what I do, you would know I can't stay."
>
> On looking at the same place again, she said with a rather puzzled expression, "He has Vida with him,"

turning again to me saying, "Vida is with him." Then she said, "You do want me, Dad, I am coming." Then, Doris died.[6]

I asked Miller, "Who was Vida?"

"That was her sister," he replied. "She had died three weeks earlier, a fact that everyone had kept from Doris because they didn't want to upset her."

"What's your assessment of that account?" I asked.

"You can see why Barrett felt motivated to collect and study deathbed visions for the rest of his life," he said. "From a naturalistic standpoint, why would a young wife with a family, who is experiencing painful physical trauma, suddenly seem perfectly at peace, determined to leave this world and go to another realm, and to see someone in the afterlife she didn't know had died?"

As for Barrett, he said that the evidential value of these visions "is greatly enhanced when the fact is undeniably established that the dying person was wholly ignorant of the decease of the person he or she so vividly sees." His conclusion? "These cases form, perhaps, one of the most cogent arguments for survival after death."[7]

I asked Miller, "Are there characteristics that are common among deathbed visions?"

"They aren't the result of deep meditation or patients seeking a religious experience," Miller said. "They come unexpectedly and yet are taken as real. In fact, people often stress that these are far more vivid than a dream. People report visiting with deceased relatives, angels, God—or whatever name their worldview gives to the ultimate deity—and Jesus. The closer they are to death, the more likely they are to report that those on the other side have come to accompany them to the afterlife.

"Many people report celestial scenes of great beauty," he continued. "While some are distressing in nature, the positive visions result in peace and joy at a time when you would expect only despair.

Some who have been comatose revive to say their goodbyes just prior to death. Children, who may not have been told they are dying, will often comfort their parents, announcing that they're looking forward to going to the other side."

The Power of Dying Declarations

I pointed out that the possibility of false or fabricated accounts cannot be ruled out.

Miller agreed. "Yes, that's to be expected, because some people may have mental illness or be in the throes of dementia. It's safest to stick with the demonstrated core experiences as reported in respected research."

"What gives these experiences credibility to you?"

"In my book, I spell out eleven characteristics of these experiences that seem more compatible with the afterlife hypothesis than the dying brain hypothesis."

"For instance?"

"First of all, because of your legal expertise, you know that statements made by people on their deathbeds, by their very nature, are generally considered to have special credibility in both civil and criminal courtroom cases," he said.

I knew that was correct. Under the Federal Rules of Evidence, a declaration made by a dying person, which typically would be barred as hearsay, may nonetheless be admissible as legal evidence in trials.[8] The assumption is that people on the cusp of death, or who believe they're about to die, are unlikely to fabricate stories.

"Who tries to lie in their dying moments?" asked Miller. "They have no time to profit from a book or enhance their social media following. So when millions of people—including those in our circles of trust—testify on their deathbeds that a deceased relative or angel has come to take them to the afterlife, I have reason to take their testimonies seriously."

"What about corroboration?" I asked. "Many of these cases seem to have aspects that can be confirmed by outside factors."

"Yes, for example, perfectly healthy people see an apparition of a person they didn't know had just died. Or people are made aware of something they could not have known naturalistically, such as the timing of their own death."

"What do you mean?"

"A couple years ago, my mom told me out of the blue, 'I think I'm about to die and want to make sure you know what I want for my funeral.' I asked if she was feeling especially bad, and she responded, 'No.' But I went ahead and helped her pick out what to wear in the casket and listened to all her instructions. She hadn't been diagnosed with a terminal disease. Her heartbeat and blood oxygen levels were fine. But she died from unknown causes within a couple weeks.

"And this isn't a rare occurrence," he added. "How do people know their time of death? It's not as if they have died before and can recall the feeling."

Visions Experienced by Children

I was intrigued that so many youngsters report having glimpses of the afterlife before they pass from this world. I asked Miller, "Is there special credibility to the deathbed experiences of children?"

He began by telling the story of a physician named Diane Komp, who was a professor of pediatrics at the Yale University School of Medicine and specialized in treating children who have cancer.

"Early in her career, she vacillated between agnosticism and atheism," he said. "Yet as she began to treat dying children, they convinced her of the existence of God and the afterlife because of their experiences of death. Rather than being scared to leave their families and all that is familiar, many dying children reported visions that made them excited or peaceful about leaving."

For instance, one of Komp's cancer patients was six-year-old Mary Beth. Her dire diagnosis wasn't discussed in her presence. But she told her mother she had a vivid dream in which one of her grandfathers, who had died before she was born, came to her along with Jesus. They told her she would be dying soon but encouraged her not to be afraid. She woke with a great sense of peace and reassurance, and she died on Christmas Eve.

"Here we have a little girl who wasn't expecting to die or to meet a grandfather, and yet she has an experience so unlike a normal dream that she awakes with absolute peace about dying," Miller said. "Typically, death for a child would be a thoroughly frightening prospect. Many kids react with horror when they're left briefly with a babysitter or at day care. Imagine them contemplating permanent separation from all they're familiar with."

Another one of Komp's young patients suddenly sat up in bed just before she died, exclaiming, "The angels—they're so beautiful! Mommy, can you see them? Do you hear their singing? I've never heard such beautiful singing!"[9] In fact, encountering visions of angels isn't uncommon among children facing death.

Explained Miller, "In our culture, artwork for children typically shows all angels as having wings, even though the Bible doesn't teach that. Consequently, we'd assume that if expectations were informing the content of these visions—in other words, if children were simply imagining things they had already been told—then they would describe angels as having wings. But Barrett noted that in his cases of children's visions, often the angels had no wings.

"As an example, in her doctoral dissertation on children's deathbed visions, Angela Ethier reported the case of a dying preschool girl who asked her mom if she could see the angels in the room. The mother bluffed by saying yes and then described them as having big wings. Her little daughter scoffed. 'Mama, you don't have to lie.' She went on to describe the angels in vivid detail, emphasizing, 'They don't have wings!'"[10]

Concluded Miller, "So if expectations, informed by culture and upbringing, aren't causing the content of children's deathbed visions, it makes sense that they're coming from elsewhere. The most consistent explanation is that these really are encounters with a spiritual realm."

Seeking Naturalistic Explanations

I asked Miller whether there are any naturalistic explanations for deathbed experiences that make sense to him.

"I try to objectively and dispassionately assess naturalistic explanations, but I found that none are consistent with the findings of almost fifty years of near-death studies and 130 years of deathbed research," he said.

"Skeptics keep suggesting that a lack of oxygen to the brain explain these phenomena. But sincere researchers should simply examine good summaries of past research to see how such explanations have been found wanting. For example, in her doctoral research, Penny Sartori compared hallucinations to NDEs and found them to be quite different."[11]

"Are all predeath experiences positive, or are some negative?" I asked. "If the Bible is correct, shouldn't some folks expect a less than blissful eternity?"

Miller sighed. "First, note that deathbed visions are experienced *prior* to a person's final death. The Bible teaches that judgment, heaven, and hell occur *after* final death," he replied. "Why should Christians expect *prior* to death what the Bible says will happen *after* death?"

He collected his thoughts and then added, "Let's imagine that God's main purpose in either causing or allowing such visions is to give people a final chance to get their hearts right with him. Since 2 Peter 3:9 says God is patient, wanting all to come to repentance, it makes sense that even those who resisted God to life's end might get a final chance. And since Paul taught that the kindness of God leads us to repentance,[12] why would it seem odd for God to continue to woo people with his kindness, even until the end? So even if nobody ever reported a scary deathbed experience, I wouldn't take this as contradictory to Scripture."

"Still, there are distressing deathbed visions, aren't there?"

"Yes, certainly. Karlis Osis and Erlendur Haraldsson found that 14 percent of those reporting an otherworldly deathbed vision reacted with negative emotions. When another team interviewed dying patients directly, they found 18 percent of the reports to be distressing. Still, I personally believe that God gives each person what they need to complete any unresolved soul work before life's end."

Evidence from Multiple Witnesses

Corroboration of deathbed experiences can prove difficult if the dying person is the only individual who sees the vision. On the other hand, there are cases where other people share in the experience, which adds immeasurably to the credibility of the phenomenon. I asked Miller to provide an example.

"Dr. Raymond Moody reported what happened with the Anderson family in suburban Atlanta," came his reply. "Three siblings and a sister-in-law all witnessed an unearthly light as their mother took her last breath."

With that, he flipped open Moody's book, *Glimpses of Eternity*, and read an excerpt from their account:

At that moment, we saw vivid bright lights that seemed to gather around and shape up into . . . I don't know what to call it except for an entranceway. . . . We saw my mother lift up out of her body and go through that entranceway. Being by the entranceway, incidentally, was a feeling of complete joy. My brother called it a chorus of joyful feelings, and my sister heard beautiful music, although none of the rest of us did. . . . The lights were so vivid we had no choice but to tell our story to the hospice nurse. She listened and then told us that she knew of similar things happening and that it was not uncommon for the dying process to encompass people nearby.[13]

That's consistent with what Barrett said he found in his research. "Many well authenticated cases are on record where the relatives of a person, watching by the death-bed, have seen at the moment of death a cloudy form rising from the body of the deceased and hovering for a time in the room and then passing away," Barrett wrote.[14]

When I asked Miller about the frequency of these shared experiences, he said, "Some research indicates they happen in 2 to 4 percent of the population."

I let out a whistle. "If that's true, then we're talking about potentially *millions* of cases," I said.

"That's right. And it's important to point out that these cases are entirely consistent with Christianity's teaching that our soul separates from our body at the time of death."

Visits by the Deceased

I turned to another area of afterlife research—instances in which a deceased person appears to a living individual, who sometimes hasn't even been told yet that the person has died. "How often do these occur?" I asked.

"In her doctoral dissertation, Jenny Streit-Horn did a systematic review of related research and concluded that one out of three people will experience an afterdeath communication of some sort in their lifetime."[15]

That number staggered me—that's over two *billion* people worldwide. "Can you give me an example?" I asked.

"In the Guggenheim collection of more than 3,300 afterdeath communications, they tell the story of Leslie, who turned off her light to go to bed when she suddenly saw her father, who had died of cancer four years earlier." Miller pulled out some notes and began quoting what the woman reported:

> All the lights were out in the house, yet I could see him very clearly because there was a glow around him. I kept thinking, "This is really Daddy! This is really him!" . . . I wanted to go over and touch him, and I started to get out of bed.
>
> He smiled and said, "No, you cannot touch me now. . . . But I want you to know that I am all right. Everything is fine. I am always with you."
>
> Then he paused and said, "I have to go look in on your mother and Curtis now." Curtis is my son, and he and my mother were in the next room. I got up and followed my father to the hallway. But he disappeared—he just faded away.
>
> So I went to bed and kept saying to myself, "This is just your grief. Daddy wasn't really there." Then I finally fell asleep. . . .
>
> The next morning I got up, and Curtis, who was three, almost four at the time, came out in the hallway. He said, "Mommy, I saw Granddaddy last night!" My mouth fell open and I said, "You did?" He said, "Yes! He came in my room. He was standing by my bed."
>
> How could a three-year-old come up with that? I questioned him, "Were you dreaming?" He said, "No, Mommy, I had my eyes open. I was awake. I saw him!"
>
> So then I knew that Daddy had to have actually been there. . . . It was a wonderful experience for me because I learned that love continues on.[16]

"Surely," said Miller, "she was warranted in concluding that she actually saw her deceased father, fully conscious, visiting from some sort of afterlife realm. After all, her experience was backed up by the independent testimony of her son."

In a strikingly similar case, a forty-five-year-old business executive named Blair was in a hotel with her five-year-old son when suddenly her deceased father appeared to her. "He seemed very, very solid," she said. "There were colors radiating from him and surrounding him—a combination of bluish white, rose, and gold."

He told her, "Be strong and take care of your mother. Remember, I love you!" The entire experience lasted just a few seconds.

She thought her son was asleep, but he got up and ran to her, exclaiming, "My granddaddy! My granddaddy!" She said, "Your granddaddy is gone." And he replied: "No! My granddaddy was right here!"[17]

Revealing Secrets to the Living

Miller brought up another intriguing category of afterlife cases—instances where a deceased person comes to tell a living individual something they otherwise would not have known.

"For instance," he said, "there are cases in which a deceased individual returns to tell a surviving spouse where hidden money is located or where there's a will that nobody knew about."

In one report, the family of a sixty-four-year-old woman who died of a heart attack couldn't find a stash of savings bonds they had been told was in the house. That is, until the deceased woman's grandson said he heard her voice distinctly telling him they were hidden in the false bottom of a garment bag in the closet. He checked there, and, sure enough, that's where he found them.[18]

Miller said there's also the account of a nurse from Florida named Anita. "Her grandfather, who died of heart failure at age eighty-seven, appeared to her on the night of his funeral and told her in his Hungarian accent, 'I will be a great-grandfather in the spring.' She said she had a great feeling of comfort and warmth. She immediately told her husband. The next day, she took a pregnancy test—and she was surprised to find out she was pregnant. When their son, Tyler, was born in May, she kept saying, 'Grandpa, you were right!'"[19]

"Are there cases in which a deceased person passes along false information?" I asked.

"We can get false reports about such instances, coming from the mentally ill, people on drugs, or people trying to profit from their stories," he said. "Again, that's why I encourage seekers to go to the best studies rather than dredging up uncorroborated stories from the internet."

I ventured to ask, "Might more sinister forces be at work?"

"Well, prominent psychiatry professor Richard Gallagher didn't believe in personal forces of evil until he began observing people who suddenly exhibited superhuman strength, knew private details of his life, and were seemingly possessed by evil entities. He found that these entities often posed as deceased relatives, later admitting they were demons with the apparent intent of leading others astray. In distressing near-death experiences, people often report hearing lies from these entities, such as telling them God can't rescue them or that their entire existence is an illusion."

My mind flashed back to my interview with Douglas Potter about Satan and demons—and Miller's comments made perfect sense to me. Perhaps visions of deceased individuals are actually demons in disguise. That's when a realization popped into my mind: Even if they were demons, this would nevertheless be further evidence for the existence of a supernatural realm.

Afterlife Reports and the Bible

I was curious how Miller reconciled deathbed experiences with his Christian faith, since some theologians attribute them to satanic influence. Miller has given the issue a lot of thought, as illustrated by an entire book he wrote on this subject.

"I don't believe that all deathbed experiences are of God," he began, "but rather than dismiss or accept all of them, I want to follow Paul's exhortation in 1 Thessalonians 5—that we should examine everything carefully and hold fast to what is good. God doesn't contradict himself, so if a reported experience goes against what God has already told us, we have good reason to red-flag that story. And the experience also should bear good fruit."

"Let's talk specifics," I said. "What about the claim that it's unbiblical to suggest that anyone should get visited by a deceased person?"

"I'd say look at the transfiguration, where Jesus and three of his disciples received a visit from the long-deceased Moses and Elijah."

"What about deathbed visions? Is there a biblical precedent for those?"

"Consider the vision that Stephen experienced in Acts 7. At the peak of his confrontation with the Pharisees, just before they stoned him to death, verse 55 reads, 'Stephen, full of the Holy Spirit, looked up to heaven and saw the glory of God, and Jesus standing at the right hand of God.'"

Miller went on. "There's also biblical warrant for people being made aware of the timing of their imminent deaths. Consider Moses in Deuteronomy 34, Jesus in Mark 8, Paul in 2 Timothy 4, and Peter in 2 Peter 1."

"When you systematically compare Christian doctrine with the results of the best studies of near-death experiences and deathbed accounts, what do you find?"

"I found forty-seven points of correspondence," came his reply. "For example, God exists and is personal and loving and knows us intimately. Angels exist. Our words and deeds are known to God, and they matter. Conscious life continues after death."

"What do you say to those who claim that visions are reserved for special dispensations, such as the giving of the law, the coming of Jesus, and the start of the church, and therefore we no longer need them after the completion of the New Testament?"

"It's an interesting hypothesis," he replied. "But honestly, I don't see it taught in Scripture. And since visions had purposes beyond the giving of doctrine, how can we say dogmatically that there's no longer a need for them?"

He gestured toward the Bible on his desk. "I've gone through Scripture and reflected on the characteristics and purposes of visions," he said. "My first observation is that they're not on the periphery of God's work. Instead, they're central, starting with Genesis and ending with Revelation.

"Secondly, they have many purposes—sometimes to comfort, other times to warn, and sometimes to give very specific personal instructions. Thirdly, they come in great variety, as if God is saying, 'Don't put me in a box. I reveal myself in many different ways!' He spoke to some while they were awake and to others in dreams— apparently *vivid* dreams as distinguished from ordinary ones. He revealed himself through a burning bush and a donkey, through a gentle whisper and a thundering voice, visually and audibly, received by one and received by many."

Then Miller added with intensity, "The Bible never says these are the only ways he will ever reveal himself or interact with human-kind. So why would it seem odd that God would continue to use a variety of visions for a variety of purposes?"

Miller's answer made me think of what my ministry partner Mark Mittelberg often points out when we teach together: "Don't forget that on the Day of Pentecost in Acts 2:17, Peter declared that 'in the last days, God says, I will pour out my Spirit on all people. Your sons and daughters will prophesy, your young men will see visions, your old men will dream dreams.'

"Peter was describing things that were already happening at that time and that certainly would continue as we get closer to the end of history. This included dreams and visions among his followers, both young and old. So, yes, we should expect supernatural manifesta-tions like these among God's people today as well."

Confirming the Afterlife Hypothesis

Miller has spent more than a decade delving into deathbed experiences and how they open a window to a supernatural realm. He has combed through mountains of scholarly research going back more than a century, reviewed compelling individual accounts of visions and otherworldly encounters, and subjected the mystical to rigorous investigation and scrutiny. He pressed for answers—and found that they point toward the reality that there's more to our existence than what we can analyze in a laboratory.

As we moved toward the end of our conversation, I asked him about his conclusion that the afterlife hypothesis—in other words, that a supernatural world awaits us—is the most logical inference based on the evidence.

He sat back in his chair and spoke in a sincere and reflective tone. "Most convincing to me," he said, "was the convergence of multiple streams of evidence. I can reflect on thousands of deathbed experiences collected globally by competent researchers, with case after case testifying to extremely real encounters with God, the afterlife, deceased relatives, and angels. Then we can reasonably project that millions of people will have such experiences.

"Beyond that," he continued, "I can bring the research back home to my circles of trust and hear from my wife, family, friends, colleagues, and students, many of them testifying that they've experienced extraordinary events pointing to the afterlife, often with compelling corroboration.

"So in personally investigating these cases for many years, the preponderance of the evidence convinces me that what the Bible has taught us all along is true: Death is not the end of life. Just as we can say that the observations of modern physics dovetail with the biblical view that the universe had a beginning, so I can say that observations of the dying confirm the biblical view of the afterlife.

The bottom line is that death isn't the destruction of self; it's a transition to another form of existence."

"How has this affected you personally?"

"My own faith has been taken to new levels," he answered. "And I'm more motivated than ever to live for things that last beyond the grave. As Jesus said, 'What good will it be for someone to gain the whole world, yet forfeit their soul?'"[20]

It was a good reminder to end on. But I knew these deathbed visions were only one type of evidence for life beyond this world. For people who are clinically dead and yet destined to be revived and live on, sometimes there are near-death experiences that give them a peek into the life to come—and in many such cases, there is corroboration that bolsters the credibility of the account.

Turn the page and I'll tell you more.

CHAPTER 8

EXTRAORDINARY
NEAR-DEATH
EXPERIENCES

The evidence of near-death experiences points to an afterlife and a universe guided by a vastly loving intelligence.

Physician and NDE researcher Jeffrey Long,

Evidence of the Afterlife

A single mother named Mary, who was dying from severe bleeding, was wheeled unconscious into an operating room at Memorial Hospital in London. But as she would say later, she was fully conscious the whole time as her spirit watched everything from a vantage point near the ceiling.

"As the blood drained from my body, so did my will to live," she said later. "I heard a 'pop' sound and suddenly the pain stopped. . . . I had a very clear view of my body as they ferociously worked on

—·■·—

145

me, hooking up a transfusion and other tubes. I recalled thinking that I just wished they would stop."

Suddenly a tunnel appeared, and she felt herself being pulled toward it. Her spirit passed through a ceiling fan and then through the ceiling. "I was happy to be away from that tense scene below," she said.

She felt a presence that kept her calm with a sense of love and wisdom as she picked up speed and headed toward a bright light in the distance. "I didn't see anyone," she said, "but I felt the essence of my grandpa who had died when I was 13."

At the end of the tunnel, she was overwhelmed by a radiant white light that "seemed to embody all the concepts of love. A love which was unconditional and like a mother has for a child. . . . I knew in my heart that this was God. Words cannot describe my awe in his presence. . . . I could tell he knew my every thought and feeling."

The next thing she saw was a sleeping baby who "I knew to be me." That's when a review of her life began as she reexperienced highlights from childhood to adulthood. "I felt every good or bad deed I had ever done and its consequences upon others. It was a difficult time for me, but I was supported by unconditional love and weathered the painful parts. I was asked telepathically about whether I wanted to stay or return."

With that, she popped back into her body and felt searing pain. A nurse in a blue smock gave her an injection of pain medicine. "It seemed as if I had not been unconscious for more than a few minutes, yet my visit to the 'Other Side' seemed to last hours," Mary said.

It's a compelling story, but did Mary actually catch a glimpse of a supernatural world and the existence of an omniscient deity? Well, there's one other detail that seems to provide extra credibility to her account.

When Mary's spirit floated out of her body, she noticed a red label on the top side of a blade on the ceiling fan, hidden from view for people in the room. She later described the sticker in great detail.

At Nancy's urging, a nurse got a tall ladder so she could inspect the top of the blade—and, sure enough, there was the red sticker, just as Mary had described it.[1]

Is There Life after Life?

Raymond Moody, a physician with doctorates in philosophy and psychology, coined the term "near-death experience" (NDE) in his 1975 bestselling book *Life after Life*.[2] His interviews with 150 people who experienced NDEs inspired Kenneth Ring, a longtime professor of psychology at the University of Connecticut, to become a prominent NDE researcher and founding editor of the *Journal of Near-Death Studies*.

"The stories Moody's respondents told were so captivating and enthralling and depicted the experience of dying in such radiantly glorious language that people reading about it could scarcely believe that what they had always feared as their greatest enemy, when seen up close, had the face of the beloved," Ring said. "And more—when Moody's interviewees attempted to describe the experience of dying, they often mentioned a light of unceasing supernatural brilliance that exuded a feeling of pure, unconditional, *absolute* love and was associated with such an overwhelming sensation of peace that they sometimes could only liken it to 'the peace that passeth all understanding.'"[3]

It's no wonder that the public was thrilled with Moody's writings and subsequent books by others about afterdeath encounters. "It seemed clear evidence," Ring said, "that what our Western religions, at least, taught was true: that life continues after death, that heaven is no fantasy, and that those who die do, indeed, see the face of God."[4]

According to a 2019 study, as many as one in ten people across thirty-five countries have undergone some sort of NDE.[5] But could these experiences be explained away as hallucinations or the electrical glitches of a brain in its last gasps? Might they be the product of oxygen deprivation or some little-understood neurological phenomenon? Could they be fraudulent—after all, one youngster did fabricate his account in a bestselling book.[6] Is there any corroboration—like, perhaps, the red sticker on the top of a blade on a ceiling fan—to support claims of a supernatural afterdeath existence?

Fortunately, I knew where I could get answers. A longtime friend of mine—himself a former spiritual skeptic—has researched more than a thousand cases of near-death experiences and had written a bestselling book on the topic. An email message yielded an appointment with him. Leslie and I packed our suitcases at our Houston home and headed west in our car toward Austin.

Honestly, I couldn't wait to get to the bottom of this. In my view—echoing what neuroscientist Sharon Dirckx told me during our interview for the first chapter of this book—all that is needed would be just one well-documented case of a near-death experience. For me, that would constitute strong evidence that our consciousness continues even after clinical death and that there really is an otherworldly realm of the supernatural.

Just *one* case.

INTERVIEW *with*

JOHN BURKE

John Burke was sixteen years old when his father, an engineer for an oil company in Houston, was dying of cancer. One day, John noticed a book on his dad's nightstand—it was Raymond Moody's groundbreaking report on NDEs. Curious, John picked it up and read it from cover to cover.

"At the end—I'll never forget—I was sitting on my bed with

tears streaming down my face," he recalls. "I was an agnostic at the time, but I remember thinking, *Oh my gosh, this Jesus stuff might be true—and if he's real, I want to be with him.*"

Shortly afterward, a friend led him in a prayer of commitment to Christ. John went on to get his engineering degree at the University of Texas, worked for a couple large oil companies, and then completed his master's level work in theology and philosophy at Trinity International University near Chicago.

I met John when he was executive director of ministries at a church where I was a teaching pastor. In 1998, he and his wife, Kathy, left to start Gateway Church in Austin, Texas, growing it to five thousand attenders.

Over the years, John has written several influential books, including *No Perfect People Allowed*, *Soul Revolution*, and *Unshockable Love*. His curiosity over NDEs, sparked by Raymond Moody's book, only increased through the decades. In 2015, his research resulted in *Imagine Heaven*, which has sold nearly a million copies. He followed that in 2023 with *Imagine the God of Heaven*.

John and I settled into a conference room at the church. He was casually dressed, his dark brown hair a bit tousled. He is athletic (an amateur sailor and soccer player) and quick-witted, with an easy smile and enthusiastic voice.

What NDEs Hold in Common

"In all of your research," I asked, "what was your most surprising discovery about near-death experiences?"

"First, I'm not particularly fond of the term *near-death experiences*," he began. "As one survivor said, 'I wasn't *near* dead; I was *dead dead*.' Some of these cases involve people with no heartbeat or brain waves. There are instances where doctors had already declared them dead. They may not have been *eternally* dead, but many were certainly *clinically* dead."

"Okay, good point," I said.

"Now, let me answer your question," he continued. "What surprised me the most is that even though they vary a fair amount, these accounts have a common core—and incredibly, it's entirely consistent with what we're told about the afterlife in the Bible."

"Yet a lot of Christians associate NDEs with the occult or New Age thinking," I said.

"Not all Christians think that way. Many take the approach of the late theologian R.C. Sproul, who tried to keep an open mind about NDEs and encouraged more research and analysis.[1] Christian philosophers J. P. Moreland and Gary Habermas have been writing about the implications of NDEs as far back as the early 1990s."[2]

"Why is there such a wide variation in how people describe their NDE?"

"Well, I noticed there's a difference between what people *report* they experienced and how they *interpret* it," he said. "The interpretations vary, but when you dig down to what they actually experienced, there's a core that's consistent with what Scripture tells us about the life to come."

I cocked my head. "As a pastor, you're not basing your theology about heaven on these NDEs, are you?" I asked.

"Not at all. I'm basing my beliefs on the Bible. That's our most reliable source. I'm merely saying that the Bible contains black-and-white words about the afterlife, and these NDEs tend to add color to the picture. They don't contradict; they complement."

"What do NDEs hold in common?" I asked.

"Three-quarters of people experience the separation of consciousness from the physical body," he replied.

"An out-of-body experience."

"That's right. About the same number have heightened senses and intense emotions."

"Positive ones?"

"Generally, yes. Two out of three encounter a mystical or

brilliant light, and more than half meet other beings, either mystical ones or deceased relatives or friends. More than half describe unworldly or heavenly realms. A quarter say they undergo a life review. A third say they encounter a barrier or boundary, and more than half were aware of a decision to return to their physical body."

"Isn't it true that many people find it difficult to describe the experience?"

"For sure," he said. "A girl named Crystal said, 'There are no human words that even come close.' A guy named Gary said nothing could adequately describe the divine presence he encountered."[3]

"More Brilliant Than the Sun"

"Tell me about that so-called divine presence," I said. "What do people typically say about him?"

"They talk about a brilliant light—brighter than anything they've ever seen," Burke said.

Then he told the story of an atheist named Ian McCormack from New Zealand, who went scuba diving off the coast of Mauritius in the Indian Ocean and was stung four times by box jellyfish.

I recoiled when Burke said that. I knew from my travels that these jellyfish are often called the world's most venomous creature. One sting can result in cardiovascular collapse and death in two to five minutes.[4] And Ian was stung *four* times.

"Ian was dying," Burke said. "He saw visions of his mother, who had told him to call out to God if he ever needed help. He was in utter darkness and felt terrified. He prayed for God to forgive his sins—and a bright line shone on him and literally drew him out of the darkness. He described the light as 'unspeakably bright, as if it was the center of the universe . . . more brilliant than the sun, more radiant than any diamond, brighter than a laser beam. Yet you could look right into it.'

"He said this presence knew everything about him, which made him feel terribly ashamed. But instead of judgment, he felt 'pure, unadulterated, clean, uninhibited, undeserved love.' He began weeping uncontrollably. Ian asked if he could 'step into the light.' As he did, he saw in the middle of the light a man with dazzling white robes—garments literally woven from light—who offered his arms to welcome him. He said, 'I knew that I was standing in the presence of Almighty God.'"[5]

Burke paused and then continued. "Remember the transfiguration? In Matthew 17:2, it says that Jesus' face 'shone like the sun, and his clothes became as white as the light.'" He smiled. "Reminds me of that."

"But if Ian had been a Hindu, might he have encountered a god from that faith?"

"In all my research, I've never read of people describing anything like Krishna, who has blue skin, or Shiva, who has three eyes, or descriptions of the dissolving of the individual self in the impersonal Supreme Brahma, which is the ultimate Hindu reality. In fact, two researchers studied five hundred Americans and five hundred Indians to see how much their cultural conditioning may have affected their NDE."

"What did they find?"

"That several basic Hindu ideas of the afterlife were never portrayed in the visions of the Indian patients. No reincarnation. They did describe encountering a white-robed man with a book of accounts. To them, that might vaguely suggest Karma, or the record of merits and demerits. But again, that's an interpretation, because it's also very consistent with what we find in the Bible. Bruce Greyson, who studied cross-cultural NDEs, agreed that it's not the core experience that differs, but the ways in which people interpret what they have experienced."[6]

"Everything Is Exposed"

I asked Burke to elaborate on the life review that so many people go through during their near-death experience.

"It occurs in the presence of the Being of Light, and it often begins with him asking something like, 'What have you done with the life I gave you?' It's not said in judgment, but in love—to prompt reflection and learning.

"Everything is exposed from a person's life—every thought, every motive, every deed. Nothing is hidden. What's interesting is that the focus isn't on your accomplishments or trophies or résumé, but on how you loved others. It's all about relationships. People actually see and feel how their actions—even small, seemingly insignificant ones—ripple through the lives of other people, even four or five steps down the road, in ways they never knew.

"Through it all, there's no judgment. What happens is that people tend to judge themselves. One man said he was so ashamed by his cruel and selfish behavior that he begged them to stop the review.[7] Yet here's the thing—Jesus continued to communicate only unconditional love for him."

"Do people from different cultures experience it differently?"

"Actually, it's pretty consistent. Steve Miller studied non-Western, non-Christian NDEs and said, 'In my non-Western sample, I saw no significant difference in life reviews compared to Western life reviews.'[8] And remember that Jesus said in the Bible, 'There is nothing concealed that will not be disclosed, or hidden that will not be made known.'"[9]

I put up my hand to stop him. "Wait a second," I said. "This is what concerns a lot of Christians. The Bible says God will judge each of us, but that doesn't sound like what these life reviews are about. It sounds more like universalism—everybody is saved, regardless of how they lived or whether they ever sought forgiveness through Christ."

Burke's response was a smile. "That's based on a big misunderstanding," he answered. "First, Jesus himself said, 'By your words you will be acquitted, and by your words you will be condemned.'[10] That's what people experience—God loves them, and they judge themselves. Plus, the Bible talks about two judgments.

One determines whether we've accepted or rejected God's free gift of love, forgiveness, adoption, and salvation; the other is to reward his followers for how they lived.

"But this life review isn't either of those," he said. "The author of Hebrews tells us that 'people are destined to die *once*, and after that to face judgment.'[11] Remember, these people are not *irreversibly* dead; they may be *clinically* dead, but they will be returning to life at some point. This life review seems to be a clarifying reminder that God knows everything about us, and that one day we all will give an account. Keep in mind that the Bible teaches there's no judgment at all until human history comes to its conclusion."[12]

"So you don't see any conflict between these life reviews and Christian doctrine," I said, the words coming out more as a statement than a question.

"No," he said. "I really don't. Throughout my book *Imagine Heaven*, I cite chapter and verse for how the core of NDEs tracks with the Christian faith."

Descending into Hell

Most near-death experiences involve positive encounters—but not all. Twelve different studies involving 1,369 subjects revealed that 23 percent reported NDEs ranging from disturbing to terrifying or despairing.[13] In fact, a 2019 study by the European Academy of Neurology Congress of 1,034 people across thirty-five countries showed that one out of ten people had undergone a near-death experience—and 73 percent of them rated it as having been "unpleasant."[14]

I said to Burke, "In the early days of NDE research, very few people reported having a hellish experience. Why is that?"

"Embarrassment. Wanting to suppress the memory. Fear of social ostracism. Some suffer long-term psychological trauma. Today people are more willing to talk about it, like Howard Storm, who has become a friend of mine."

Storm, an atheist, was a professor of art at Northern Kentucky University when he "died" from a stomach ulcer that perforated his duodenum. Oddly, he found himself standing up next to the bed, feeling better than ever. He began following some mysterious but friendly visitors who beckoned him down the hallway. This turned into a trek of miles, with conditions getting darker and darker.

Suddenly, the strangers who had greeted him so warmly became rude and hostile. Now it was pitch-black and Storm felt stark terror. They began pushing, hitting, pulling, kicking, biting, and tearing with their fingernails and hands as they laughed and swore at him. He fought back as best he could, but he was mauled—physically and emotionally—in the struggle.

"There has never been a horror movie or book that can begin to describe their cruelty," Storm recalled. "Eventually, I was eviscerated. I definitely lost one of my eyes, my ears were gone, and I'm lying on the floor of that place.

"So now I have eternity—time without measure—to think about my situation. . . . Because I had lived a garbage life, I had gone down the toilet. And I realized, this is the horrible part: that the people that had met me were my kindred spirits. They denied God; they lived for themselves; and their lives were about manipulation and control of other people. My life was devoted to building a monument to my ego. My family, my sculptures, my paintings—all of those were gone now, and what did they matter? I wasn't far from becoming like one of my own tormentors for all eternity."

Eventually, Storm called out for help. "I yelled into the darkness, 'Jesus, save me!' I have never meant anything more strongly in my life."

A small light appeared—"way brighter than the sun"—and hands and arms came out. "When they touched me, in that light, I could see me and all the gore. I was roadkill. And that gore began to just dissolve and I came back whole."

He felt a love far beyond words. "If I took all my experience of love in my entire life and could condense it into a moment, it still wouldn't begin to measure up to the intensity of this love that I was feeling. And that love is the foundation of my life from that moment on."

So transformational was this experience that when Storm was healed of his medical condition, he resigned his tenured professorship and chairmanship of the university's art department to become the pastor of a small church, where he serves to this day.[15]

"Sometimes," Burke said to me, "people suggest that NDEs are merely hallucinations of some sort. But hallucinations are typically scattered and confused, while NDEs are lucid and cohesive. Besides, I don't see people completely changing the direction of their life based on a mere hallucination. Often, though, people who've gone through an NDE are changed forever.

"Like my friend Howard."

The Boy Who *Didn't* Come Back

In 2010, the inspiring book *The Boy Who Came Back from Heaven* described how young Alex Malarkey was critically injured in a traffic accident and met Jesus in heaven during a near-death experience.[16] It became an instant hit in Christian circles, with more than a million copies sold, and was the basis of a television film.

Later, Malarkey made a startling confession: "I did not die. I did not go to heaven. I said I went to heaven because I thought it would get me attention."[17] The scandal rocked the Christian publishing industry. The lesson was clear: It was remarkably easy for someone to fabricate claims of an NDE.

I recapped that incident to Burke and asked, "Isn't this an ever-present danger in researching NDEs?"

"No question about it, but I've tried to guard against it in my research," he said.

"How so?"

"By focusing on stories from people who lack a profit motive. These are orthopedic surgeons, oncologists, bank presidents, cardiologists, commercial airline pilots, professors, neurosurgeons. They don't need the money and, frankly, they risk having their credibility tarnished if they make up wild tales. Very few of the more than a thousand people studied have written a book. Plus, think about the fact that around the globe—in all kinds of culturally diverse places—basically the same story is emerging from NDE survivors. There's no way everyone conspired together to concoct something."

"How convinced are you that there are no physiological or neurological explanations for NDEs?" I asked. "A lot of theories have been put forth over the years."

Burke shrugged. "I just don't think any of them explain everything away," he replied. "For example, it's been shown that when you try to induce experiences, you don't completely replicate an NDE."

He picked up his book and flipped to its conclusion. "Pim van Lommel is a Dutch cardiologist who did a large-scale prospective study into NDEs that was published in the respected British medical journal, the *Lancet*," Burke said.

He scanned the text for its relevant portions and then quoted them to me. "After examining possible alternate explanations for NDEs, van Lommel conceded that although 'various physiological and psychological factors could all play a role, none can fully explain the phenomenon.' His bottom line was that these theories 'fail to explain the experience of an enhanced consciousness, with lucid thoughts, emotions, memories from earliest childhood, visions of the future, and the possibility of perception from a position outside and above the body.'"[18]

"There's still controversy about NDEs though—isn't that right?"

"Certainly the debate continues," Burke said. "An increasing amount of research is being done. More than nine hundred articles have been published in scholarly journals. But many skeptical researchers have now concluded that NDEs give us a peek into the afterlife. None of the alternative explanations make as much logical sense as the straightforward conclusion that there really is life after death."

The Errant Tennis Shoe

Personally, I was hungry for further corroboration. I can't verify that Ian McCormack stood in the presence of Almighty God or that Jesus rescued Howard Storm from torment. On the positive side, I have their testimony, their changed lives, and the evidence of similar encounters reported around the globe. All of that is intriguing. But, of course, I don't have independent eyewitnesses who can vouch for what happened. The investigative journalist in me wanted something that could be checked out.

"I was impressed by the case in which the dying woman left her body, drifted toward the ceiling, and was able to see a red sticker on the hidden side of the fan blade," I said. "Her description of the sticker was later confirmed to be correct. That kind of independent corroboration is helpful. Are there other cases like that?"

"Oh, sure," came his reply. "Quite a few."

"Give me some examples."

"There are many cases where NDE patients leave their body, watch doctors try to resuscitate them, and are able to later describe the exact procedures and tools the doctors used. Cardiologist Michael Sabom was a skeptic until he investigated those kinds of cases. For instance, his patient Peter Morton underwent cardiac arrest and yet described the resuscitation efforts in such precise and accurate detail that Sabom said he could have used the tape to train other physicians."

"Hold on," I said. "Couldn't the patient have been guessing? Maybe he was simply recalling what he had seen on medical shows on television."

"That's been investigated," Burke replied. "Dr. Penny Sartori did a five-year study and found that patients who claimed to be out of their bodies were surprisingly accurate in their observations. She compared that with patients who were asked to guess what happened during their resuscitations."

"How did those folks fare?"

"Not well. She said they all had errors and misconceptions of the equipment used, and incorrect procedures were described. For example, she said many guessed that the defibrillator had been used when, in fact, it had not."[19]

"Interesting," I said.

"One of the most famous cases comes from researcher Kimberly Clark Sharp, who describes the out-of-body experience of a heart-attack patient named Maria. During the time Maria was unconscious, she drifted through the ceiling and outside the hospital. When she did, she saw a tennis shoe on the hospital's third-story window ledge."

"How did she describe it?"

"A man's shoe, left-footed, dark blue, with a wear mark over the little toe and a shoelace tucked under the heel. Sharp investigated, and sure enough—she eventually found the shoe, exactly as Maria had described it."[20]

I pondered the story for a moment. "Well, that's impressive," I said. "How often does this kind of corroboration occur?"

"Janice Holden studied ninety-three NDE patients who claimed to make multiple verifiable observations while out of their physical bodies. She said a remarkable 92 percent of the observations were 'completely accurate.' Think of that—nearly everyone was totally correct. Another 6 percent contained just 'some error.' Only 2 percent were 'completely erroneous.'"[21]

I had to concede. "That's a pretty amazing track record."

And the Blind Can See

I gestured toward Burke to continue with examples of corroborated cases. He thought for a second and then began rattling them off, occasionally picking up his book and flipping through it for details to refresh his recollection.

"The *Lancet* published an account of a patient who was brought into the hospital comatose and not breathing after cardiac arrest. A male nurse removed the man's dentures and tucked them into the drawer of a crash cart. A week later, in another room, the patient regained consciousness. When the nurse came in, the patient recognized him, saying, 'You took my dentures out of my mouth,' and he proceeded to precisely describe how the nurse had put them in the bottom drawer of a specific cart.

"The nurse said, 'I was especially amazed because I remembered this happening while the man was in a deep coma and in the process of CPR. When I asked further, it appeared the man had seen himself lying in bed, that he had perceived from above how nurses and doctors had been busy with CPR.'"

In another case, a seven-year-old girl named Katie was found floating facedown in a swimming pool. She was profoundly comatose, with massive brain swelling and no measurable brain activity. She didn't have a heartbeat for nearly twenty minutes. She was hooked up to an artificial lung to keep her breathing. Somehow, though, she made a miraculous recovery in just three days—and stunned doctors by saying, "I met Jesus and the heavenly Father."

Intrigued, the doctors questioned her at length. In fact, they had her draw a picture of the emergency room, and she succeeded in correctly placing everything. Then she said that in her out-of-body state, she followed her family home one night. She was able to give specific details about what she observed, including what her father was reading, how her brother was pushing a toy soldier in a Jeep, and her mother was cooking roast chicken and rice. She even knew what clothes each family member wore that night.

"Everything checked out," said Burke.

I further researched Katie's story and found that the pediatrician who resuscitated her, Melvin Morse, published her case in the *American Journal of Diseases of Children* and then gathered eight researchers to conduct a study of children's near-death experiences at Seattle Children's Hospital.

"After looking at all the other explanations for near-death

experiences, I think the simplest explanation is that NDEs are actually glimpses into the world beyond," Morse concluded. "I've read all the convoluted psychological and physiological explanations for NDEs, and none of them seem very satisfying."[22]

In my interview with Burke, he went on to say there are cases where congenitally blind people can see during their NDE. For example, Vicki had never visually seen anything in her twenty-two years. Then she was in a car accident and found herself looking down on the crumbled vehicle, and later she watched doctors working on her body as she floated toward the ceiling.

After going down a tunnel to a wondrous place, Vicki encountered two schoolmates who had died years before. Though mentally disabled in life, they were now fully healthy. She then saw a playback of her earthly years. She was later able to provide various accurate observations, including about her childhood friends, which she could not have witnessed at the time but claimed to have seen in the life review.

Among the conclusions of Kenneth Ring, who interviewed twenty-one blind people who reported NDEs, are that "blind and visually impaired descriptions of the experience show visual, or 'visual-like' perceptions, and some of these reports have been validated by outside witnesses."[23]

A Parade of the Improbable

The more I investigated NDEs, the more documented cases of corroboration I found, including several reported by Moreland and Habermas:

- A woman registered an absence of brain waves, had no vital signs, was declared dead, and was being wheeled to the morgue when she regained consciousness. She accurately described the exact resuscitation procedures used on her by doctors, repeated a joke one of them had told to relieve tension, and even recalled the designs on the doctors' ties.

- A young woman on her deathbed left her body and went to another room at the hospital, where she overheard her brother-in-law say he was going to wait around to see if she was going to "kick the bucket." She later embarrassed him by telling him what she had heard.

- Five-year-old Rick was comatose with meningitis before he was taken by ambulance to the hospital. He remained unresponsive for several days. Yet he described leaving his body and seeing grief-stricken relatives during that time—and he even watched as a twelve-year-old girl was moved out of the room he was to occupy. His specific observations were confirmed by others.

- On her deathbed, a woman named Eleanor began calling out the names of deceased loved ones she was seeing. Suddenly, she saw a cousin named Ruth. "What's she doing here?" Eleanor blurted out. It turns out that Ruth had died unexpectedly the week before, but Eleanor, because of her illness, had never been told.

- Another girl, who had an NDE during heart surgery, said she met her brother in the afterlife—which surprised her because she didn't have a brother. When she later recovered and told her father, he revealed to her for the first time that she did, indeed, have a brother, but he had died before she was born.[24]

- A five-year-old Dutch girl contracted meningitis and fell into a coma. In her NDE, she met a girl, about ten years old, who told her, "I'm your sister. Our parents called me Rietje for short." Rietje kissed her and said, "You must go now," and the girl returned to her body. She later shocked her parents by relaying the story. They confirmed she did have a sister named Rietje who had died of poisoning, but they decided not to tell the other children until they were old enough to understand.[25]

Head-scratchers, all of them. And just the tip of the iceberg. I'm not surprised that NDE researcher Jeffrey Long, a seasoned radiation oncologist, concluded, "NDEs provide such powerful scientific evidence that it is reasonable to accept the existence of an afterlife."[26]

The Culmination of What We Seek

Fair or not, there are stereotypes about engineers—for instance, that they're relentlessly rational rather than syrupy or sentimental, and that they favor facts and logic over feelings and emotions. I live in a Houston neighborhood populated by oil company engineers, and frankly, those perceptions aren't far off the mark. And I did detect some of these traits in Burke—until we came toward the end of our conversation.

The exchange began with a rather innocuous question. "What do you want people to walk away with from reading your book *Imagine Heaven?*" I asked. I anticipated a perfunctory answer.

Burke thought for a few moments. "I want them first to fall in love with Jesus, and to see"—his voice caught, then he halted. His eyes flooded. Emotions overwhelmed him. "I'm sorry," he muttered as he fought to regain his composure.

"It's all right," I assured him.

He took a breath. "It's just that"—he stopped to gather himself before he resumed. "It's just that I want people to see that Jesus is everything we want. He's the culmination of all we seek," he said finally.

"Many people I've interviewed try to describe the astonishing beauty they've seen in heaven," he continued. "Scenery that takes your breath away. A fragrance so gentle and sweet. Colors like nothing on earth. One person said, 'The colors seemed to be alive.'[27] But then they say, 'Yes, it was amazing, but I didn't even care about it.'

I'd ask why. And they would say, 'Because I couldn't take my eyes off Jesus. He's beyond beautiful. He's everything I've ever longed for.'"

Burke's eyes met mine. "That helped crystalize something that has profoundly changed me."

"What is it?"

"That everything I've ever enjoyed in life—the beauty of the outdoors, the love of a parent, the laughter of a child, the fulfillment of marriage—all of that is just a speck compared to the greater reality that's found in him."

Now *my* eyes moistened. I clicked off my recorder.

Enough said.

A Peek into the Afterlife

That evening, Leslie and I sat across from each other in a booth as we ate dinner at an Austin seafood restaurant. I described my interview with Burke at length, giving her all the salient details.

"What's your conclusion?" she asked.

I put down my fork. "These descriptions of an afterlife are fascinating," I said. "And John's right—a lot of these core experiences do match up with biblical accounts of what happens after we die. Still, there's quite a variation among the stories."

"And," Leslie added, "there's really no way to verify all these details about heaven and hell."

"True," I said. "But are they making this stuff up? So many people have had NDEs that it's hard to believe they could all be fabricated. What are these accounts, really? Are these people sincerely describing an experience like a dream or hallucination that's been produced by some medical phenomenon, like oxygen deprivation? Well, no alternate explanations have been able to account for all the features of NDEs. But let's set aside these descriptions of the afterlife and just focus on what we can know for sure."

"And what's that?" Leslie asked.

"At a minimum, these cases demonstrate convincingly that consciousness really does continue after clinical death. For how long? The evidence doesn't establish that. But we have corroboration of a lot of things that people could never have otherwise known unless they'd had an authentic out-of-body experience."

I let that statement stand for a while as we ate. "I guess what I'm saying," I added, "is that the best explanation for the totality of the evidence is that there is a postmortem existence of some sort. After our brain stops working, after our heart stops beating, after the doctors declare us dead—we still live on. Our consciousness survives. We survive."

CHAPTER 9

WHAT CAN WE KNOW ABOUT
HEAVEN?

Joy is the serious business of Heaven.

C. S. Lewis, *Letters to Malcolm*

God made this world of space, time, and matter; he loves it, and he is going to renew it.

N. T. Wright, *Simply Good News*

The Star Wars movies, the original *Star Trek*, and the TV program *Cosmos* captivated the imagination of Sarah Salviander as she was growing up in Canada. "By the time I was nine years old, I knew I would be a space scientist someday," she said.

Soon Salviander became an atheist like her parents. Though she had never read the Bible, she thought Christianity was "philosophically trivial" and made people "weak and foolish." Ultimately, she earned her doctorate in astrophysics. But there were unexpected twists. For instance, her early physics professors were Christians, and their influence tempered her antipathy toward the faith.

Then as she was studying deuterium abundances in relation to the Big Bang, she was "completely and utterly awed" by the underlying order of the universe and the fact that it could be explored scientifically. "Without knowing it," she said, "I was awakened to what Psalm 19 tells us so clearly: 'The heavens declare the glory of God; the skies proclaim the work of his hands.'"[1]

After that, a physicist and theologian convinced her that the Bible's creation account was "scientifically sound and not just a 'silly myth' as atheists believed."[2] And if Genesis is true, what about the Gospels? That led her to investigate the life of Jesus. Like Albert Einstein, she became "enthralled by the luminous figure of the Nazarene."[3] Based on her cerebral analysis of the evidence, Salviander put her trust in Christ. And yet it was a subsequent personal tragedy that truly solidified her faith.

Her first child, a girl named Ellinor, was stillborn—a heartbreaking experience for Salviander and her husband. Nurses allowed them to stay in the hospital room most of the day to hold their deceased baby.

"I bonded with Ellinor during that time," Salviander told me. "Sadly, though, what I had bonded with was a tiny lifeless body. Grief does a lot to twist our thinking, and as awful and crazy as it sounds, I felt like it was my motherly duty to be buried with Ellinor."

What rescued her from this morbid impulse? It was nothing less than the reality of heaven. If the evidence was sufficient to convince Salviander that Christianity is true, then its teachings about heaven aren't based on wishful thinking but are truly grounded in reality— and that meant Ellinor would be parented by none other than her heavenly Father himself.

"Knowing she was safe in a realm of indescribable love, joy, peace, and beauty—and that this would be the place in which we would eventually be reunited—I was finally freed from despair," she said. "I experienced a vision of Ellinor's body being gently taken from my arms by God and carried up to heaven, and that was the precise moment I had peace. There was no better place for her to be, and as a mother, that was the only way I could really let her go."[4]

Her confidence in the existence of heaven made all the difference for Salviander. But how much can we really know in advance about what our experience in eternity will be like? As it turns out, the Bible provides precious few concrete details. In fact, it actually declares, "No eye has seen, no ear has heard, and no mind has imagined what God has prepared for those who love him."[5]

As Martin Luther said, "As little as children know in their mother's womb about their birth, so little do we know about life everlasting."[6] J. Todd Billings, a Christian theologian suffering from incurable cancer, said that although we know that Christ "will be the center of the life to come," nevertheless "the *information* we have about life everlasting is tiny, minuscule."[7]

As a result, myths and misconceptions abound. "Nearly every Christian I have spoken with has some idea that eternity is an unending church service," said author John Eldredge. "We have settled on an image of the never-ending sing-along in the sky, one great hymn after another, forever and ever, amen. And our heart sinks. *Forever and ever? That's it? That's the good news?* And then we sigh and feel guilty that we are not more 'spiritual.' We lose heart, and we turn once more to the present to find what life we can."[8]

Yet there are some facts we *can* know about heaven—and that's what drew me to a modest Anglican church in the northern suburbs of Chicago on a balmy summer afternoon. I was anxious to have a discussion with a noted New Testament scholar whose book on heaven debunks several popular myths about the afterlife and sets the record straight, based on what we can responsibly glean from the biblical accounts.

SCOT MCKNIGHT, PHD

Scot McKnight is a highly influential and prolific New Testament scholar, with particular expertise in historical Jesus studies, the Gospels, early Christianity, and contemporary issues involving the church. Having grown up as the son of a Baptist deacon in Freeport, Illinois, he came to faith in Christ as a youngster and later had a transformative experience with the Holy Spirit at a church camp.

Asked about his career in theology, he told me, "That's all I ever wanted to do my whole life."

He earned his master's degree from Trinity Evangelical Divinity School and his doctorate from the University of Nottingham, where he studied under the eminent scholar James D. G. Dunn. After serving as a professor at Trinity and North Park University, he now teaches at Northern Baptist Theological Seminary in Lisle, Illinois.

McKnight has become a force in Christian culture through his highly successful blog, Jesus Creed; through media exposure on television and in such magazines as *Time* and *Newsweek*; and through his lectures in places around the world, including South Korea, Australia, and South Africa.

Among the more than eighty books he has authored are the award-winning *The Jesus Creed, The Blue Parakeet: Rethinking How You Read the Bible, The King Jesus Gospel*, commentaries on various New Testament books, texts on how to interpret the New Testament generally and the Synoptic Gospels specifically, and even a book on Jesus' mother called *The Real Mary*.

It was McKnight's book on the afterlife, called *The Heaven Promise*, that prompted me to get together with him near Chicago, not far from where he and his wife, Kristen, a psychologist who was his childhood sweetheart, have resided for years.

With a fringe of graying hair and wire-rimmed glasses, McKnight has a professorial demeanor, though not in an off-putting way. His smile is quick, his eyes are inquisitive, and his manner is engaging and empathetic—in short, he seems like the kind of professor who would hang out with students at a coffee shop to chat about their lives outside of the classroom.

I began by asking McKnight why he believes in an afterlife with God. Like any good theologian, he laid out his thoughts crisply and systematically, saying he had nine reasons in all.

"First," said McKnight, "I believe in heaven because Jesus and the apostles did. Jesus said, 'For my Father's will is that everyone who looks to the Son and believes in him shall have eternal life, and I will raise them up at the last day.'[1] Peter promised his churches they would 'receive a rich welcome into the eternal kingdom of our Lord and Savior Jesus Christ.'[2] As for John, he said, 'And this is what [God] promised us—eternal life.'[3] Paul talked about our frail bodies, saying, 'For we know that if the earthly tent we live in is destroyed, we have a building from God, an eternal house in heaven, not built by human hands.'[4] If all of them believed in heaven, then it's good enough for me."

"What's your second reason?" I asked.

"Because Jesus was raised from the dead—to me, that's the big one," he replied. "Not only was he resurrected, but people saw his body; they talked with him; they ate with him; and then he returned to the Father with the promise that he will come back to consummate history. This gives great credibility to an afterlife—and as N. T. Wright said, 'The resurrection of Jesus is the *launching of God's new world*.'[5]

"My third reason for believing in heaven is that the overall Bible believes in it."

"Wait a second," I said. "The agnostic scholar Bart Ehrman says the earliest biblical books don't teach anything about heaven, and he seems to suggest that the concepts of heaven and hell were simply made up over the centuries."[6]

"Well, let's look at some facts," responded McKnight. "It's true that there's very little interest in heaven or the afterlife in the Old Testament. It speaks of death—or *sheol*—the way that other Near Eastern and Mediterranean cultures did at the time, which is that death seems to be permanent. *Sheol* is a dark, deep, and miry pit. In fact, the Old Testament's only statements about the afterlife are found in its latest books.[7] It's the New Testament that ushers in a new hope for eternal life and heaven."

"Should that bother Christians?" I asked.

"Not in the slightest, because this is how divine revelation works. It unfolds over time," he explained. "The Bible's major themes develop and grow and expand and take us to the very precipice of eternity. It's like watching a play, where the whole story isn't clear until the end. Once we get to Jesus, and especially his resurrection, the Old Testament's images of *sheol* give way to his glorious teachings of immortality, eternal life, and the kingdom of God."

Beauty, Desire, Justice, Science

"What's your fourth reason for believing in heaven?" I asked McKnight.

"Because the church has taught it consistently," he said. Christian theology from the very beginning has believed in an afterlife, especially because of the resurrection. There has never been an era in which the church hasn't believed in heaven.

"Then there's my fifth reason for believing in heaven—because of beauty."

That sounded intriguing. "How so?"

"Even atheists get awestruck by the grandeur of the world—visiting the Grand Canyon, strolling among the California redwoods, hearing Bach, or seeing a painting by van Gogh. These point us toward something beyond. You see, many of us believe in heaven because we see in the present world a glimpse of something far grander—the world as we think it *ought* to be. Where do we get that sense of *ought*? Could it indicate a future reality—a new heaven and a new earth? If God made a world this good, doesn't it make sense he would make a world where it will all be even better?"

McKnight let that question linger for a minute. Then he moved on to his next reason for believing in heaven—namely, because most people do. He cited statistics showing that 84 percent of Americans believe in some kind of heaven, with nearly seven out of ten convinced that it's "absolutely true."[8]

Indeed, Todd Billings points out that even a third of those who *don't* believe in God *still* believe in life after death. In fact, he said, "belief in the afterlife appears to be on the rise" over recent years in America.[9] Said a researcher at San Diego State University, "It was interesting that fewer people participated in religion or prayed but more believed in an afterlife."[10]

McKnight told me, "Essentially, humans down through history and across the spectrum of religions and philosophies have always believed in an afterlife. Why is that? Is there something inherent in humans, a kind of innate intuition from God, that there's life beyond the grave? The Bible says God has 'set eternity in the human heart.'[11] I believe the history of human belief in heaven is an argument for believing it's true."

"What's your seventh reason?"

"Because of desire," he replied. "C. S. Lewis said, 'If we are made for heaven, the desire for our proper place will be already in us.' He said this is a desire that 'no natural happiness will satisfy.'[12] Elsewhere he explained, 'If I find in myself a desire which no experience in this world can satisfy, the most probable explanation is that I was made for another world.'[13] As philosopher Jerry Walls put it, 'A good God would not create us with the kind of aspirations we have and then leave those aspirations unsatisfied.'[14]

"I believe that the ongoing lack of fulfillment in possessing what we desire—the love of another, family, beauty, work—indicates there is a true home that will ultimately satisfy all our desires fully—and that home is heaven. In other words, the fleeting satisfactions of this world point beyond us toward a place of final and lasting fulfillment."

With that, McKnight went on to his eighth reason for believing in heaven—the desire for justice to be done.

"This world reeks of injustice. We've been told since childhood that life isn't fair." He gestured in the direction of the city of Chicago. "Not far from here, innocent kids in the inner city are getting shot. Sexual abuse and exploitation flourish around the world. When I was in high school, I thought racial discrimination would end in my generation, but it obviously didn't. We seem to have an innate sense of what's right and wrong, and we long to see justice done.

"I believe in heaven because I believe God wants to make all things right. He wants justice to be finally and fully established. That means victims of injustice will someday sit under the shade tree of justice and know that God makes all things so new that past injustices are swallowed up in the joy of the new creation."

"And what's your final reason?"

"Because science doesn't provide all the answers. We have an empirical mindset today. A lot of people believe scientific knowledge is superior to any other form of knowledge. But that's simply not true. Science can tell us how the world works and behaves, but it can't probe meaning and purpose. It can map brain function, but it can't explain love.

"The point is that science can't prove heaven, but not everything has to be subjected to scientific scrutiny. For instance, we have excellent historical evidence for Jesus' resurrection, and that ought to be sufficient to point toward the reality of an afterlife with God."

A New Heaven and a New Earth

Among the misconceptions about heaven is that it's an ethereal existence, up in the clouds somewhere, a purely spiritual place where we are ghostly souls who spend every waking hour singing hymns to God. When I asked McKnight to respond to those ideas, his eyes widened. "Well, there's a lot to set straight there," he said.

"Let's start at the beginning."

"Okay," he said. "We need to see heaven as being in two phases. First, there's the present heaven, which is where we go when we die. This is a temporary situation—I liken it to a dormitory where students don't expect to stay forever. Eventually, they'll move into a more permanent condo or house."

"This would be the so-called 'intermediate state,'" I said.

"Correct. Jesus said to the thief on the cross, 'Today you will be with me in paradise.'[15] When Stephen was being stoned to death, he looked up to heaven, or paradise, and saw the glory of God.[16] We don't have a lot of information to go on, but in this intermediate state we will be consciously present with God."

I said, "When Jesus talks about the death of his friend Lazarus, he says Lazarus has 'fallen asleep.'[17] Doesn't that mean the intermediate state is a place of slumber where we're unaware of what's happening?"

"No, Jesus used that term to suggest Lazarus was in a place of rest in the presence of God. This was a temporary situation, as sleep is. Ultimately, this present heaven is going to give way to a new heaven and a new earth. That's the second phase."

"So in the end heaven isn't some far-off place, but it's *here*," I said.

"Right. It's the complete renewal of our world, a very earthy, physical place, not just for spirits or souls, but for resurrected bodies designed for the kingdom of God. John says in Revelation, 'Then I saw "a new heaven and a new earth," for the first heaven and the first earth had passed away, and there was no longer any sea. I saw the Holy City, the new Jerusalem, coming down out of heaven from God, prepared as a bride beautifully dressed for her husband.'"[18]

"Does that suggest that the new heaven will be situated over the current Jerusalem?"

"Some people think so, and that God will dwell in the

reconstructed temple. But I think that's too wooden of an interpretation. The Bible says this is a *new* Jerusalem. In other words, this world will resemble our present earth, but it will be a transformed place for transformed people. There will be no temple, because John tells us that 'the Lord God Almighty and the Lamb are its temple.'[19]

"We're talking about a glorious redemption and restoration of all creation," he continued, his voice getting more animated. "Jesus described it as a place with multitudes of rooms for his followers.[20] God will dwell with us, and we will dwell with God. We will actually see God's face. Can you imagine that? All of creation will be set free and turn to God in praise. It will be creation on steroids, the way it was designed to be.

"The Hebrew word for *good* is *tov*. So whatever is truly *tov* about our world today will be enhanced in the new heaven and the new earth. It will be a place of celebrations, music and songs, festivals and festivities." He winked as he added, "And the Cubs will always win the World Series."

That *did* sound extraordinary!

"How will all of this unfold?" I asked.

"Paul says in 1 Corinthians 15 that first is the resurrection of Jesus, after which he will return to triumph over the powers of evil that are at work in the world. Then he will conquer death itself before he hands over the kingdom to the Father. With that, the mission of history is accomplished. Paul ends with the expression 'so that God may be all in all.'[21] That's the goal of history. God is the Alpha and Omega—he is the beginning and end of all existence and at the center of all its meaning."[22]

Theocentric versus Kingdom-Centric

"According to the Bible, what will our bodies be like in this new heaven and new earth?" I asked.

"Our souls will be reembodied, only this time our bodies will be transformed and imperishable," McKnight explained. "In fact, whatever can be said about Jesus' resurrected body could be said about ours. Our bodies will be perfected for a new kind of existence in eternity."

He patted his bald head. "I'll even have hair in heaven," he added with a chuckle.

"How old do you think we'll be in heaven?" I asked.

"There have been long debates about that. Some think it will be the age of Jesus at his resurrection, but we don't really know. I think we'll age without aging; in other words, we won't degrade over time, but we'll continue to grow and expand intellectually as we learn and develop further. It's important to note that this isn't a *new* body; it's a transformation of our *current* body. There's a one-to-one correspondence, or continuity, between the two. People in heaven will recognize us. They'll say, 'Hey, it's Lee Strobel. I'm surprised he made it!'"

Which evoked a hearty laugh.

McKnight continued. "Paul says we are 'sown a natural body' and 'raised a spiritual body.'[23] By that, he meant we'll have a body made for a perfectly Spirit-driven world. In one sense, our body will be ordinary. When the disciples met Jesus on the road to Emmaus, for example, they didn't see anything weird about him. It was a body that needed food and had marks from his earlier life. But in another sense, our body will be extraordinary—it can appear in a room without opening the door, or even glow with the glory of God."

I said, "Americans tend to be pretty individualistic, and our tendency is to see the final heaven as a place where we'll have a singular experience with God. But it's much more than that, isn't it?"

"Yes, Christians tend to go to one of two extremes in thinking about heaven," came his answer. "Some people see heaven as purely *theocentric*, or God-centered, focusing on individuals worshiping him and bringing him glory."

"We can't deny the centrality of God in heaven," I said.

"Absolutely, he will be fully exalted, but that can come from more than just an endless and ecstatic worship service. God is glorified when we're caring, when we're being good parents, when we're nurturing our garden. Sometimes this theocentric view pictures heaven as a spiritual experience rather than an embodied one.

"On the other side is a *kingdom-centric* view of heaven, which stresses the community aspect of the afterlife. Here the emphasis is on God and his people, on worship and fellowship, on justice and peace, on social engagement. It's an embodied existence where relationships flourish amidst our total devotion to God."

"Do you think this view can get carried too far as well?"

"Yes, the descriptions of heaven can become almost too mundane. One person complained about too much emphasis on the social aspects of heaven by saying, 'Who wants a parade and a barbecue every day?'[24]

"The answer, it seems to me, is in the middle," he concluded. "We need a balance between the two views. Heaven will be a place of both worship *and* fellowship. It will be a glorious union of delight in God *and* delight in one another. We have a king *and* we will be citizens of his kingdom, who are in a flourishing society together."

"How," I asked, "will people in heaven enjoy themselves if they know there are others, perhaps relatives, who are suffering in hell?"

McKnight acknowledged the question with a nod. "That issue has spurred a lot of debate through the years," he said. "A bunch of theories have been offered. We don't know how God will do it, but somehow he will deal with this. We can have confidence in that. C. S. Lewis said that God won't allow hell to have veto power over people rightfully enjoying themselves in eternity with him."[25]

The Heavenly Veranda

For me, the community aspect of heaven has been especially intriguing. I asked McKnight to elaborate further.

"The final heaven will be a global village," McKnight said. "It's a place designed for those who want to be in relationship with God and in fellowship with others. After all, what happened after Jesus rose from the dead? He immediately renewed fellowship with his disciples. In the eternal heaven, God will be on his throne, but at the same time the new creation will be filled with loving relationships among his people."

McKnight paused to remind me that the Bible doesn't give us a high-resolution picture of heaven. Rather, it uses metaphors and images to stoke our imagination by suggesting what eternal life with God will be like. One such picture is that Jesus is preparing rooms for us in heavenly homes.[26]

"When I use my imagination," McKnight said, "I picture our homes as having a veranda for fellowship and a garden for retreat."

"A veranda?" I asked.

"Yes, it's a sign of hospitality," he replied. "A church leader studied the history of architecture in New Zealand and found that before World War II, homes were built with verandas, where people would sit in the evening with their family to greet passersby and invite them to stop and chat. But verandas tended to disappear after the war. They were replaced by gardens in the back of the property, where people would retreat from the rest of the world."[27]

Interestingly, Leslie and I had been spending our spare time looking at houses to downsize, and one of our priorities has been a roomy front porch where we can sit and interact with neighbors. I was surprised that even in so-called retirement communities, few homes offer such a feature.

"I like the vision of the veranda," I said to McKnight.

"Me too," he replied. "When I was growing up, we didn't have air-conditioning, so after dinner we'd go out in the front yard to cool off and neighbors would come up and chat and hang out. It was great. I believe heaven will strike the perfect balance of privacy and devoted love of God, as well as fellowship and devoted love of family and others.

"And there will be parties—oh, will there be parties!" he added. "The Bible uses the metaphors of banquets and feasts—in fact, the first image of the kingdom of God in the final vision of Revelation is a wedding celebration of love and friendship and community.[28] Heaven will be a fellowship of differents—everyone reconciled and forgiven, all relationships characterized by trust and joy, and everyone with a story to tell—one that all of us will want to hear."

The First Hour in Heaven

If there will be an authentic—indeed, transcendent—sense of community among people in the final heaven, what about all of the petty conflicts, testy arguments, and relational quarrels that exist between us in this world? Won't they carry into eternity and frustrate God's plan for us to live in harmony forever?

"That's a good question," McKnight said. "And that brings me to what I believe will transpire in our first hour of heaven."

"What's that?"

"Reconciliation," he replied. "I believe we will have face-to-face meetings with everyone we've been in conflict with—and there will be truth telling, confession, honesty, and repentance. No equivocation, no excuses, no pretending. Friendships will be repaired; relationships will be set right. We'll lock arms and slap backs and give hugs and shed tears of relief and joy."

"You really think so?"

"How else can we carry on in peace and harmony if these rifts aren't healed?" he asked. "Obviously, I don't know the mechanics of how this will take place. Maybe it will be instantaneous. But take place it must. And we will *want* it to happen. God will fill us with the desire and ability to reconcile with each other. Tutsis will sit down with Hutus; unfaithful husbands will sit down with their wounded wives; rebellious children will settle up with their parents."

That last comment triggered a personal thought. My father and

I had a rocky relationship. He told me at the height of an argument on the eve of my high school graduation, "I don't have enough love for you to fill my little finger." We never really reconciled after that; instead, we swept our conflict under the rug.

I believe my father, who died in 1979, was a genuine believer and that we will meet again someday in heaven. In recent years, through prayer and introspection, I've come to grips with the many ways my own rebellion, dishonesty, and selfishness contributed to the schism between us. I've longed to admit all this to him and express my regret and repentance. I've wanted to get past the ill will we both harbored for so many years.

I mentioned this briefly to McKnight, who listened with the patience of a counselor. "Well," he said, "I do think that your father is already more conscious of these things than you are."

"Really?"

"He has the perfect desire to reconcile. I'm guessing he has already repented of his side in the conflict. And one day, your relationship will be healed. It will be a beautiful moment for the both of you. Think of it—after that, you'll spend forever with him in the kind of father-son relationship that both of you have always wanted."

I smiled and reached down to check the recorder as if to make sure it was still working properly. It was a ruse, of course. I didn't want McKnight to see that my eyes were glistening.

Seeing the Face of God

Scripture has several references to the hope of seeing God face-to-face in eternity, often called the *beatific vision*, a doctrine that has inexplicably faded in much of contemporary Protestant theology.

Scholar Hans Boersma, in tracing the beatific vision through Christian tradition, said, "We are true to the way God has made us when we make the vision of God our ultimate desire."[29] Andrew Louth, professor emeritus at the University of Durham, said that "the 'beatific vision,' gazing on God in utmost joy, is the ultimate goal of Christian living, the fulfillment of our Christian discipleship."[30]

In the Psalms, David wrote, "One thing I ask from the LORD, this only do I seek . . . to gaze on the beauty of the LORD and to seek him in his temple."[31] Paul said that although we see things dimly now, someday in eternity "we shall see face to face."[32] Jesus said in the Sermon on the Mount, "Blessed are the pure in heart, for they will see God."[33]

"This seems confusing," I said to McKnight. "The Bible says God told Moses, 'You cannot see my face, for no one may see me and live.'"[34]

"Yes, the Bible says people cannot gaze on God and survive his glorious brilliance," McKnight said. "But while God's full presence is unendurable for humans here and now, in eternity all of his followers will get face time with him. The apostle John specifically confirms that all those in heaven 'will see his face.'[35] When we're there, we won't merely be able to *survive* his glorious presence, but we will *revel* in it forever."

He pointed out that Jesus said, "Anyone who has seen me has seen the Father."[36] At one point, Jesus was transfigured before his disciples, and "his face shone like the sun." Even his clothes "became as white as the light."[37]

"They saw him as he manifested his essential glory—the resurrected body—and the book of Revelation opens with John catching a glimpse of this same glorious Jesus," McKnight said. "When we see God in eternity, it will fill us to overflowing with happiness and joy. We will be fully alive, with a profound relational knowledge of the Almighty."

McKnight said that when his children were young, they enjoyed "Magic Eye" books, where you stare at a bundle of dots until they morph into a three-dimensional picture, all while you lose peripheral vision. In a sense, you enter into the scene as your eyes adjust and are transformed for the image.

"Being with God will be like that, except greater. Our everyday life of devotion to God is like that bundle of dots—sometimes it's wonderful, sometimes it's not," he said. "When we encounter God fully under the power of a transformed body, all the dots will suddenly make sense—and we will have been absorbed into the depth of who God is. Saint John of the Cross called God's presence a 'living flame of love'[38]—that means our dwelling with God will be a wonderfully warm and intimate encounter."

He pursed his lips. "We're not ready for that yet," he said, a hint of longing in his voice. "Someday, yes. Then the veil will be torn away, and we will have the capacity to experience God face-to-face. You see, Lee, that's what heaven is for. Heaven will exist for those who long to gaze upon the luminous and beautiful face of God."

In the words of the towering eighteenth-century theologian Jonathan Edwards, "How good is God, that he has created man for this very end, to make him happy in the enjoyment of himself, the Almighty."[39]

Charles Spurgeon couldn't contain himself at the thought: "The very glory of heaven is that we shall see him, that same Christ who once died upon Calvary's cross, that we shall fall down, and worship at his feet, nay more, that he shall kiss us with the kisses of his mouth, and welcome us to dwell with him forever."[40]

"No man hath seen God at any time," says the King James Version of John 1:18. "The only begotten Son, which is in the bosom of the Father, he hath declared him." In the original Greek, the idiom "in the bosom" describes the closeness of God and his Son.

In effect, says Michael Reeves in his book *Delighting in the Trinity*, John is painting a picture of Jesus as being eternally in the lap of the Father. "One would never dare imagine it," said Reeves, "but Jesus declares [John 17:24] that his desire is that believers might be with him there."[41]

Go ahead—for just a moment, *dare*.

It's a staggering thought—heaven will be *here*, in this world, a re-created and renewed environment free from sin and decay, a bustling place full of commerce and friendships and beautiful nature, all focused on the community of God's people glorifying their triune Creator.

As the apostle John wrote in Revelation 21:5, "He who was seated on the throne said, 'I am making everything new!' Then he said, 'Write this down, for these words are trustworthy and true.'"

Wrote author John Eldredge, "If God were wiping away reality as we know it and ushering in a new reality, the phrase would have been, 'I am making all *new things*!' But that's not what he says."[42] Rather, he said he is making "everything new."

"The early Christians," said N. T. Wright, "believed that God was going to do for the whole cosmos what he had done for Jesus at Easter."[43]

Fully seeing the supernatural—that is, personally experiencing God's glorious world to come—will bring the kind of joy and fulfillment we can't even imagine today. All of which stoked in me an ever-deepening desire to encounter God face-to-face.

CHAPTER 10

THE LOGIC OF
DAMNATION

Few biblical teachings evoke as much emotion as the theology of hell. For example, theologian David Bentley Hart of the University of Notre Dame declared that the idea of conscious eternal torment is "morally corrupt, contrary to justice, perverse, inexcusably cruel, deeply irrational, and essentially wicked."[1] Ukrainian philosopher Nikolai Berdyaev reached a similar conclusion: "I can conceive of no more powerful and irrefutable argument in favor of atheism than the eternal torments of hell."[2]

In his book *Why Hell*, Steve Gregg concedes that "hell, as traditionally conceived, has few friends, it seems."[3] And certainly that's true. Even scholars who endorse the traditional teaching of eternal torment wince at its implications. The topic of hell rarely comes up in polite conversation—or even in many sermons these days.

Maybe that explains why just a bare majority (58 percent) of Americans believe in hell, down from 71 percent in recent years,[4] and a mere 2 percent believe they will end up there,[5] even though Jesus warned that "broad is the road that leads to destruction, and many enter through it."[6]

Speaking of Jesus, he talked more about judgment and hell than anyone else in the Bible, referring to it as *Gehenna* (transliterated, *Geenna*), or the Valley of Hinnom, which was located just south and west of Jerusalem.[7] Once thought to have been a smoldering garbage dump during Jesus' time, scholars now recognize Gehenna as having been "actually far worse: a place where the most horrible things take place, such as the willful sacrifice of children," said pastor and professor Mark Jones.

"Evil at its worst is associated with Gehenna," he added. "Hell is a place of pure evil, a place as scary as it is destitute of all hope. And it is an everlasting place."[8]

Under Christianity's traditional teaching, the impenitent endure eternity in conscious torment and separation from God in hell—a truly horrifying prospect. Harvard-educated church historian John Gerstner insists that there's "one essential reason" that evangelicals hold tenaciously to this doctrine: "God's Word teaches it."[9]

But does it, *really*? Or is the issue more nuanced than many Christians suppose? While the Bible does tell us there's a place called hell, some of the specifics remain open to controversy. "The Bible is arguably less clear on the nature of hell than on the existence of hell," said author Preston Sprinkle.[10]

The traditional interpretation irks many scholars. For instance, in the view of Bible teacher Grady Brown, "The doctrine of 'endless punishment' has for centuries been the 'crazy uncle' that the Church, with justifiable embarrassment, has kept locked in the back bedroom."[11]

Canadian theologian Clark Pinnock didn't mince words. "Everlasting torture is intolerable from a moral point of view because it makes God into a bloodthirsty monster who maintains an everlasting Auschwitz for victims whom He does not even allow to die," he said.[12]

In recent years, an increasing number of professors and preachers are opting for alternatives to the traditional understanding of hell. Some maintain that the unrepentant are simply eradicated by God, perhaps after a limited period of suffering, rather than enduring endless torment. Others believe "love wins," a clever way of saying that everyone will be saved in the end—including, presumably, Adolf Hitler—so if hell does exist, eventually it's going to be vacant.

These are significant issues that demand thoughtful responses. "When it comes to hell, we can't afford to be wrong," Sprinkle and Francis Chan said in their book *Erasing Hell*. "This is not one of those doctrines where you can toss in your two cents, shrug your shoulders, and move on. Too much is at stake. Too many *people* are at stake. And the Bible has too much to say."[13]

To pursue solid answers, I sat down with a noted scholar who is an adherent of the conventional view of hell—and where better to find such an advocate than in South Florida in the depths of summer, where the sweltering heat is often likened to Hades itself.

Not unreasonably, it seemed to me.

INTERVIEW *with*

PAUL COPAN, PHD

Soft-spoken and sincere, mild-mannered and unfailingly polite, philosopher Paul Copan comes off as a consummate gentleman and the kindly father of six. While all of that's accurate, he's also a rigorous scholar with an incisive mind who is not afraid to wade boldly into controversial waters. For example, his books *Is God a Moral Monster?* and *Did God Really Command Genocide?* have become go-to resources for his penetrating analysis of troubling Old Testament texts.[1]

Copan has authored or edited nearly forty books, including popular-level works and academic tomes. He is a professor at Palm Beach Atlantic University in West Palm Beach, has been a visiting scholar at Oxford University, and served as president of the Evangelical Philosophical Society for six years. Copan writes about hell in one of his most recent books, the second edition of *Loving Wisdom: A Guide to Philosophy and Christian Faith*, which is what initially caught my attention.[2]

"You opened your chapter by saying the doctrine of hell has troubled both believers and unbelievers alike," I began. "Purely on an emotional level, do you personally find the traditional view of hell to be disquieting?"

Copan adjusted his glasses as he acknowledged the question with a slight nod. "Yes, at some level I do," he replied. "C. S. Lewis said he would love to discard the doctrine of hell, but if Christianity is the story of reality, we can't pick and choose which bit of reality to believe and which to reject."

I was familiar with Lewis's words: "There is no doctrine which I would more willingly remove from Christianity than this, if it lay in my power. But it has the full support of Scripture and, specially, of Our Lord's own words; it has always been held by Christendom; and it has the support of reason."[3]

Copan continued. "The Bible says the judge of all the earth will do what is right.[4] So if it turns out that our understanding of hell is truly unjust, then we would have to reject it. The goodness and justice of God are more fundamental than our limited interpretations of hell, which are sometimes colored by centuries of tradition, going back to Dante's *Inferno*."

"All the more reason," I said, "to carefully sort out what's biblical and what isn't."

"That's right."

"We Can Do What We Wish"

"Do you think the traditional view of hell drives a lot of people from God?" I asked.

"To a certain point, yes, but that needs qualification," he said. "For some people, no matter what philosophical perspective we give about hell, their visceral rejection of it—perhaps based on caricatures or misunderstandings—will nevertheless prevail."

"Can you elaborate?"

"Sociologist Robert Bellah and educator Alan Bloom pointed out that freedom has become the new absolute and relativism has become the default position in our culture.[5] So if this is the average person's worldview, it's not surprising that the doctrine of hell would offend them. Hell violates the 'absolute' of relativism, and to many in our culture, the existence of hell would undermine an individual's own freedom. More recently," he added, "we encounter another challenge in talking about hell, which Greg Lukianoff and Jonathan Haidt discuss in their book *The Coddling of the American Mind*."[6]

I chuckled. "That's an intriguing title."

"Intriguing, yes, and accurate," Copan replied. "They point out that a growing number of universities are protecting students from words and ideas they don't like, they're creating safety zones, and they're barring professors from uttering microaggressive statements, such as 'America is a land of opportunity.' The authors argue that universities are contributing to the infantilization of our culture by prohibiting any speech that causes offense or discomfort."

"And," I said, "hell is certainly a topic that can make people extremely uncomfortable."

"Exactly right."

"How would you push back against all of this?"

"First, by noting that Jesus is considered by many to be *the* outstanding moral and spiritual authority in history—and yet he taught extensively on hell. If God is the cosmic authority, we should expect his ways and standards to be infinitely more finely tuned than our own limited moral perceptions. Our perspective may be skewed by our own self-interest or because our cultural lenses cloud our notions of justice or fairness.

"Second, other cultures may not find the notion of hell morally problematic. So why are we imposing our individualistic Western judgment on those non-Western cultures?

"Third, the fact that God and hell both exist serves as a reminder that cosmic justice will ultimately be done. Human beings will not get away with evil but will be held accountable for their actions—and that's a good thing. Finally, fourth, remember that if any view of hell truly diminishes the goodness and justice of God, then it must be rejected. That means we may need to hold certain conceptions of hell tentatively."

"For some people, hell might be a wake-up call," I observed.

"Right. Jesus said to repent or perish.[7] The doctrine of hell can remind us that there is an accountability before God, and the consequences of separating ourselves from him are, indeed, dire and miserable."

Flames, Darkness, Gnashing of Teeth

"The description of hell typically includes eternal flames," I said. "Some theologians see this as literal, while others insist the flames are metaphorical. What's your assessment?"

"I don't believe hell is a place of intense thermal output," came his answer. "These images of hell are metaphorical. If two key images of hell—flames and darkness—were taken literally, they would cancel each other out. The flames would illuminate the place. Also, the flame imagery is associated with the lake of fire in Revelation 19 and 20, which is where the devil and his angels will be cast. Literal fire affects physical bodies with nerve endings, not spirit beings like them, so physical fire would be pointless."

I raised my hand to slow him. "Isn't the idea that the flames are metaphorical just a modern attempt to soften the picture of hell for those repulsed by it?"

Copan shook his head. "Not at all," he insisted. "Even the

Reformers Martin Luther and John Calvin took this metaphorical view."[8]

"A metaphor always points toward a reality that it's trying to illustrate," I said. "What's the point of the imagery of the flames and darkness?"

"Both images represent existence away from the Lord's presence.[9] This is the real essence of hell—being cut off from our source of life and joy and separated from God's blessings forever. Darkness evokes this sense of separation and removal. The reference to flames represents severe, holy judgment. Even in a state of separation, God sustains in existence those who have chosen to separate themselves from him. To be away from the presence of the Lord—the 'great divorce,' as C. S. Lewis put it—is the worst loss possible for any human being. That's torment."

"Is hell a torture chamber for eternity?" I asked.

"There's a difference between *torture*, which is externally imposed, and *torment*, which is internally generated. Torment, in effect, is self-inflicted. It's because people have resisted the initiating grace of God that they end up having their own way forever. God isn't willing that any perish; hell is the result of humans freely separating themselves from him and his love."

"What's the nature of the torment?"

"Revelation 14:11 speaks of 'the smoke of their torment' and that they have 'no rest day or night' forever. To be tormented means not being at rest. Just two verses later, we see that this torment is the opposite of the 'rest from their labor' that's experienced by faithful saints."[10]

"Seven times in Matthew and Luke we see references to 'gnashing of teeth,'" I said. "What's that imagery about?"

"New Testament scholar Craig Blomberg said this reflects anger at God. For example, those who were about to stone Stephen were gnashing their teeth in anger.[11] Again, this imagery is meant to warn us that hell is spiritual misery. This misery is a natural consequence of a life lived apart from God, as well as the punishment of those who don't want to be in God's presence. Indeed, God's presence would actually be *greater* misery for them."

"You mean they wouldn't *want* to be in heaven?"

"Right. They would have to repent in order to be in God's holy presence. That's why philosopher Dallas Willard said that 'the fires of heaven burn hotter than the fires of hell.'[12] They'd be much more content in their own self-absorbed misery away from God, rather than to face the discomfort of God's glorious presence."

I asked the question that arises in the minds of so many people. "Why would a good God send people to hell?"

"I think that question is framed incorrectly," Copan said.

"How so?"

"The operative word is *send*. Each choice we make in this life moves us closer to our ultimate destination—whether toward or away from God. We set our spiritual and moral compasses. That means that those who reject the rule of God *send themselves* to hell. Humans bring misery upon themselves by separating themselves from him. People consign themselves to hell—and God reluctantly lets them go. As the musician Michael Card says, God 'simply speaks the sentence that they have passed upon themselves.'"[13]

Willard agrees. "Some people not only want to hide from God but want to be as far away from God as possible. . . . The best place for them to be is wherever God is not, and that's what hell is," he wrote. "This is like the teacher who finally sends the trouble-making student out of the classroom, as it were, and says, 'Okay, if you want to go away, you can go away.'"[14]

Finite Sins, Infinite Punishment?

For many critics, the everlasting nature of hell is a disproportionate consequence of a limited lifetime of wrongdoing. Asks former pastor Rob Bell, "Have billions of people been created only to spend eternity in conscious punishment and torment, suffering infinitely for the finite sins they committed in the few years they spent on earth?"[15]

I posed the question to Copan, "Wouldn't infinite torment be an injustice that would be inconsistent with God's character?"

"The amount of time it takes to commit a sin isn't commensurate with the seriousness of the sin," Copan answered. "If I were to pick up a gun and kill you right now, how much time does that take? A few seconds? Yet the impact would be catastrophic and would reverberate through time, down the generations of your family. It might take many years for me to defraud you of your savings, but a murder committed in a flash would be the more serious offense and deserving of the greater punishment.

"You see," he continued, "everlasting hell is warranted for those who have deliberately rejected the infinite God—the infinite Good—and spurred the knowledge of God and the boundless gift of salvation he offers. God is more concerned with the direction of one's heart than the number of sins committed. People aren't consigned to be away from God because they committed a string of finite sins, but because they have spurned the greatest Good. Also, consider that people commit these sins against an infinite God—that's relevant too."

Centuries ago, Thomas Aquinas put it this way in his *Summa Theologiae*: "Now a sin that is against God is infinite; the higher the person against whom it is committed, the graver the sin—it is more criminal to strike a head of state than a private citizen—and God is of infinite greatness. Therefore, an infinite punishment is deserved for a sin committed against him."[16]

Copan added: "I'll mention one other factor as well."

"What's that?"

"It's the fact that the rebellion against God isn't just confined to a limited time on earth, but it continues unabated in hell—and therefore warrants ongoing judgment," he said. "The prominent theologian D. A. Carson has written that the Bible doesn't suggest there will be repentance in hell."

He rustled through some notes before finding this quote from Carson: "Perhaps, then, we should think of hell as a place where people continue to rebel, continue to insist on their own way, continue societal structures of prejudice and hate, continue to defy the living God. And as they continue to defy God, so he continues to punish them. And the cycle goes on and on and on."[17]

Said Copan, "As we discussed earlier, the gnashing of teeth in hell reflects continued anger at God. And if people continue to resist and hate God, then continuing judgment is certainly warranted."

Hell Isn't "One Size Fits All"

Two decades ago, when I was personally struggling to reconcile the doctrine of hell with the justice of God, I sought out philosopher J. P. Moreland and questioned him about the topic.[18]

One of his points that helped my understanding was that not everyone in hell will suffer the same way. Adolf Hitler won't have the same experience as my narcissistic neighbor who turned up his nose at God for his entire life but who didn't murder anyone. As evidence, Moreland cited Matthew 11:20–24, where Jesus said certain cities would suffer more than others because they refused to repent despite miracles he had performed there.

Blomberg said Luke 12:42–48 ranks "among the clearest in the entire Bible in support of degrees of punishment in hell."[19] This parable includes Jesus saying: "The servant who knows the master's will and does not get ready or does not do what the master wants will be beaten with many blows. But the one who does not know and does things deserving punishment will be beaten with few blows."

Augustine believed in degrees of punishment, saying in the fifth century: "We must not, however, deny that even the eternal fire will be proportioned to the deserts of the wicked."[20]

I asked Copan, "Do you agree that justice in eternity won't be 'one size fits all'?"

"Yes, absolutely, just as there are degrees of sin, so there are degrees of punishment. For example, Numbers 15 refers to intentional sins and unintentional sins. Jesus speaks of the blasphemy against the Holy Spirit, which won't be forgiven in the present life or the life to come, in contrast to any other sin or blasphemy, which can be forgiven.[21] Or consider the Jewish leaders of his day committing the 'greater sin,' whereas the sin of Roman authorities was a lesser one."[22]

"It makes sense to me that God's justice would be proportional," I said.

"Me too. The fact that the degreed nature of sin spills over into the afterlife—that each person is judged according to his deeds—does significantly address the challenge of hell's unreasonableness," he replied. "As I said earlier, the Bible asks, 'Will not the Judge of all the earth do right?'[23] And the answer is, yes, of course he will. In hell, the degree of misery will be correlated to the degree of responsibility."

From Sméagol to Gollum

Even so, Copan said, as people in hell continue to hate and resist God, over time the divine image in many of them may very well become eclipsed so that they turn into mere wisps and shadows of what they once were.

"Notice how Revelation reveals an irrational human hostility despite God's severe judgments," he said. "The text refers to people being seared by the intense heat, the beast's kingdom becoming darkened, and huge hailstones falling from the sky. People gnawed their tongues because of pain. And yet nevertheless—despite all this—they continue to curse and blaspheme God.[24] What's going on here could be called *corrosivism*."

"What do you mean by that?"

"I mean the end state of the unredeemed is the diminishing

of their humanity, something akin to the deterioration of J. R. R. Tolkien's hobbit Sméagol. Over time, he turned into the diminished, corroded, corrupted, wisp-like 'sub-hobbit' creature Gollum.

"Some theologians claim that unredeemed people who resist God to the end will eventually be extinguished from existence. In a way, this kind of diminished humanity bears some resemblance to that view. Who they were once has faded away."

Copan pulled out a quote from N. T. Wright: "It seems . . . it is possible . . . for human beings to choose to live more and more out of tune with the divine intention, to reflect the image of God less and less, [such that] there is nothing to stop them finally ceasing to bear that image, and so to be, as it were, beings who were once human but are not now," he wrote.

"Those who persistently refuse to follow Jesus, the true Image of God, will by their own choice become less and less like him, that is, less and less truly human. We sometimes say, even of living people, that they have become inhuman . . . I see nothing in the New Testament to make me reject the possibility that some, perhaps many, of God's human creatures do choose, and will choose, to dehumanize themselves completely."[25]

Copan put down the paper. His look was at once sober and sad. "And so," he said, "we end up not with human beings in hell, but with human 'remains,' as C. S. Lewis put it.[26] Human debris. Subhuman creatures in whom the light of the image of God has effectively been extinguished. That's so very, very tragic."

Escaping from Hell

What if there were an escape hatch—a valid biblical alternative to the traditional view of hell? What if God cut short the torment of the unrepentant by snuffing them out and thus ending their suffering?

For example, some annihilationists (or conditionalists) emphasize that humans are not intrinsically immortal. They say God, who alone is inherently immortal, grants eternal life to those who embrace Jesus as their forgiver and leader.[27] But lacking immortality, the unsaved simply cease to exist when they die, or they are resurrected for the final judgment and then consigned to hell for a limited period of punishment, after which their lives are extinguished forever. Either way, there's no everlasting torment in unquenchable fires.

"My prediction is that, even within conservative evangelical circles, the annihilation view of hell will be the dominant view in 10 or 15 years," said Sprinkle, coauthor of *Erasing Hell*. "I base that on how many well-known pastors secretly hold that view."[28]

Southern California pastor Gregory G. Stump said the case for conditional immortality is compelling. "This view seemed to be derived from the clear and consistent language of Scripture, it had an internal coherence that made sense of the overarching narrative of redemptive history, and it resolved philosophical and intuitive difficulties that have plagued generations of Christians and non-Christians alike for centuries."[29]

I asked Copan, "Is annihilationism heretical, or does it fall under the umbrella of orthodoxy?"

"I believe it's a secondary issue," came his response. "It's not a major doctrinal deviation, even if I disagree with it. There's some precedent among a few early church fathers who held this view, and there are some solid evangelical scholars who embrace it."

"How strong is their case?"

"They rally significant biblical support," he said. "They cite such biblical language as *destruction*, *perish*, and *death*, as well as images of trees being cut down or chaff and branches being burned.[30] The New Testament talks about God's judgment being a raging fire that will consume the enemies of God.[31] Jude refers to the destruction of Sodom and Gomorrah[32] as an example in undergoing the punishment of eternal fire.[33] If these cities were incinerated, shouldn't that foreshadow the fate of the unrepentant? Second Peter 2:6 suggests this—these cities were burned to ashes and made to be an example of what is going to happen to the ungodly."

I raised an eyebrow. "You sound sympathetic to their cause."

"A number of biblical texts appear to support their position. *However*," he said, raising his index finger and drawing out that word, "we have to consider the entire range of biblical teaching. Personally, their treatment of certain passages doesn't go far enough to convince me. That's why I still endorse the traditional view. The case for conditionalism, in my opinion, falls short."

Was Jesus an Annihilationist?

I pointed out that agnostic New Testament professor Bart Ehrman thinks Jesus was an annihilationist. "A close reading of Jesus's words shows that in fact he had no idea of torment for sinners after death," writes the controversial scholar. "Their punishment is that they will be annihilated, never allowed to exist again."[34] As an example, Jesus talks of two gates through which a person can pass—the broad gate leading to destruction. Said Ehrman: "Jesus does not say it leads to eternal torture."

"What's your assessment?" I asked Copan.

"Granted, Jesus doesn't say 'eternal torture,' but he does talk about the wailing and gnashing of teeth. The idea that Jesus had no idea of torment for sinners after death is problematic for several reasons."

"For instance?"

"For one thing, there was a variety of Jewish views about the afterlife, including everlasting conscious torment. The first-century Jewish historian Josephus refers to the Pharisees as holding that the wicked are 'punished with eternal torment' and experience 'eternal imprisonment.'[35] Second, there's the story Jesus tells about the rich man and Lazarus in Luke 16, which clearly presupposes torment for the wicked."

I interrupted. "Ehrman claims the author of the gospel put this known rabbinic story into Jesus' mouth."

Copan smiled. "That's disputed," he replied. "But nevertheless, Jesus uses images of weeping and gnashing of teeth to describe the state of separation from God, which doesn't sound like immediate extinction to me.[36] What's more, Jesus was clearly familiar with such texts as Daniel 12:2, which speak of those who would be resurrected to everlasting contempt."

That verse reads, "Multitudes who sleep in the dust of the earth will awake: some to everlasting life, others to shame and everlasting contempt." As one author observed, "There is no way to escape the obvious grammatical contrast between the unending well-being of the righteous and the unending shame and contempt of the wicked. To limit the suffering of the wicked without limiting the bliss of the righteous is grammatically impossible."[37]

"So you don't think Jesus was an annihilationist," I said, more as a statement than a question.

"No, I don't. Consider his teaching about sheep and goats in Matthew 25, where Jesus says in verse 46 that the unredeemed 'will go away to eternal punishment.' Jesus not only says in verse 41 that the *fire* for the unredeemed will be eternal, but here he emphasizes that the *punishment itself* will be eternal. That's a formidable challenge for annihilationists."

Copan also noted that Jesus says in verse 41 that the cursed will be thrown "into the eternal fire prepared for the devil and his angels." Asked Copan, "What happens to the devil and his minions? Revelation 20:10 says they will be cast into the lake of fire and tormented day and night for ever and ever—a fate, it appears, that will be shared by the unrepentant."

He added, "The Greek verb for *torment—basanismo—*indicates conscious suffering. We see this throughout the New Testament. Revelation 14:11 says that the smoke of unbelievers' torment will rise for ever and ever. As New Testament scholar G. K. Beale said, the word for torment is used nowhere in Revelation or biblical liter-ature in the sense of annihilation of personal existence; the book of Revelation, without exception, uses it of conscious suffering on the part of people."[38]

I looked up from the notes I was furiously scribbling. "These are serious challenges to the annihilation theory," I said.

"They are—and there are others too."

Other Obstacles to Annihilationism

I asked Copan about the verses that talk about the destruction of the unredeemed. "As Ehrman pointed out, Jesus said the broad gate leads to destruction.[39] On the surface, that sounds an awful lot like annihilation."

"Hold on a moment," Copan replied. "Destruction doesn't always mean 'cease to exist.' Second Peter 3:6 says that the world in Noah's day was destroyed. But we know it actually continued to endure. The same Greek word for *destroy*—*apollymi*—can be trans-lated as 'lost,' as in the story about the lost—but existing—coin in Luke 15:9. Also, a second death doesn't necessarily suggest being extinguished. After all, we were once dead in our trespasses and sins, though physically alive."[40]

"What other passages argue against annihilationism?"

"There's 2 Thessalonians 1:9–10, which says the unrepentant will be punished with an everlasting destruction and shut out from the presence of the Lord. Why mention being excluded from God's presence if 'everlasting destruction' means they have totally per-ished? In contrast, 1 Thessalonians 4:17 says believers will be with the Lord forever. Again, we see a parallel, indicating ongoing exis-tence for both the redeemed and the unredeemed."

Copan stressed again that while annihilationists can present a good case for their position, "to me it's insufficient to overcome the historic understanding of hell within the Christian tradition. This goes back to the earliest church fathers. For example, the apostle John's disciple Polycarp said just before he was burned alive for his faith, 'You threaten me with fire which burns for an hour, and is then extinguished, but you know nothing of the fire of the coming judgment and eternal punishment, reserved for the ungodly. Why are you waiting? Bring on whatever you want.'"[41]

All of which leaves universalism—the idea that everyone is redeemed in the end—as the remaining logical alternative to an eternal hell. I wanted to quiz Copan to see whether this theological view makes any biblical sense.

Universalism: Will All Be Saved?

If everlasting hell were true, "Christianity should be dismissed as a self-evidentially morally obtuse and logically incoherent faith."[42] So says influential academic theologian David Bentley Hart in his acerbic 2019 book *That All Shall Be Saved*, a 214-page screed with 118 derogatory comments about theologians who disagree with him, their views, their God, and their understanding of hell.[43]

Former pastor Rob Bell puts it in a kinder, gentler way in his bestseller *Love Wins*, where he writes approvingly of universalism. "At the heart of this perspective is the belief that, given enough time, everybody will turn to God and find themselves in the joy and peace of God's presence," he said.[44]

Christian universalism says in the end God will forgive and adopt all people through Christ—perhaps after a limited period of restorative punishment in hell for some. Thus, says Hart, "I for one do not object in the least to Hitler being purged of his sins and saved."[45]

In recent decades there has been an uptick in interest about universalism, driven among academics by the writings of Swiss theologian Karl Barth and among the broader public by Bell's high-profile ministry, which attained the heights of Oprah.

Copan's reaction was firm. "I believe universalism is an aberrant and dangerous doctrine," he said flatly. "You certainly get no hint of it in the Old Testament, where Psalm 1:6 reads, 'For the LORD watches over the way of the righteous, but the way of the wicked leads to destruction.'"

"Can a person be both a Christian and a universalist?" I asked.

"Universalists can be authentic Christians. Still, universalism falls outside the pale of the mainstream Christian tradition, although there are pockets of it in church history."

"Certainly, there's an emotional tug to it," I commented.

"Yes, who doesn't want everyone to be saved? Even God desires it!" he declared, his eyes widening. "As 1 Timothy 2:4 and 2 Peter 3:9 say, he wants all to come to a knowledge of the truth. But Christ is the *potential* Savior of all, not the *actual* Savior of all.[46] In other words, salvation is *universal in intent*—that is, God's desired will—but it's not achieved *in fact*—that is, God's permissive will. While salvation is *potentially* offered to all, not all freely accept it.[47]

"The Scriptures," he continued, "repeatedly indicate there will always be creatures who fully and finally say *no* to God. Finite, moral agents—whether angelic or human—have the capacity to choose contrary to God's moral order. Only God is necessarily good; he cannot do what is wrong. The same isn't true for contingent moral creatures like us who can choose lesser finite goods over the Ultimate Good. They can turn a good thing into a God substitute and fall prey to idolatry."

Are "All Things" Reconciled?

I interrupted to say, "In Colossians 1:16, Christ is said to have been the agent through whom *all things* were created. Four verses later, he is called the agent through whom *all things* are to be reconciled. Doesn't that sound suspiciously like universalism?"

"You have to keep reading to get the full picture," he answered. "Paul goes on to say, 'Now he has reconciled you . . . *if* you continue in your faith, established and firm, and do not move from the hope held out in the gospel."[48] So there's a condition there."

I nodded. "In other words, you're in one camp or the other."

"Right. And you can't disconnect these texts from what Paul says elsewhere—that some will end up shut out from the presence of the Lord,[49] or that those who preach a false gospel are condemned."[50]

"What about the Bible's use of the word *all* to describe those who are ultimately redeemed, as in 1 Timothy 2:6, which says Jesus gave himself as a ransom for all people?"

"Again, we need to examine that word closely. When the gospel of Mark says 'all the people of Jerusalem' flocked to be baptized by John, he doesn't mean every single individual was doing that. It simply meant a lot of people.[51] In this case, Jesus did pay for all the sins of the world and make grace available to all sinners, but we have to accept that payment on our behalf if we're going to benefit from it. Not everyone will do that."

"What about Jesus' mission, which was 'to seek and to save the lost.'[52] If some were actually left behind, did he fail?"

"No, he didn't consider it to be a failure just because there would be those who refused to take the narrow road. Jesus acknowledged that the eleven disciples the Father had given to him were preserved, even though 'the son of perdition'—Judas—didn't truly belong to Jesus.[53]

"At the cross, Jesus completed his mission: 'It is finished.'[54] Isaiah 53 says God would see the anguished death of his Suffering Servant as an atoning work that would justify many[55]—even if not all would embrace the Messiah. Jesus identified with us in life and death in order to save those who would choose the narrow path."

The Freedom to Say *No*

I scanned through some notes before finding the quote I was searching for. "The commentary author William Barclay said, 'If one man remains outside the love of God at the end of time, it means that that one man has defeated the love of God—and that is impossible.'"[56]

I barely completed the sentence before Copan jumped in. "But," he said, "we can't ignore the many Scriptures that indicate some will have their own way and get their divorce from God, despite his best efforts. God doesn't force his love on people. Jude 21 reminds us that we must keep ourselves in the love of God. This suggests that we can remove ourselves from God's loving influence. If God's undefeatable sovereignty means that all will be saved, how is this accomplished since it's up to human beings whether to accept or reject God's initiating grace? Even divine love can be resisted.

"We routinely read in Scripture that God does his utmost to reach people, only to be rebuffed. God actually appears exasperated at the rebellion of his people. For example, in the parable of the vineyard in Isaiah 5, when Israel produces worthless grapes, God asks, 'What more could have been done for my vineyard'—that is, Israel—'than I have done for it?'

"In Matthew 23, Jesus weeps over Jerusalem, longing to gather the city as a hen gathers her chicks, but Jerusalem refused. In Acts 7:51, before he was stoned, Stephen accuses his stiff-necked persecutors of always resisting the Holy Spirit. For stubborn rebels, the more God pours out his grace, the more they want to flee. They want to find happiness on their own terms."

"Still," I said, "Philippians 2:9–11 says, 'Every knee should bow . . . and every tongue acknowledge that Jesus Christ is Lord.' Doesn't this suggest that everyone will eventually come to faith?"

"But will they bow *willingly*?" Copan responded. "Paul is citing Isaiah 45:23 there, and he's aware that not all bowing before God springs from a humble, repentant heart. God's defeated foes will bow before him in shameful, reluctant acknowledgment that he is Lord.[57] Just a few chapters later, Isaiah 49:23 indicates that some will prostrate themselves before God and lick the dust from his feet. His enemies exhibit a feigned obedience.[58] Psalm 81:15 says, 'Those who hate the LORD would cringe before him, and their punishment would last forever.'"

For a magazine article in 2019, Copan interviewed Michael McClymond, professor of modern Christianity at St. Louis University, about his masterful two-volume historical and theological analysis of universalism called *The Devil's Redemption*,[59] a 1,325-page tome with 3,500 footnotes, written partly in response to Rob Bell's popularization of the discredited doctrine.

"Universalism isn't just a mistake," McClymond said. "It's also a symptom of deeper problems. In a culture characterized by moralistic therapeutic deism, universalism fits the age we inhabit. Universalism is the opiate of the theologians. It's the way we would want the world to be. Some imagine that a more loving and less judgmental church would be better positioned to win new adherents. Yet perfect love appeared in history—and he was crucified."[60]

I sat back in my chair and asked myself, *Where does all of this leave us?* Clearly, what remains is the traditional view of hell, which should chasten us and motivate us to tell as many people as we can that there is indeed a judgment, but there's also a divinely ordained escape route—that is, the gift of eternal life that God freely offers to everyone who will receive it in repentance and faith.[61]

Wrote Augustine in *The City of God*, "Those who desire to be rid of eternal punishment ought to abstain from arguing against God."[62]

CHAPTER 11

LIFE AFTER DEATH: EVIDENCE FOR THE
RESURRECTION

Even for a decorated cold-case homicide investigator, this was a formidable challenge. J. Warner Wallace typically used his considerable detective skills to solve murders that were decades old, but he had never tackled a case that stretched back for two millennia.

What's more, this time he wasn't merely attempting to identify the perpetrator of a long-ago crime; instead, he was trying to determine whether the victim was truly deceased—and whether he defied all naturalistic explanations by supernaturally rising from the dead on the third day.

Quite an assignment for a hyper-skeptical atheist.

Wallace is the son of a cop and the father of a cop. Initially, Wallace resisted the temptation to follow in his father's footsteps. He started out with a career in the arts, earning a degree in design and a master's degree in architecture, but before long the lure of the badge proved too strong.

After doing training through the Los Angeles Sheriff's department, Wallace joined the force in Torrance, California, working on the SWAT team, collaborating with the gang detail, and investigating robbery and homicide cases. Later he became a founding member of the department's cold-case homicide unit, assigned to crack murders that nobody else had been able to solve.

His success brought accolades and opportunities. Soon he was being featured on NBC's *Dateline* and news outlets seeking expertise on what it takes to arrest killers who thought they had gotten away with murder.

Through the years, Wallace's street-honed skepticism served him well. "As a cop, if you believe everything people tell you, you'd never arrest anyone," he said. For him, facts need to be solid, witnesses have to be credible, evidence must be persuasive, corroboration is crucial, and alibis have to be dismantled.

As an adolescent, Wallace's skepticism cemented him into atheism. His parents divorced when he was young. His father, at his mother's insistence, would drop him off at the Catholic church on Sundays, where he would attend a Latin Mass by himself.

"I didn't understand a word, but it didn't matter," he said. "I didn't believe any of it. Plus, I didn't have any Christian role models who could explain why they accepted this stuff."

It wasn't until Wallace was thirty-five that he subjected the gospels to months of painstaking analysis through various investigative techniques, including what detectives call "forensic statement analysis." This skill involves critically analyzing a person's account of events—including word choice and structure—to determine whether they are being truthful or deceptive.[1] Eventually, Wallace became convinced that Christianity is true beyond a reasonable doubt.

"In a sense, it was my skepticism that led to faith," he said, "because it pushed me to question everything, to doubt my own doubts, and to demand answers that could stand up to scrutiny."

The answers ended up convincing him that Jesus, in time and space, did conquer his tomb and thereby provide convincing evidence of his divinity. It was that meticulous investigation of the miraculous resurrection that prompted me to jump on a plane and fly to Southern California, where I met with Wallace at his ranch-style house in Orange County.

INTERVIEW *with*

J. WARNER WALLACE, MTS

"I'm an all-in kind of guy," Wallace said to me. "C. S. Lewis said if Christianity isn't true, it's of no importance, but if it is true, nothing is more important—and I agree.[1] That's why I've jumped in with both feet."

After becoming a Christian in 1996, Wallace earned a master's degree in theological studies from Golden Gate Baptist Theological Seminary, served as a youth pastor, and planted a church. Currently, he is an adjunct professor of apologetics at Biola University, is a senior fellow at the Colson Center for Christian Worldview, and teaches at Summit Ministries in Colorado.

I have been a friend of Wallace's for several years, ever since I wrote the foreword to his book *Cold-Case Christianity*, in which he offers ten principles from his detective work that can be used to examine the reliability of the Gospels.

His other books include *God's Crime Scene*, in which he examines eight pieces of evidence from the universe that make the case for the existence of God; *Alive*, which focuses on the resurrection; and *Forensic Faith*, which helps readers become better defenders of Christianity. Ever the artist, Wallace creates his own drawings to illustrate his books.

Although now retired from the police force, he still consults on cold-case homicides and acts as an investigative consultant for television networks.

Wallace is a bundle of crackling energy, speaking in fast, clipped sentences, sometimes verbally machine-gunning others with a flurry of facts. He's constantly taking his eyeglasses off and putting them back on as he speaks, almost using them as a prop. Slender and fit, he looks as though he's still in good enough shape to run down a burglar, although at the same time his close-cropped silver hair gives him the air of a senior investigator.

I've always appreciated Wallace's no-nonsense "just give me the facts" exterior, which syncs well with my own journalistic bent, but I also admire what's underneath—an exceedingly compassionate and gracious heart toward others.

Oddly, though, I had never talked at length with Wallace about his journey from atheism to faith. After we sat in his recreation room and chatted for a while about family, I asked, "What prompted you to start checking out the Gospels?"

"My wife, Susie, was raised with a cultural Catholicism, so she thought it was important to take the kids to church, and I went along," he explained. "One Sunday, the pastor said, 'Jesus was the smartest guy who ever lived, and our Western culture is grounded in his moral teaching.'"

"How did you react?"

"I thought, *I'm a cop enforcing the penal code, but I know there's a universal moral law above that.* After all, adultery is legal, but it isn't right. So it got me thinking about where that moral code came from. That's why I went out and bought this."

He pulled a red pew Bible from the shelf and handed it to me. "I got this for six bucks," he said.

I flipped it open to a random page and saw that it was very neatly but quite thoroughly marked up. There were homemade tabs, notes in small print in the narrow margins, and color-coded underlining throughout. I went to the gospel of Mark and saw that it was densely annotated.

"I was using forensic statement analysis to analyze the Gospels—for instance, here in the gospel of Mark, I was looking for the influence of Peter, so that's what one of the colors represents," he explained. "I was nitpicking the details. By the time I was done, I had gone through three Bibles."

"How long did your analysis take?"

"Six months."

"What was your verdict?"

"That the Gospels reliably recorded true events," he said. "But that presented a problem for me."

"Why?"

"Because they talk about the resurrection and other miracles," he said. "I could believe the Gospels if they said Jesus ate bread, but what if they said the loaf levitated? C'mon, I couldn't believe that. I didn't believe miracles could happen, so I rejected them out of hand."

Getting Past Stubborn Presuppositions

I could relate to the impediment of the supernatural since it was a stubborn obstruction in my own spiritual investigation. "What changed your mind?" I inquired.

"I asked myself, *Do I believe* anything *supernatural?* And I concluded that, well, yes, even as an atheist, I did believe something extra-natural occurred."

"For instance?"

"The big bang," he replied. "Everything came from nothing. If nature is defined as everything we see in our environment, then there had to be something before that, a first cause that was beyond space, matter, and time. That meant the cause couldn't be spatial, material, or temporal. I realized that if there was something extra-natural that caused the beginning of all space, time, and matter as recorded in Genesis 1:1, then that same cause could accomplish all miracles recorded in the Gospels. In other words, if there is a God, miracles are reasonable, maybe even expected."

"So you got past your presupposition against the miraculous," I said.

"I did. As a detective, I knew presuppositions can derail an investigation. I remember a case in which a woman was found dead in her bed. She was a locally notorious drug addict, and there was drug paraphernalia on her nightstand. The patrol officers got there and didn't even bother to pull down the sheets, since this was so obviously an overdose. But when investigators got there, they pulled down the sheets—and they saw she had been stabbed to death."

He paused as the implications registered with me. "Presuppositions can be impediments to truth," he said. "The resurrection was the most reasonable inference from the evidence, but I was ruling out miracles from the outset."

"What led you to conclude that this first cause of the universe was personal and not just some force?"

"I recognized that there are universal moral laws," he replied. "For example, it's wrong to torture a baby for fun in any culture, anywhere, any time. And transcendent moral laws are more than simply *truths*—they are obligations between *persons*. If there are objective, transcendent moral obligations, the best explanation for them is an objective, transcendent moral person."

"Okay, you concluded that the Gospels contain reliable eyewitness accounts, even of the miraculous," I said. "What came next?"

"I was stuck on the 'why' question: Why did Jesus come, die, and return from the dead? I started analyzing Paul's writings, and I was amazed by his insights into what he called natural man or sinful people. His description fit me in an uncanny way," he replied.

"Plus, the message of grace is so counterintuitive. Every other religion is based on performance, which makes sense because humans love to achieve and compete to get a reward. This message of grace—of unearned forgiveness—didn't sound like it had human origins. It came off as either ridiculous or divine. This doesn't prove anything in and of itself, but it was one more piece of the puzzle."

"In the end, then, it was a cumulative case," I said.

"Bingo," he said crisply. "The totality of the evidence overwhelmed me. When we're trying to solve a homicide, we typically put all the facts on a whiteboard and see if we can make the case. I didn't have to do that here. The case made itself."

The Eyewitness Gospels

As someone who covered criminal justice as a journalist for years, I'm fascinated by how DNA evidence has been used to solve crimes that happened decades earlier. For Wallace, though, DNA hasn't been a factor in any cold case he has solved.

"Typically, we've solved them through the analysis of eyewitness testimony," he said. "And that's the way I tested the Gospels."

"The skeptic Michael Shermer believes the Gospels are just moral stories that don't have a historical core to them," I said.[2] "Why are you convinced they're based on eyewitness accounts?"

"There's good evidence that John and Matthew wrote their gospels based on their eyewitness testimony as disciples of Jesus. While Luke wasn't a witness himself, he said he carefully investigated everything from the beginning,[3] presumably by interviewing eyewitnesses. According to Papias, who was the bishop of Hierapolis, Mark was the scribe of the apostle Peter—and my forensic analysis of Mark's gospel bears that out."

"In what ways?"

"Mark treats Peter with the utmost respect and includes details that can best be attributed to Peter," Wallace replied. "Mark also makes a disproportionate number of references to Peter. And unlike the other gospels, Mark's first and last mention of a disciple is Peter, which is an ancient bookending technique where a piece of history is attributed to a particular eyewitness.

"Of course," he continued, "Peter called himself an eyewitness,[4] and John said he was reporting what we have seen with our eyes.[5] In fact, when they were arrested for testifying about the resurrection, they said, 'We cannot help speaking about what we have seen and heard.'[6] Over and over, the apostles identified themselves as 'witnesses of everything he [Jesus] did in the country of the Jews and in Jerusalem.'"[7]

"Nevertheless," I interjected, "you and I both know that eyewitness testimony has been challenged in recent years. In fact, some defendants convicted by eyewitness testimony have been exonerated through new DNA evidence."

"No question—all eyewitness accounts have to be tested for reliability. In California, judges give jurors more than a dozen factors to weigh in evaluating an eyewitness account," he said. "We can apply these tests to the Gospels—for instance, is there any corroboration, did the witnesses have a motive to lie, did their stories change over time? When we do, we find they hold up well."

"How early do you date the Gospels?"

"Acts doesn't report several major events that occurred in the AD 60s—including the martyrdoms of Paul, Peter, and James— apparently because it was written before they occurred. We know Luke's gospel came before Acts, and we know Mark was written before Luke, because he uses it as one of his sources. Even before that, Paul confirms the resurrection in material that goes back to within a few years of Jesus' execution.[8] When you consider Jesus died in AD 30 or 33, the gap shrinks to where it's not a problem."

"So it doesn't bother you that the Gospels were passed along verbally before being written down?" I asked.

"Not at all. I've seen witnesses in cold cases say their memories from thirty-five years ago are like it happened yesterday. Why? Because not all memories are created the same."

"What do you mean?"

"If you asked me what I did on Valentine's Day five years ago, I probably couldn't recall very much. That's because it's only one of many Valentine's Days I've celebrated with Susie. But if you asked me about Valentine's Day of 1988, I can give you a detailed report of what took place."

I narrowed my eyes. "Why's that?"

Wallace smiled. "Because that's the day Susie and I got married," he replied. "When witnesses experience something that's unique, unrepeated, and personally important or powerful, they're much more likely to remember it. Of course, many of the disciples' experiences with Jesus met those criteria.

"Can they remember all the times their boat got stuck in a storm?" he asked. "Probably not, but they could remember the time Jesus quieted the squall. And think of the resurrection—as much as anything they experienced, that was unique, unrepeated, and extremely powerful."

Dealing with Gospel Discrepancies

"But what about the conflicts between the various gospel accounts—don't they cast doubt on the reliability of the eyewitness testimony?" I asked.

"Based on my years as a detective, I would expect the four gospels to have variances," he replied. "Think of this—the early believers could have destroyed all but one of the Gospels in order to eliminate any differences between them. But they didn't. Why? Because they knew the Gospels were true and that they told the story from different perspectives, emphasizing different things."

"The conflicts aren't evidence they were lying?"

"People might assume that if they've never worked with eyewitnesses before. In my experience, eyewitness accounts can be reliable despite discrepancies. Besides, if they meshed too perfectly, it would be evidence of collusion."

That echoed the assessment of Simon Greenleaf of Harvard Law School, one of America's most important legal figures, after he studied the gospels. "There is enough of a discrepancy to show that there could have been no previous concert among them," he said, "and at the same time such substantial agreement as to show that they all were independent narrators of the same great transaction."[9]

Interestingly, while writing this chapter I was reading a breakthrough book by New Testament scholar Michael Licona called *Why Are There Differences in the Gospels?*[10] Licona, who earned his doctorate at the University of Pretoria, is a noted resurrection scholar and professor at Houston Christian University.

His research shows that many apparent discrepancies between the Gospels can be explained by the standard compositional techniques that Greco-Roman biographers typically used in that era. The Gospels fall into the genre of ancient biography.

For example, one common technique, modeled by the historian Plutarch, is called "literary spotlighting," which Licona likened to a theatrical performance where there are multiple actors on stage but the lights go out and a spotlight shines on only one of them.

"You know other actors are on the stage," he said, "but you can't see them because the spotlight is focused on one person."

Applying this to the Gospels, he noted that Matthew, Mark, and Luke say multiple women visited Jesus' tomb and discovered it empty. However, John's gospel only mentions Mary Magdalene. Is that a discrepancy that casts doubt on the Gospels?

"It seems likely that John is aware of the presence of other women while shining his spotlight on Mary," he said. "After all, he reports Mary announcing to Peter and the beloved disciple, 'They have taken the Lord out of the tomb, and we don't know where they have put him.'[11] Who's the 'we' to whom Mary refers? Probably the other women who were present.

"Then observe what happens next," Licona continued. "In John, Peter and the beloved disciple run to the tomb and discover it empty, whereas Luke 24:12 mentions Peter running to the tomb and no mention is made of the beloved disciple. However, just twelve verses later, Luke reports there were more than one who had made the trip to the tomb.[12] These observations strongly suggest Luke and John were employing literary spotlighting in their resurrection narratives."

Based on exhaustive analysis of the Gospels, Licona reaches this conclusion: "If what I'm suggesting is correct—that an overwhelming number of Gospel differences are . . . most plausibly accounted for by reading the Gospels in view of their biographical genre—*the tensions resulting from nearly all of the differences disappear* and arguing that the Gospels are historically unreliable in view of their differences is no longer sustainable."[13]

Gospel Mysteries Solved

Wallace then made the counterintuitive statement that some of the differences between the Gospels actually show their cohesion in a way that would be expected if they were based on independent eyewitness accounts.

"I noticed that sometimes one of the Gospels would describe an event but leave out a detail that raised a question in my mind—and then this question gets unintentionally answered by another gospel writer," he explained.

"You're referring to what have been described as *undesigned coincidences*," I said.

"Right," he replied. "There are more than forty places in the New Testament where we see this kind of unintentional eyewitness support."[14]

"What are some examples?"

"In Matthew's gospel, Jesus encounters Peter, Andrew, James, and John for the first time. They are fishermen mending nets. He says, 'Follow me,' and, sure enough, they spontaneously do.[15] Now, doesn't that seem odd—that they would drop everything and immediately follow this person they've never met?"

"That does create a mystery," I conceded.

"Fortunately, we have Luke's gospel. He says Jesus got into Peter's boat and preached from it. Then he told Peter to put out his nets, and Peter reluctantly did so even though they had worked all night and caught nothing. Miraculously, the nets emerged teeming with so many fish that they began to break. In fact, the catch filled two boats. Luke says Peter and the others were astonished and Peter recognized Jesus as Lord."[16]

"All of a sudden," I said, "Matthew's account makes more sense."

"Exactly. When the testimony is put together, we get a complete picture. The disciples heard Jesus preach and saw the miracle of the abundant fish. After they returned to shore, Jesus said to follow him—and they did, based on his revolutionary teachings and his display of supernatural power."

"Have you seen unintentional coincidences in your police work?"

"I've had instances where a witness's account leaves questions unanswered until we find an additional witness later," he said. "This is a common characteristic of true eyewitness accounts."

"What are some other examples?"

"Matthew says that during Jesus' trial, the chief priests and members of the council struck him and said, 'Prophesy to us, Messiah. Who hit you?'[17] Now, that's a strange request. Couldn't Jesus just look at his attackers and identify them? But when Luke describes the same scene, he mentions one other detail—Jesus was blindfolded."

"There," Wallace said, snapping his fingers. "Mystery solved."

"What's your conclusion?" I asked.

"The most reasonable explanation is that the Gospels were penned by different eyewitnesses who were just reporting what they saw and unintentionally including these unplanned supporting details," he said.

"So this was one more piece to the puzzle for you," I said.

"One of many. We have archaeology corroborating certain points of the Gospels. We have non-Christian accounts outside the Bible that provide confirmation of key gospel claims. We have students of the apostles who give a consistent account of what the disciples were teaching. And we have a proliferation of ancient manuscripts that help us get back to what the original Gospels said."

"Okay then, Mr. Detective. What's your verdict?"

"That the Gospels can be messy, that they're filled with idiosyncrasies, that they're each told from a different perspective and have variances between them—just like you'd expect from a collection of eyewitness accounts," he said. "I became convinced that they constitute reliable testimony to the life, teachings, death, and—yes—the resurrection of Jesus."

Did Jesus Really Die on the Cross?

Ah, the resurrection.

Even skeptics agree with the apostle Paul's assertion that if the resurrection were disproved, then the entire Christian faith would collapse into irrelevancy.[18] Consequently, opponents are constantly minting fresh objections to undermine this central tenet of Christianity. In recent years, for example, agnostic New Testament scholar Bart Ehrman and others have advanced new efforts to cast doubt on whether Jesus died and escaped his grave alive.

I said to Wallace: "Even if we concede the gospel accounts are rooted in eyewitness testimony, we're still faced with the issue of whether a miracle the magnitude of the resurrection makes sense. Let me challenge you with some of the most potent objections to Jesus rising from the dead."

"Shoot," he said, quickly catching himself with a chuckle. "Maybe that's not the best terminology for a cop. Anyway, yes, go ahead."

"It seems to me the two relevant issues are, first, whether Jesus was actually dead from crucifixion, and, second, whether he was encountered alive afterward, necessitating an empty tomb," I said.

Wallace folded his arms. "Agreed," he replied.

"So how do we know he was really dead? Is it reasonable that he would succumb that soon? The thieves on either side of him were still alive."

"But the path to the cross for Jesus was dramatically different than the path for the thieves," he said.

"How so?"

"Pilate didn't want to crucify Jesus, as the crowd was demanding, so he kind of makes an offer. He says, in effect, 'I'll tell you what I'll do—I'll beat him to within an inch of his life. Will that satisfy you?' Consequently, Jesus was given an especially horrific flogging. That didn't satisfy the crowds, and he was crucified. But he was already in such extremely bad shape that he couldn't even carry his cross."

"But these soldiers weren't medical doctors," I said. "Maybe they thought Jesus had died when he hadn't."

"That objection usually comes from people who've never been around dead bodies. As a cop, I've witnessed a lot of autopsies. Let me tell you, dead people aren't like corpses in movies. They look different. They feel different. They get cold, they get rigid, their blood pools. These soldiers knew what death looked like; in fact, they were motivated to make sure he was deceased because they would be executed if a prisoner escaped alive. Plus, the apostle John unwittingly gave us a major clue."

"What's that?"

"He says that when Jesus was stabbed with a spear to make sure he was dead, water and blood came out. In those days, nobody understood that. Some early church leaders thought this was a metaphor for baptism or something. Today, we know this is consistent with what we would expect, because the torture would have caused fluid to collect around his heart and lungs. So without even realizing it, John was giving us a corroborating detail."

I reached into my briefcase and removed a copy of the Qur'an, which I placed on the table between us. "Yet," I said, "there are more than a billion Muslims who don't believe Jesus was crucified.[19] Many of them believe God substituted Judas for Jesus on the cross."

Wallace picked up the Qur'an and paged through it. "Here's the problem," he said, handing it back to me. "This was written six hundred years after Jesus lived. Compare that to the first-century sources that are uniform in reporting Jesus was dead. Not only do we have the gospel accounts, but we also have five ancient sources *outside* the Bible."[20]

"Still, how can you disprove the claim that God supernaturally switched people on the cross?" I asked.

"That would mean Jesus was being deceptive when he appeared to people afterward. No, that would contradict what we know about his character. And how would you explain him showing the nail holes in his hands and the wound in his side to Thomas?"

"You have no doubt, then, that he was dead."

"No, I don't. When scholars Gary Habermas and Michael Licona surveyed all the scholarly literature on the resurrection going back thirty years, Jesus' death was among the facts that were virtually unanimously accepted," he said.[21]

"Besides," he added, "crucifixion was humiliating—it's not something the early church would have invented. And we have no record of anyone ever surviving a full Roman crucifixion."

Tombs, Ossuaries, and Conspiracies

Even the skeptical Bart Ehrman concedes Jesus was killed by crucifixion, but he recently wrote a book saying it's "unlikely" that Jesus was buried in a tomb, saying that "what *normally* happened to a criminal's body is that it was left to decompose and serve as food for scavenging animals."[22]

"Of course, if Jesus was never buried, then that would neatly explain why the tomb was unoccupied," I said.

Wallace smiled and cited the eminent New Testament scholar Craig Evans, who wrote that Ehrman's description of Roman policy on crucifixion and nonburial is "unnuanced and incomplete."[23]

"It is simply erroneous to assert that the Romans did not permit the burial of the executed, including the crucified," Evans wrote.[24] "The gospel narratives are completely in step with Jewish practice, which Roman authorities during peacetime respected."[25]

Declared Evans, "I conclude that the burial of the body of Jesus in a known tomb, according to Jewish law and custom, is highly probable."[26]

"I'll add one thing," Wallace said to me. "An ossuary with the remains of a crucifixion victim was discovered in 1968, with part of an iron spike still in his heel bone. This is evidence that at least some crucifixion victims were buried, as the earliest account of Jesus' death tells us he was."[27]

Ironically, one of Ehrman's own colleagues at the University of North Carolina at Chapel Hill, a Jewish archaeologist named Jodi Magness, confirmed, "The Gospel accounts describing Jesus' removal from the cross and burial are consistent with archaeological evidence and with Jewish law."[28]

Whatever occurred two thousand years ago, there's little dispute that the disciples *believed* the once-dead Jesus appeared to them alive. Not only do the four gospels report this, but there's confirmation from students of the apostles (Clement and Polycarp), as well as an early creed of the church found in 1 Corinthians 15:3–8 and a speech by Peter in Acts 2.

"You've broken a lot of conspiracy cases as a cop," I said. "Do you see any way these people could have been lying about this?"

"For a conspiracy to succeed, you need a small number of conspirators, good communication between them, a short time span, significant relational connections between the conspirators to bind them together, and little or no pressure. That's not the situation with the resurrection witnesses.

"On top of that," he added, "they had no motive to be deceitful. In fact, we have at least seven ancient sources that tell us the disciples were willing to suffer and even die for their conviction that they encountered the risen Jesus."[29]

"But," I interjected, "new research has shown that history is murky on what actually happened to some of them."[30]

"True, but what's important is their *willingness* to die. That's well established. They knew the truth about what occurred, and my experience is that people aren't willing to suffer or die for what they know is a lie.

"Even more importantly, there isn't a single ancient document or claim in which any of the eyewitnesses ever recanted their statement. Think about that for a minute. We have ancient accounts in which second-, third-, and fourth-generation Christians were forced to recant, but *no* record of an eyewitness ever disavowing their testimony. I think that helps establish the truthfulness of the eyewitnesses."

From One Miracle to Another

I tried another approach. "I'm sure you've seen cases where people close to a murder victim are so full of grief that it colors their recollections about what happened," I said.

"To some degree," he replied. "But I sense where you're going with this: Did the sorrow of the disciples cause them to have a vision of the risen Jesus? That's a different matter altogether."

"Why?"

"First, groups don't have hallucinations, and the earliest report of the resurrection said five hundred people saw him. Second, Jesus was encountered on numerous occasions and by a number of different groups. The vision theory doesn't seem likely in those varying circumstances. And I can think of at least one person who *wasn't* inclined toward a vision."

"Paul?"

"Yeah, he was as skeptical as—well, Michael Shermer," he said, referring to the editor of *Skeptic* magazine.

"What if one of the disciples—maybe Peter—experienced a vision due to his sorrow and then convinced the others that Jesus had returned? As you know, Peter had a strong personality and could be persuasive."

"I've had murder cases where one emphatic witness persuaded others that something happened," Wallace conceded. "Inevitably, the persuader has all the details in their most robust form, while the others tend to generalize because they didn't actually see the event for themselves. But this theory can't account for the numerous, divergent, and separate group sightings of Jesus, which are described with a lot of specificity. Also, Peter wasn't the first to see the risen Jesus."

"Good point," I said.

"I'll add one last point," said Wallace. "With all these theories of visions or hallucinations, the body is still in the tomb."

I asked Wallace, "What happened when you finally concluded that none of the escape hatches would let you avoid the conclusion that the resurrection really happened?"

"I remember being in church one Sunday," he said. "I leaned over and whispered to Susie that I was a believer."

"As easy as that?"

He chuckled. "Not that easy," he said. "Yes, the evidence broke through my philosophical naturalism, and the Gospels passed all the tests we use to evaluate eyewitness accounts. So I came to believe *that* Jesus is who he claimed to be. But then there was another step—believing *in* Jesus as my forgiver and leader."

"How did that happen?"

"The more I understood the true nature of Jesus, the more *my* true nature was exposed—and I didn't like what I saw. Being a cop had led me to lose faith in people. My heart had shriveled. To me, everyone was a liar capable of depraved behavior. I saw myself as superior to everyone else. I was cynical, cocky, and distant."

Honestly, I was surprised by his description of himself. I have only known Wallace as a warm, sincere, and generous person—but then, I have only known him since he has been a follower of Jesus.

"I know it sounds like a cliché," Wallace continued, "but coming to faith in Christ changed me drastically over time. As someone forgiven much, I learned to forgive others. After receiving God's grace, I was better able to show compassion. Now my life is consumed by letting others know that faith in Christ isn't just a subjective emotion, but it's grounded in the truth of the resurrection."

I thought of the words of the apostle Paul, himself a hardened law enforcer who was transformed after encountering the risen Jesus: "Therefore, if anyone is in Christ, the new creation has come: the old has gone, the new is here!"[31]

One supernatural event—the resurrection of Jesus—leads to another event that's just as extraordinary, just as jaw-dropping, just as worship-inducing: a profound spiritual rebirth into a new life that's simply inexplicable in mere human terms.

That's the supernatural power of God to revolutionize the lives and eternities of sinners like J. Warner Wallace, Lee Strobel, and countless others who exchanged their rebellion for God's amazing grace.

CHAPTER 12

GHOST STORIES, PSYCHICS, AND THE
PARANORMAL

Kathy moved to a Spanish-style house in the high desert town of Adelanto, California, in 2006. Before long, mysterious things began happening. A putrid smell would come and go. The dog would stare at the rooftop and bark. There was the sound of shuffling feet on the bedroom carpet. Doorknobs jiggled. Kathy's young daughter, jumping rope outside, let out a bloodcurdling scream when she saw a hairy, hunched-over creature with glowing eyes on the roof. It didn't take long for the family to leave the area.

A middle school student was on the second floor of his family's Canadian house at about 10:00 p.m. when he felt a sensation of someone watching him through one of the small windows beside the couch. Looking out, he saw the apparition of a man's face. He had a wide, toothy grin, bloodshot eyes, and his neck looked injured. The young man then glimpsed him through a second window as the ghostly figure drifted off and disappeared.

Troubled by the sensation that someone was watching him as he slept, another young man used a "spirit box"—an electronic device designed to communicate with the dead—to seek out Timothy, an invisible friend he'd had since he was four. Sure enough, he said he was able to chat in short snippets with the ghost, eventually piecing together the tragic story that Timothy and his family had drowned in a car accident when their vehicle plunged into a river.

These are among thousands of experiences submitted to a website that solicits accounts of personal ghost stories and other paranormal encounters from around the world.[1] Each person claims their report is true. There's no confirmation of that, though the sincerity of many stories seems hard to deny.

So far in our journey together, we have examined evidence that there really is an unseen world, a supernatural dominion created by God. We have encountered credible accounts of miracles and other phenomena that point toward the existence of a realm beyond our five senses. Importantly, it's a world that's consistent with what is taught in the Bible, which itself has been shown to be trustworthy.[2]

Then there is the *paranormal*—literally, "beyond the normal." These are claims about ghosts and goblins that haunt houses; psychics, clairvoyants, and mediums who communicate with the dead; and occultists who practice dark magic, consult crystal balls, and host séances.

Much of this is related to an unbiblical belief system called *spiritism*, also known as spiritualism, which centers on the attempt to communicate with deceased human beings or extra-human intelligences through a human medium, psychic, or channeler—practices that the Bible warns against.

Many people scoff at paranormal claims, and yet there's often something in us that wonders whether any of it could be true. I remember seeing a Ziggy cartoon in which he was seated in a commercial airliner, with all of the other seats empty. "You've got the whole plane to yourself," the cheery flight attendant told him. "The large group going to the psychic convention all canceled at the last moment." Ziggy looked puzzled—and highly concerned.

Some paranormal reports are particularly eerie. Like the incident described by former president Jimmy Carter in which an American twin-engine plane crashed in Africa and couldn't be located. Satellites were reoriented to shoot photos of the area without success.

"So the director of the CIA (Stansfield Turner) came and told me that he had contacted a woman in California that claimed to have supernatural capabilities," Carter said. "She went into a trance, and she wrote down latitudes and longitudes, and we sent our satellites over that latitude and longitude and there was the plane."[3]

Was that a lucky guess? A parlor trick of some sort, akin to an illusion that a magician would pull off? Or did this psychic really tap into some otherworldly source of information—perhaps even a demonic spirit seeking to bolster its credibility?

Fueled by popular culture, belief in the paranormal flourishes in the United States. According to Gallup, three in four Americans profess at least one paranormal belief, including one-third who believe in ghosts.[4] In fact, Pew Research found that 18 percent of Americans say they have either seen or been in the presence of a ghost.[5] What's more, 41 percent believe in psychics.[6]

While there's no shortage of stories on such topics, I decided to focus on popular paranormal claims about the dead—for example, that ghosts routinely return from the grave on their own and that psychics can communicate with the deceased. What principles can be learned that can be applied to evaluating other paranormal phenomena? For answers, I reached out to one of the most popular apologists in America—someone whose many books include the intriguingly titled *The Truth Behind Ghosts, Mediums and Psychic Phenomena.*

RON RHODES, THD

Through the years, I have interviewed scores of theologians, historians, scientists, and others, but I have seldom come across a more fascinating spiritual journey than the one described by author and speaker Ron Rhodes. His road to faith was paved with nothing less than good old-fashioned rock 'n' roll.

When Rhodes was growing up in Texas, his family attended a liberal church, where he went through religious rituals but never heard about how to have a personal relationship with Jesus. "I thought I was a Christian," he said, "but in reality, I wasn't."

Then in his teens, he and his seven siblings started The Rhodes Kids, a soft rock band in which he strummed guitar and sang. Through the unlikely intervention of singer Wayne Newton, whose manager was a friend of their manager, they ended up performing in front of more than thirty million television viewers on the national Jerry Lewis Telethon.

This propelled them to a highly successful musical career, appearing on everything from *The Tonight Show* with Jack Paar to *American Bandstand* with Dick Clark, and working with such celebrities as Ann-Margret, guitarist B. B. King, Barbara Eden, Peter Falk, and many others.

Before their appearance on *The Merv Griffin Show*, they were sharing a green room with Christian singer Pat Boone, his wife Shirley, and their daughters. Backstage, Shirley was describing her personal relationship with Jesus when tears of joy flooded her eyes.

"I had never seen anything like it," Ron would say later. "I was used to a liberal church, but here was a person—and a family—who had such a close relationship with the Lord that tears were flowing. Wow! This was completely foreign to my experience."

This prompted him to delve deeply into the Bible. What did he find? "It's plain as day that I am a sinner and that salvation comes only through faith in Jesus Christ, who died on the cross for me," he said. "Why didn't my church teach this? Anyway, I became a Christian—a true believer—and my life was changed forever."

He went on to study at Dallas Theological Seminary, where he earned both a Master of Theology and a Doctor of Theology degree. After getting into discussions with some relatives who were Jehovah's Witnesses, he got interested in apologetics, especially dealing with cults. The legendary counter-cult apologist Walter Martin later invited him to work at the Christian Research Institute, which produced the national *Bible Answer Man* radio show and published the *Christian Research Journal*.

Since then, he has taught as an adjunct at five seminaries and universities and has written nearly one hundred books, with millions of copies in multiple languages around the world. Included are *Reasoning from the Scriptures with Jehovah's Witnesses* and *The End Times in Chronological Order*, as well as his latest book, *The Complete Reference Guide to Bible Prophecy*.

Now in his early seventies, with gray hair and an impressive white mustache, Rhodes and his wife, Kerri, live alongside a lake in East Texas. He has an engaging personality and an encyclopedic memory, and he tends to lay out answers in a thorough and logical way. Recent throat surgery made speaking a challenge for him, so our interview over Zoom was augmented with written answers that he provided to my questions about ghosts, psychics, and the paranormal in general.

Spirits That Shun the Tunnel

"You have said that interest in ghosts and contacting the dead was once relegated mainly to fringe cultic groups but that belief in paranormal phenomena has infiltrated popular culture and crossed religious spectrums," I began. "Why is that? What factors are driving the popularity of the paranormal in our society?"

"At its core, many people turn to the paranormal due to burn-out with traditional religion," came his response. "They feel that church has become lifeless and barren, failing to meet their needs and losing its relevance. Today's popular psychics address this in their books. They highlight a common theme—people are increasingly disillusioned with organized religion and are in search of something authentic. They crave a spirituality that feels genuine and effective."

"Did a lot of these psychics abandon church themselves?"

Rhodes nodded. "Many of them share stories of past involvement with organized religion. Their experience was profoundly off-putting. They were repelled by the guilt, judgmentalism, and the concept of a loving God who could condemn souls to hell. Consequently, they abandoned the church and welcomed spiritism with open arms."

I noted that the tenets of spiritism are contrary to Christianity. "What is it about spiritism that attracts people?" I asked.

"Regardless of your philosophy or religious beliefs, or even if you reject Christianity entirely, spiritism promises that everyone crosses over to the other side, which they see as a joyful existence in the afterlife. Even more enticing, it offers the possibility of communicating with those who have already crossed over. If there ever were a feel-good religion, this is it!"

Seeking to get past misconceptions, I asked Rhodes for clarity on a basic question: "Exactly what is a ghost?"

He kicked into his professorial gear. "Every person possesses a spirit or soul, often described by occultists as an *astral body*," he replied. "At death, this spirit departs from the physical form. Psychics claim that after death most people choose to enter a tunnel that leads them to a spiritual realm they refer to as 'the other side.' But some spirits supposedly choose to stay on earth instead, and these entities are known as ghosts. To clarify, if a person traverses through the tunnel, they are *not* considered to be a ghost."

"What supposedly happens to these ghosts that linger on earth?"

"Occultists say they may suffer the bewildering delusion of still being alive. They grow increasingly perplexed as the world seemingly ignores their existence. Every time they talk to someone, they are overlooked. Psychics say these ghosts are the easiest spirits to contact, since they haven't crossed over to the other side yet. Once a spirit moves on, communication becomes more challenging, akin to trying to tune in to a more distant radio station."

"What about the spirits that do go through the tunnel?" I asked. "What happens to them?"

"Psychics say they can continue to evolve," Rhodes said. "When spirits first enter the astral plane, they start at the initial level. But the astral plane has multiple levels, and, over time, spirits can evolve and ascend to higher levels. With each level they attain, it becomes increasingly challenging for a psychic to make contact with them. Practically speaking, psychics claim it's easiest to communicate with the spirits of people who have recently died."

"Why would some spirits refuse to go through the tunnel?"

"They may prefer to stay close to a beloved family member or a familiar place, such as their home. Psychics often highlight that the love connection never dies. In other words, they say a ghost will continue to love their spouse who's still alive.

"In other cases," he continued, "the spirit may stay behind to comfort their grieving loved ones. They may try to convey messages like, 'I'm in a good place,' or 'Feel free to move on with your life.' Some spirits allegedly stay behind because they want to protect loved ones from danger, because they're greedy and can't let go of their earthly possessions, because they have unfinished business, or because they have lived a vile life and fear that if they go through the tunnel, it will lead to hell."

He took a moment as I processed his answer. He might have seen the skepticism on my face. Then Rhodes added, "You and I might wonder how people can believe ideas like these. Remember the biblical teaching that Satan can blind the minds of human beings.[1] He is a master of deception."

Without question, these beliefs are contrary to Scripture. I was anxious to explore a biblical perspective of these things, but first I needed to hear a bit more about the precepts of spiritism.

The Experience of Ghosts

I asked Rhodes how psychics claim that ghosts typically manifest themselves.

"They'll point to things like unusual sounds you might hear in your home—the echo of footsteps, mysterious knocks on the wall, or the chime of a bell," he said. "More chillingly, they'll claim you could hear laughter, screams, or a whisper just behind you. Objects may inexplicably move around. For example, the hairbrush you typically leave by the bathroom sink may suddenly appear on the kitchen counter. There might be a drop in temperature or a peculiar smell. Lights may flicker on and off. Electrical appliances could spring to life. Many describe the eerie sensation of being watched. Some psychics say you can detect a ghost by seeing a shadow or a sudden fleck of light shooting across the room. Some people claim to have witnessed a foglike apparition of a deceased person."

I consulted my notes. "What are electronic voice phenomena?"

"This is when a voice can supposedly be discerned amidst the white noise of a radio that's not tuned to any particular station. Also, faces have been detected in the white noise on untuned TV screens. Thermal imaging cameras can reveal cold spots in a room, which are interpreted as ghostly presences. Typically, ghostly phenomena are said to occur so quickly that witnesses are left uncertain as to whether they truly saw or heard anything."

"You said in your book that ghostly phenomena are experience-based," I said. "What do you mean by that?"

"All reports we have about ghosts are based on subjective

personal experiences, such as, 'I heard a knocking sound in the wall,' 'My dog barked at something in the room,' or 'I thought I saw a shadow or a beam of light shooting across the room.' These are in contrast to objective observations, like, 'I saw him walk out of the store and get into a BMW' or 'He knocked on the door and I invited him in. He brought me roses.'

"These subjective experiences are shaped by personal perspectives and emotions, while the objective observations are based on concrete facts and external reality. The distinction is significant. People attribute their subjective experiences to a supernatural cause—the presence of ghosts—without solid evidence. A light bulb flickering or a fleeting shadow doesn't definitively prove the presence of a ghost, since there are plausible alternative explanations."

"Such as?"

"Someone claims they saw a ghost because a beam of light darted across a room. But perhaps a car passed by and sunlight reflected off it, briefly shining into the room and hitting a mirror, creating the appearance of light shooting across the place. There are always more plausible explanations for such subjective experiences."

"What about the suspicious sounds some people hear in their house and attribute to ghosts?" I asked.

"More often than not, there are far more likely explanations," he said. "In my current house, for instance, there's a consistent knocking sound in the master bedroom closet. But this is *not* a ghost! A bit of investigation uncovered that this only occurs when the air conditioner is running, apparently due to air pressure in the ducts."

The Science of Ghosts

Rhodes's comments brought to mind an article by science writer Kathryn Hulick, who said a psychological phenomenon called absorption explains why some people believe, for instance, that a window somehow opened by itself. Absorption is when a person becomes so focused on a task that they tune out everything else and remember only what they're paying attention to.

For example, a person might see an open window but not recall opening it. "What if someone had opened it and you just didn't notice because you were so absorbed by something else?" Hulick asked. "That's a lot more likely than a ghost."

In her article "The Science of Ghosts," she cites a prominent psychologist as saying some people are more likely to become absorbed than others—and these people also report higher levels of paranormal beliefs, including a belief in ghosts.[2]

I said to Rhodes, "Some ghost-hunting TV shows use scientific equipment in an attempt to measure spirit activity."

"Yes, this can plant the idea that there might be scientific evidence supporting the presence of ghosts," said Rhodes. "But this is where someone's worldview plays a crucial role. When ghost enthusiasts observe the world, they see everything in terms of 'ghosts among us' or 'spirits among us.' A cold room, knocking noises, a beam of light darting around—these and other subjective phenomena are viewed through the filter of their ghost-affirming worldview.

"When ghost hunters use audio recorders and cameras to seek evidence of ghosts, they interpret the sounds and images through their ghost-affirming worldview. For example, if a brief human voice is detected within the white noise of an untuned radio, the immediate assumption is that the voice originates from the spirit world around us."

"But there are more plausible explanations," I said.

"Right," he replied. "For example, it might be a case of auditory *pareidolia*, the phenomenon where people perceive faint conversations or whispers while listening to white noise. Our brains attempt to interpret random sounds by attributing familiar patterns to them. That's a common occurrence."

"What about cameras?"

"Some investigators claim to capture ghost orbs on cameras,

supposedly representing the souls of the deceased. Also, some investigators share photos featuring what appears to be a person, although with a semitransparent, ethereal appearance. I've checked these things out."

"How?"

"I took a collection of these so-called ghost photos to a professional photographer, who examined them, grinned, and then said creating photos like these would be a piece of cake. So a skilled photographer can produce convincing ghost images without there being any actual ghosts involved."

Then he added, "In fact, there are 231 million iPhones worldwide, each with a built-in high-resolution camera. Why aren't we flooded with high-resolution images of ghosts and other paranormal phenomena if they are indeed so ubiquitous?"

A Charade by Demonic Spirits

I have noticed that many claims of ghost sightings occur as people are waking up in bed. "Why is that significant?" I asked Rhodes.

"When you awaken, your mind isn't at its sharpest. Your cognitive and perceptual abilities can be sluggish. In this half-awake state, you might perceive things that aren't real, like hearing a voice or seeing an apparition. Experts call this cognitive distortion."

"What other factors can account for ghost sightings?"

"Fraud tops my list," he said. "This is exemplified by the modern spiritualist movement, which began in 1848 at the home of a New York farmer named John Fox. Fox had three daughters who claimed to hear tapping sounds in their house, which they believed were communications from the spirit of a murdered man. The Fox sisters quickly rose to prominence within the spiritualist movement."

"Then what happened?"

"In 1886, one of the sisters admitted she had produced the tapping sounds by cracking her toe joints. She later tried to retract her confession, but the momentum of spiritualism had already become unstoppable. To this day, psychics frequently engage in various fraudulent activities. A close second to outright fabrication is the misinterpretation of data. As I mentioned earlier, experiences are often misconstrued as being the work of ghosts, even though there are more logical explanations."

"According to the Bible, what really happens when we die—and how does this impact the idea of ghosts?" I asked.

Rhodes's answer began with this declaration: "The biblical viewpoint on the afterlife thoroughly dismantles the idea that ghosts wander among us."

"How so?"

"The Bible states that the dead do not return to earth as spirits. Instead, upon death, a believer's spirit leaves the physical body and immediately enters the presence of the Lord in heaven. This is why the apostle Paul longed to 'depart and be with Christ.'³ In 2 Corinthians 5:8, we are taught that Christians are away from the body in death and are at home with the Lord in heaven. The text emphasizes an instantaneous transition from earthly life to heavenly life."

"What about unbelievers?"

"At death, the spirit of an unbeliever is involuntarily confined to a place of suffering, as described in Luke 16:19–31, which is where Jesus tells about a rich man and Lazarus, who had both died, with the rich man in a place of suffering and Lazarus in a place of bliss."

I asked, "What lessons can we glean from that story?"

"First, both the rich man and Lazarus were fully aware of their deaths and entry into the afterlife. Second, at death their eternal destinies were sealed. Third, after death they could not remain on earth as ghosts. Fourth, the dead and the living on earth could not contact each other. Visiting earth, even to warn loved ones, was not an option. And fifth, the righteous dead and the wicked dead were separated from each other, with the wicked in torment. This disproves the claim by psychics that the 'other side' is equally wonderful for everyone."

He went on. "Second Peter 2:9 reveals that the Lord knows how to hold the unrighteous for the day of judgment while continuing their punishment. This underscores that the unrighteous are no longer on earth and have no access to it. Instead, they are confined in a spiritual prison, awaiting the future judgment, which will culminate in their ultimate fate in the lake of fire."

"Based on that," I said, "continuing to hang around earth as a ghost simply isn't an option."

"That's right. In my view, paranormal experiences are certainly not encounters with the spirits of deceased people."

"So in reality, psychics are communicating with—what?"

"Demonic spirits who are pretending to be deceased humans," he said without hesitation. "The Bible says Satan disguises himself as an angel of light,[4] and if he can do that he can certainly mimic a deceased person."

"What's his endgame?"

"Deceiving millions of people," Rhodes said, "and diverting them away from Jesus Christ and the gospel that saves."

However, I brought up two cases in the Bible where God did allow the deceased to at least appear on earth—the Old Testament incident with the medium of Endor, where God miraculously permitted Samuel's spirit to appear,[5] and the New Testament event of the transfiguration, where long-deceased Elijah and Moses appeared.[6]

"Doesn't this indicate that it's not beyond God's power to allow the spirits of some deceased individuals to appear to the living on earth?" I asked.

"It's most certainly not beyond God's ability to allow deceased persons to appear," he said. Frankly, I thought that was a significant point.

"But note," Rhodes continued, "that these appearances were

not the result of a psychic's powers.[7] This was God's sovereign and miraculous intervention. I believe that both of these passages are *descriptive* and not *prescriptive*. By that, I mean they describe events that took place historically but do not necessarily prescribe things that we would expect to occur typically."

I thought back to stories I've heard from seemingly credible sources about people sensing the presence of a departed friend or family member—including some that I've described in this book. It seems that if he wanted to, God could allow some of these experiences in modern times, just as he did in the biblical examples that I cited.

But it's hard to know in each circumstance what might be a divine intervention versus some other explanation—or even spiritually deceptive spirits like those that Rhodes described. It was a reminder of the need to pray for spiritual discernment and to test all experiences and claims against biblical standards. We'll discuss more about how we can do that below.

Cold, Warm, and Hot Readings

Being a psychic can be lucrative. For instance, a successful medium in California makes an average of $104,000 a year.[8] Maybe this explains why there are four full-time psychics within a short drive of my house, not to mention numerous mediums available online.

"Let's talk about psychics," I said to Rhodes. "Are all of them involved in fakery?"

"I avoid an either-or mentality," he said. "It's unfair to categorize all of them the same way. While many may indeed engage in fraudulent activities, some could legitimately be in contact with spirit entities. I believe this to have been the case with a famous psychic I personally observed for two hours in Southern California. Again, these entities would be demonic spirits masquerading as human ones."

"Critics often accuse psychics of using a technique called *cold readings*. Tell me about that."

"These are cases where the psychic has no preexisting knowledge about the client. During the session, the psychic employs leading questions designed to elicit a response. They might say, 'I sense you are experiencing a change in your life right now. Is that correct?' Given that most people are undergoing some form of change, this question is almost guaranteed to resonate with the client.

"As the client responds, the psychic keenly observes visual clues such as clothing, body language, posture, and facial expressions. These subtle hints often guide them on what to ask next, creating the illusion of deeper insight. Psychics generally experience a lot more failures than successes during cold readings, but even an occasional correct answer can be enough to keep the client hooked."

I pointed out that *Skeptic* magazine editor Michael Shermer said that *intermittent reinforcement* explains why gamblers keep playing slot machines. If they score a hit every once in a while, it keeps them engaged. He said psychics are similar—it only takes an occasional correct statement to convince clients that they are truly psychic.[9]

"I agree," said Rhodes. "In the world of psychics, hope springs eternal. Emotions play a big role. People hope so much to contact their loved ones that they are willing to overlook the many mistakes made by psychics. I believe we're also witnessing what is known in cult studies as compartmentalization."

"What's that?"

"It's a psychological process in which individuals or groups, such as cults, selectively ignore facts that blatantly contradict their beliefs."

"Can you give me an example?"

"Jehovah's Witnesses maintain their trust in the Watchtower Society as the ultimate source of prophetic truth, even though that organization has made numerous false prophecies over the decades. The evidence against the Watchtower's credibility is substantial, yet adherents choose to believe them while continuing to ignore their mistakes."

Next I asked Rhodes about psychics using *warm readings*—where they take advantage of psychological principles that apply to most people and use those insights to make people think they have received a message from beyond. For example, when people grieve the death of a loved one, they will often keep a piece of their jewelry as a remembrance of them. Psychics use that insight in their readings.

"Does this happen often?" I asked Rhodes.

"All the time," he replied. "A typical psychic might say, 'I sense that your grandmother has crossed over to the other side and you have a piece of her jewelry. I feel that this jewelry is a closed circle.' Many people, indeed, have lost a grandmother and possess a piece of her jewelry—and often the jewelry forms a 'closed circle,' as in a ring, necklace, or bracelet.

"Also," Rhodes added, "psychics frequently fish for information about how a person died, relying heavily on the law of averages. For instance, when speaking to someone about their deceased father, a psychic might say, 'I'm sensing pain in the chest area.' If the client nods, the psychic might suggest a heart attack. If incorrect, they might pivot, saying they sense a shadow in the body, and they ask about cancer. Or they might inquire about the head, hinting at a stroke or head injury. Given that heart attacks, cancer, strokes, and head injuries are statistically common causes of death, this method often leads to success."

I also asked Rhodes about *hot readings*, where the psychic has advanced information about a circumstance but later pretends it's being revealed to them supernaturally. "Have there been documented instances of this?" I asked.

"Absolutely," he said. "I remember when a psychic was filming a segment for ABC's *20/20*. During a break, with the camera still rolling—unbeknownst to the psychic—he chatted with a woman and learned that her grandmother had passed away. An hour later, while taping the show, the psychic dramatically turned to the woman and announced that her grandmother was sitting right behind her, as if this revelation had spontaneously come from the great beyond. When the *20/20* correspondent confronted him, the psychic denied any dishonesty, but it was clear what had happened."

The Heresies of Many Psychics

I wanted to know from Rhodes how psychics typically distance themselves from claims of fraud.

"The famous psychics are clever," he said. "When they appear on television or publish their books, they're careful to warn people about psychic scams and frauds. This warning subtly conveys that while *they* are genuine, many others are not. They specifically caution against psychic hotlines advertised on TV. The underlying message is, 'Trust us, but stay away from those other guys.'"

"What if they make an incorrect prediction or offer inaccurate information during a reading, which occurs all the time?" I asked.

"There are a lot of excuses. For example, the error might be due to *trickster energy*, because some prankster spirits apparently enjoy playing tricks on psychics. Or the psychic will claim the information was meant for someone else—say, someone living nearby. Or the psychic may attribute the error to the spirits communicating in symbols, and it's hard to interpret them accurately. Or an uninvited spirit may have shown up and provided irrelevant information. There's no shortage of excuses for a psychic's failures."

I noted that some psychics say they are Christians, even promoting that claim as a way of increasing their credibility. "But generally speaking, don't most well-known psychics hold beliefs that are at odds with biblical faith?" I asked.

"Psychics who say they're Christians often attribute their psychic gift to the Holy Spirit. This is nothing more than a superficial attempt to legitimize occultism—a whitewashing of occultism," said

Rhodes. "How can anything false and unholy be derived from what is true and holy? It simply cannot."

"Yet some psychics use Christian-sounding terminology."

"Yes, but they don't define these terms according to biblical teaching. Instead, they interpret them through the lens of the occult. For example, many psychics argue that the Bible should be interpreted 'esoterically' to uncover hidden truths. But these so-called truths contradict the Bible's clear message."

"For example?"

"Many psychics deny the deity of Jesus and his bodily resurrection. According to them, Jesus is merely enlightened in the same way all humans can be. Just as they claim that Jesus embodied the Christ, they'll say everyone has the potential to do so. Some psychics ascribe to *pantheism*, the belief that God is all and all is God. Others believe in both a Father God who embodies intellect and a Mother God—Azna—who embodies emotion."

He continued. "Many psychics assert that human beings are inherently perfect and united with God, each of us possessing a divine spark. It's our journey to awaken to this divinity within. They believe sin is an illusion, and that humanity is not morally fallen. There's no offense against God that requires atonement, and so humanity doesn't need salvation. The list of heresies goes on and on. These occultic reinterpretations of doctrine echo what Paul warned about in 1 Timothy 4:1—they're the doctrine of demons."

"Sounds like a laundry list of unbiblical teachings and ideas," I said. "What are the Bible's warnings about occultic practices?"

"The Bible unequivocally condemns all forms of occultism. Leviticus 19:26 commands, 'Do not practice divination or seek omens.' Similarly, Leviticus 19:31 warns, 'Do not turn to mediums or seek out spiritists, for you will be defiled by them.'[10] The Old Testament asserts that those who associate with familiar spirits are cursed by God.[11] Furthermore, Exodus 22:18 and Leviticus 20:27 mandate that sorcerers and mediums living at that time be put to death. Deuteronomy 18:10–12 is explicit: 'Let no one be found among you . . . who is a medium or spiritist or who consults the dead. Anyone who does these things is detestable to the LORD.' Revelation 9:21 promises that all who practice sorcery will face God's judgment. Their destiny is not heaven, but rather the lake that burns with fire and sulfur. Take a look at Revelation 21:8 and 22:15."

"That's all very clear," I said. "What's the biggest danger today?"

"The widespread whitewashing of occultism," he answered. "Consider how some psychics claim they possess a gift from the Holy Spirit to communicate with the dead. Also, instead of calling themselves mediums, they prefer the term *channeler*, which sounds more palatable to many. Some even use rosary beads and pray before conducting a psychic reading. But don't be deceived—God condemns all forms of occultism."

"Do you believe any human being truly possesses innate psychic abilities?"

"No, I don't," he said. "Psychics and spiritists are always connected to a demonic spirit being. For example, in Acts 16 there's the account of a slave girl who could foretell future events.[12] When Paul drove out this spirit of divination, she lost all her psychic powers. If she had truly possessed innate psychic powers, they wouldn't have vanished when Paul cast out the spirit. Even psychics who are frauds—those who deceitfully fish for information—are under Satan's influence, for he is the father of lies, and he motivates the devious methodology employed by psychics. Check out John 8:44."

A Clarion Call to Test the Spirits

There were many other related topics I could have asked Rhodes about, including weird X-file stuff, alien abductions, horoscopes, and so forth. People often report things that don't fit our usual understanding of the world. Some supernatural phenomena, such as the miracles described earlier in this book, aren't merely subjective in nature, but they feature external corroboration or multiple and credible eyewitnesses and are consistent with the teachings of the Bible, which itself has been shown to be reliable. Consequently, it's reasonable to accept these incidents as authentic.

"But," I asked Rhodes, "how can we evaluate the credibility of paranormal claims that we see in the media or online from time to time—reports of haunted houses, for instance? What are some steps we can take in deciding whether or not to believe these accounts?"

With that, Rhodes laid out a road map for how to discern truth from falsehood. First, he said, we should already be immersing ourselves daily in Scripture. "God's Word remains our steadfast guide," he said, citing Psalm 119:105: "Your word is a lamp for my feet, a light on my path."

Second, he said to pray for discernment. "Ask God to keep you safe from false and misleading ideas" was his advice. The prayer could be as simple as this: "Father, I pray that you give me a heart of wisdom and discernment so that I might not be confused or deceived by the events being reported in the media."

Third, seek counsel when appropriate. Proverbs 15:22 says it is wise to consult counselors. "If something you saw in the media is troubling you, and you can't find answers by yourself, then seek advice from trusted, mature Christians who can provide insight and balance," he said. If such a person isn't available, he said, consult books by a reputable Christian theologian or apologist.

Fourth, always consider the source of the report. Keep in mind the source's track record for reliability; examine the source's beliefs and biases to help you assess their credibility; probe for the source's motivation—are they selling a book or promoting a TV show about the paranormal, for example; and is there any evidence that the source is anti-Christian and therefore might spin the report in a way that undermines the faith?

Fifth, remember that there may be alternative explanations for various events. Consider if the phenomena that's being reported might be better accounted for by a more mundane explanation rather than a paranormal cause.

Sixth, cross-examine the initial report of the event. Said Rhodes, "Solomon, renowned as the wisest man who ever lived, observed, 'The one who states his case first seems right, until the other comes and examines him.'"[13]

For example, Rhodes said a psychic may convincingly claim that all people—regardless of their religion—are going to heaven. But a Scripture-based cross-examination reveals the error. Jesus, who has divine credentials, affirmed, "I am the way and the truth and the life. No one comes to the Father except through me.'"[14]

Seven, be aware of "fake news." This doesn't merely involve print and broadcast reports. "Fake news also comes from Satan and demons," Rhodes said. "That's why Scripture warns us of deceitful spirits and teachings of demons.[15] Make no mistake—demons are actively trying to deceive us. This is an ongoing threat for Christians. We know this because Jesus himself warned believers about the possibility of deception,[16] as did the apostle Paul."[17]

Added Rhodes, "In today's world, we must be especially vigilant because Satan is a master at marketing false ideas to fit every niche. He offers a range of deceptive options—brimming with fake news—to satisfy people's varied desires."

"Give me some examples," I said.

"Are you intrigued by the idea of becoming a god or shaping your own reality? Try the New Age Movement. If you're seeking health and wealth, then the Word of Faith movement might be a good fit. If you dislike pain and suffering, then Christian Science may offer a solution, since it regards these things as mere errors of the mortal mind. If you're curious about communicating with departed loved ones, then try spiritism. If you lean toward hedonism, then atheism offers all sorts of sexual freedom. Enticed by the idea of multiple lives through reincarnation? Then you might find New Age beliefs or Hinduism attractive."

Each of these alternatives shares a common core. "They will distance you from the true God, the authentic Jesus, and the genuine gospel," Rhodes said. "It comes as no surprise that Scripture urges Christians to be wary of Satan's cunning schemes."[18]

The antidote in a nutshell? Rhodes concluded our time together by pointing to 1 John 4:1: "Dear friends, do not believe every spirit, but test the spirits to see whether they are from God, because many false prophets have gone out into the world."

Seeking the Real Source of Truth

People are drawn to the paranormal for a variety of reasons. Some are simply curious. That's probably natural. Others are seeking to meet deeper needs, or to find illusive answers about their life and experiences.

I get it. But the Bible warns about the dangers of pursuing answers about life from sources that aren't grounded in God's truth. Interestingly, the word *occult* comes from a Latin word meaning clandestine, hidden, or secret. Yet truth isn't shrouded in dark and murky places or left in the shadows for us to guess about and try to sort through on our own. Rather, Jesus declares, "I am the light of the world. Whoever follows me will never walk in darkness, but will have the light of life."[19]

I lived much of my life in spiritual darkness. But discovering the light of Christ has been exhilarating and exciting. Are there still some things that remain obscured from our knowledge at this point? Sure. But we know enough. There's liberation and hope in the clear teachings of Scripture. Truly, we stray from that at our own peril.

CONCLUSION

What the Unseen World Means to You Today

The king of Syria was angry. His plans to ambush Israel's king had been thwarted because the prophet Elisha, through divine insight, had been able to warn Israel's leader to avoid traps set by the Syrian troops. Seeking retribution, the Syrian king decided to send his bloodthirsty army to capture Elisha and teach him a lesson.

Under the cover of darkness, Syrian horses and chariots surrounded the city of Dothan, where Elisha was staying. The next morning, when Elisha's servant went out early, he was aghast to see in the distance a vast number of soldiers poised to pounce on them. The situation seemed hopeless.

"Oh no, my lord!" he exclaimed. "What shall we do?"

The servant knew that Elisha's fate would also be his own. He was afraid of being captured and enslaved or killed. Sensing his fear, Elisha sought to calm him down. "Don't be afraid," said the prophet. "Those who are with us are more than those who are with them."

That didn't seem to ease the trembling servant's anxiety. But Elisha knew what to do next. He offered a prayer: "Open his eyes, LORD, so that he may see."

With that, the servant's eyes were opened and he was thoroughly astounded—and profoundly grateful—for what he beheld. The hills were teeming with horses and chariots of fire all around Elisha, an army of angels that was protecting them the whole time. In the end, God answered Elisha's request to strike the Syrian troops with temporary blindness, and Elisha and his servant escaped unharmed.[1]

God gave Elisha's servant a wonderful gift that fateful day: *He allowed him to see the supernatural.* And when he caught sight of this otherwise veiled realm, suddenly his faith was restored, and his courage bolstered. The vision reassured him of the love and protection of the God who created all.

I hope something similar has happened to you as you've read the preceding pages. I trust that your eyes have been opened to the supernatural activity of God that transpires all around us every day in this otherwise hidden world. I've sought to provide clues that are clear and corroborated, evidence that is powerful and persuasive—and the end result, I hope, has been to fortify your faith.

Yes, the invisible domain is roiling with conflict right now, as the forces of evil conspire to drag as many people to hell with them as they can. But remember what Elisha said: "Those who are with us are more than those who are with them." God is mightier than all. In fact, in the end the Bible says it will take only one of his angels—just *one single angel*—to hurl Satan into the Abyss, with him and his demonic army ultimately spending forever in the lake of fire.[2]

The apostle John put it this way to all his fellow followers of Jesus: "So we fix our eyes not on what is seen, but on what is unseen, since what is seen is temporary, but what is unseen is eternal."[3]

The Evidence on the Table

You wake up in the morning and enter the kitchen, where you see a dirty plate on the table, along with a used glass and some breadcrumbs. There is also a torn and empty sugar packet, a knife with a residue of jam, and a carton of milk with nothing left inside. Your conclusion? Your roommate had an overnight snack. That seems reasonable.

Of course, it's possible that a burglar broke in and had a small feast before fleeing. Or maybe your roommate arranged the mess to make you falsely believe he'd had an overnight snack. Or perhaps a ghost took time out from haunting your house to enjoy a meal. But these hypotheses strike you as much more contrived than your original conclusion.

The *Stanford Encyclopedia of Philosophy* uses this illustration in its entry on explanatory reasoning.[4] We do this type of inference to the best explanation virtually every day of our lives, and we're typically correct in our conclusions. The stronger the evidence and the more unlikely the alternative explanations, the more confidence we can have that our inference is reasonable.

Now, let's go back to the illustration. What if your roommate had a habit of indulging in overnight snacks? What if he told you the previous night that he was planning to have a snack after midnight before catching an early flight? And what if he left a note on the table that apologized for the mess? Then you would be even *more* justified in concluding that your original hypothesis was correct.

Well, I believe that's the level of evidence we have for the existence of a supernatural realm. We've gone through a dozen chapters in describing the clear and compelling case for an existence beyond our physical world. Here's a summary that puts everything together into a cogent whole.

Our Soul Points toward the Supernatural

The evidence for an immaterial realm begins with *you*. You are not just a physical body that's destined only to die and decay, but you *are* a soul and you *have* a body. The soul is your essential core, your first-person experience of living, the locus of your introspection, volition, emotions, desires, memories, perceptions, and beliefs. The

Bible affirms the reality of the soul, which has the capability to live on even after our physical death.

Neuroscientist Sharon Dirckx said she can measure the electrical activity in a physical brain, but she can't measure what's actually in someone's mind or what it's like to be them. That's because the brain alone is not enough to explain the mind or soul. The claim that we are just a physical body that lacks free will isn't internally consistent, doesn't make sense of the world, and ultimately isn't livable. Finally, recent discoveries of neuroscience are entirely compatible with the existence of God.

Indeed, the belief that we are made in the image of a supernatural God explains a lot about us. Said Dirckx, "Because God has a mind, we have a mind; because God thinks, we think; because God is conscious, so are we."

Miracles Point toward a Supernatural Source

I personally found the accounts of modern miracles to be among the strongest evidence for the existence of God and the supernatural world. I was so captivated by the amazing story of Barbara Snyder's instantaneous healing from multiple sclerosis after she heard the voice of God beckoning her to "get up and walk" that I traveled to Virginia so I could personally interview her. With medical records from the Mayo Clinic and multiple eyewitnesses with no motive to deceive, and with her healing coming after nearly five hundred Christians prayed for her, I consider her recovery from the brink of death to be a virtual airtight case for the supernatural. No wonder her doctors labeled it a miracle.

And what about the documented case of the woman blinded by an uncurable condition whose eyesight was instantly restored after her husband prayed for her immediate recovery?

Yes, there have been instances of fraud, confirmation bias, the placebo effect, and medical mistakes throughout history, but there are also convincing healings of everything from heart defects to broken ankles to deafness to intractable epilepsy. These come after prayer and sometimes with the clear, even audible, voice of God.

Then there have been rigorous scientific studies, accepted for publication in peer-reviewed secular medical journals, that document undeniable improvement in patients after prayers to God. You can draw your own conclusions, but here's mine: God is still in the business of supernaturally intervening in our world.

Extraordinary Experiences Point toward the Supernatural

It seems logical that if God exists, he might want to reach out of his supernatural realm from time to time in order to personally encounter someone in this earthly domain—and we have innumerable examples of him doing exactly that. Because they are personal and generally uncorroborated, these experiences by themselves don't *make* the case for the supernatural, but they are undeniably *part* of the case.

The evidential value of these encounters varies. They seem most credible when they are unexpected rather than flowing out of someone's previous beliefs. For instance, the motorcycle daredevil Evel Knievel was living a wild lifestyle that would need to completely change if he became a Christian. His profound experience with God on the beach in Florida couldn't be construed as the fulfillment of his own inner desires.

These divine encounters tend to be unlike any other experience the person has ever had. They can be weighed against Scripture to see if they're consistent with its teachings. And often the ultimate outcome is the best confirmation of their divine source. For example, nobody foresaw Knievel—the drunkard, the womanizer, the gambler—turning into a radical evangelist for Jesus!

He and so many others like him—and I include myself in this category—were unlikely candidates for God's kingdom. And maybe that's the point.

Mystical Dreams Point toward a Supernatural God

I was especially intrigued by several aspects of the worldwide phenomenon of Jesus appearing in the dreams of Muslims, which is one of the most significant spiritual awakenings in the world today.

First, these experiences aren't something a typical Muslim would conjure up in their subconscious. A devout Muslim would have no incentive to imagine such an encounter with the Jesus of Christianity, who might lure them into Islamic apostasy and possibly even a death sentence in certain countries.

Second, Muslims aren't going to sleep, having a dream about Jesus, and waking as a Christian. Instead, there is typically external corroboration of the dream. In other words, they later encounter someone who had been in their dream, who then opens the Bible and tells them about God's message of grace and redemption. Or they subsequently run into a Christian who explains the gospel to them. Sometimes there's another form of corroboration—two people experience the same dream on the same night.

Third, I was struck by the fact that these are not like ordinary dreams. They're much more vibrant, more vivid, more captivating, more memorable and life-changing. And inevitably the Muslim learns something in the dream they hadn't known—they *feel* the grace and love of Jesus in a way they never would have anticipated.

For me, all of this adds up to one of the most convincing categories of evidence for the supernatural.

Angels Populate the Supernatural Realm

If we believe what the Bible teaches generally and what Jesus said specifically, then it's reasonable to conclude that the hidden realm of the supernatural is inhabited by millions of spirit beings called angels. These are immortal, highly intelligent, and personal creatures who were created to serve God and his followers.

They're not omnipresent like God (but they can travel in a flash); they aren't omniscient like God (so they can't read our minds); they can't perform miracles like God (though he can use them to do so); and yet they are awesome in their strength, their devotion, and their service in furtherance of God's plans.

We see corroboration of these angels, or "messengers," in contemporary times when they materialize in the form of humans or otherwise intervene to help or protect us. Credible individuals have offered accounts of angelic interventions. We see this in the unexpected rescue of the little boy who tumbled out of a moving car, as recounted by respected theologian Roger Olson, and in the protection of Scottish missionary John G. Paton and his wife from an angry mob, as reported by Billy Graham.

Whether there are individual guardian angels assigned to each Christian or not, this angelic army plays a crucial though unseen role in the spiritual warfare that rages in the supernatural realm.

Satan and Demons Wreak Havoc in the Supernatural Realm

Even critical scholars concede that Jesus of Nazareth was seen as an exorcist who drove out demons. To Jesus, Satan wasn't just a metaphor for evil; he was a very real adversary who was committed to thwarting him and deterring others from following him. Over half of Jesus' ministry in Mark's gospel involves delivering the demonized.

Though sketchy in details, the Bible depicts Satan as an angel whose pride caused him to rebel against his Creator and who was followed into corruption by other angels who became his army of demons.

We see corroboration of Satan's evil influence in the way credible psychiatrists have determined that some of their patients aren't merely psychologically impaired but bear the unmistakable traits of being demonically possessed. These victims speak in languages they don't know, display supernatural strength, disclose "hidden knowledge" about people, and in a few cases even levitate in full view of multiple eyewitnesses.

As a result, the hidden world of the supernatural has become a battleground between angels and demons. At particular risk are people who are outside of God's family and therefore lack the indwelling of the Holy Spirit to ward off possession. But even for Christians, Satan and his troops can mount attacks that are short of possession but are intended to dissuade them from full devotion to Christ.

That's why the apostle Paul provides guidance on how Christians can protect themselves,[5] and James urges Christians to "resist the devil, and he will flee from you."[6]

Deathbed Visions Give a Peek into the Supernatural

J. Steve Miller made a compelling case that people on the verge of death often get a peek into the otherworldly realm to which they are headed. Indeed, the ubiquity of these visions is stunning. Researchers have studied thousands upon thousands of cases with strikingly similar characteristics. Just before someone passes from this world, their eyes are opened to what—and who—awaits them.

For instance, when Jesus told the story of the rich man and Lazarus in Luke 16:22, he described how angels came to carry Lazarus to a place of bliss. Sure enough, people frequently see angels coming for them just before they close their eyes for the last time in this world. For example, it happened to Billy Graham's grandmother and to Graham's former pulpit partner Charles Templeton.

It even happens to children. "The angels—they're so beautiful! Mommy, can you see them? Do you hear their singing? I've never heard such beautiful singing!" exclaimed one child before she passed.

Interestingly, often these children don't see angels as they are routinely depicted in drawings for kids, where they have big wings. Instead, they see them without wings. If cultural expectations aren't informing their vision, "the most consistent explanation is that these really are encounters with a spiritual realm," Miller said.

In short, concluded Miller, multiple streams of evidence support what the Bible has taught all along: "Death isn't the destruction of self. It's a transition to another form of existence."

Near-Death Experiences Reveal a Supernatural Realm

Neuroscientist Sharon Dirckx said just *one* documented near-death experience (NDE) would be enough to establish that our consciousness survives death. But we have much more than one such case. Instead, there are thousands of reported NDEs, including many with astounding corroboration.

For example, there are blind people who can see for the first time during their NDE. A woman whose spirit floated from her body was able to describe a sticker on the top of a blade on a hospital ceiling fan. Another woman saw a tennis shoe on a hospital's third-floor ledge during her out-of-body experience—and it was later found just as she described it.

The spirit of a young girl followed her family home after they visited the hospital, and she accurately reported what they were doing and wearing at the time. Numerous patients have recalled with stunning accuracy how doctors tried resuscitating their dying bodies. A woman saw her cousin among the deceased she encountered during her NDE, even though she hadn't been aware of her cousin's recent death. In separate out-of-body experiences, youngsters encountered siblings they never knew they had.

Concluded a previously skeptical Yale professor who conducted a study of NDEs among children, "After looking at all the other explanations for near-death experiences, I think the simplest explanation is that NDEs are actually glimpses into the world beyond."[7]

What's more, pastor and researcher John Burke studied a thousand NDEs and said if we look at what people actually experience, as opposed to how they may interpret it, the core of these cases is consistent with Christian doctrine.

Heaven Is the Supernatural Destination of God's Family

I was captivated by theologian Scot McKnight's nine reasons for believing heaven is real. Jesus and the apostles believed in heaven. The resurrection of Jesus foreshadows it. The overall Bible points to it. The church has consistently taught about it. Earth's beauty points toward an even greater grandeur to come. The vast majority of people believe in it. The desires we feel in this world will only be satisfied by it. The injustice we see today calls out for God to make all things right. And science cannot rule out a supernatural realm beyond our existence.

My imagination was captured by the idea of a new heaven and a new earth—"the complete renewal of our world, a very earthy, physical place, not just for spirits or souls, but for resurrected bodies designed for the kingdom of God," as McKnight put it. It's a place both centered on God and where relationships between his people will flourish as never before.

Plus, McKnight's vision of the first hour in heaven being devoted to reconciliation between believers is particularly attractive, especially when I ponder how my estranged father and I will finally resolve the rift between us so that we can spend eternity in the kind of father-son relationship we have both always wanted.

But I have to say that the most awe-evoking statement I encountered about heaven came from nineteenth-century preacher Charles Spurgeon. Read it, ponder it, drink it in: "The very glory of heaven is that we shall see him, that same Christ who once died upon Calvary's cross, that we shall fall down, and worship at his feet—nay, more, that he shall kiss us with the kisses of his mouth and welcome us to dwell with him forever."[8]

Hell Is the Supernatural Destination for the Unredeemed

There's one reason traditional Christians continue to believe in the controversial doctrine that unrepentant sinners will endure conscious torment forever separate from God in hell—*Scripture teaches it.*

Yes, explained philosopher Paul Copan, there are misconceptions about hell. The imagery of flames is surely metaphorical. Hell isn't a torture chamber, though there will be torment that comes from within. And hell isn't "one size fits all." There will be degrees of punishment, meted out justly according to each person's situation.

But perhaps the biggest misconception is that God sends people to hell. "Each choice we make in this life moves us closer to our ultimate destination—whether toward or away from God," said Copan. "We set our spiritual and moral compasses. That means that those who reject the rule of God *send themselves* to hell . . . and God reluctantly lets them go."

Is there an escape hatch? Not through annihilationism, the belief that the unrepentant are snuffed out forever, perhaps after brief suffering. A pretty good biblical case can be made for this idea—but ultimately it falls short. Universalism, the heretical conviction that everyone will eventually end up in heaven, is devoid of real biblical support.

And yet there is a divinely ordained escape route available to every individual. It's the gift of eternal life that God freely offers to everyone who will receive it in repentance and faith. That's why they call it the *gospel*—it is "good news."

Jesus' Resurrection Is Supernatural Proof of His Divinity

Anyone can claim to be the Son of God, as Jesus surely did. In John 10:30, he told a crowd, "I and the Father are one." The Greek word for "one"—*heis*—is not masculine, but neuter. This means Jesus was *not* saying he and the Father are the same person, but that he and the Father are the same thing—they are one in nature or essence. The audience immediately picked up stones to kill him for claiming to be divine. Clearly, that's blasphemy.

Unless, of course, it's true.

Later, Jesus was killed by crucifixion and then was seen alive by hundreds of eyewitnesses after his resurrection—all of which provides convincing evidence that he was telling the truth about his divine identity.

Cold-case homicide detective J. Warner Wallace was an atheist until he used his formidable investigative skills to probe the credibility of Matthew, Mark, Luke, and John. His conclusion after six months of analysis was that they "reliably recorded true events."

But an obstacle remained—Wallace's presupposition against the supernatural. He had ruled out miracles at the outset, and yet here were trustworthy reports documenting them. He was flummoxed, but then he realized that even as an atheist, he believed in something extra-natural—the big bang, which sparked the origin of the universe. This evidence pointed to a transcendent and personal Creator—and if there is such a God, "then miracles are reasonable, maybe even expected."

Wallace's experience mirrors my own exploration of the resurrection as an atheist and investigative reporter trained in law. For both of us, the outcome was the same: Putting our trust in the resurrected Christ transformed our values, our character, our morality, our worldview, our attitudes, our philosophy, and, most importantly, our eternities. And that's a miracle in itself!

The Paranormal Is a Twisted Version of the Supernatural

I remember hearing ghost stories around the campfire when I was a kid. They sounded pretty convincing—*and scary*—at the time. But as the apostle Paul said in 1 Corinthians 13:11, "When I was a child, I talked like a child, I thought like a child, I reasoned like a child. When I became a man, I put the ways of childhood behind me."

Because Jesus proved his divine nature through his resurrection, we can trust what he tells us about the afterlife. And what he describes contradicts the idea of disembodied ghosts that stop short of going to "the other side" and instead decide to stay on earth and haunt people. Frankly, there are more plausible explanations for the anomalies that are typically attributed to ghostly spirits.

As for so-called psychics, the Bible condemns attempts to contact the dead. If mediums are in contact with anything, it's demonic spirits that are masquerading as deceased individuals and seeking to lure people away from biblical truth.

Fortunately, God has provided a road map to help us discern what's true and what's false. It's the Bible that gives us the ability to "test the spirits to see whether they are from God, because many false prophets have gone out into the world."[9]

Finally Arriving Full Circle

Miracles that are inexplicable apart from a divine source. Life-changing supernatural encounters. Mystical dreams with external corroboration. Deathbed visions that provide a peek into what's to come. Near-death experiences in which people see or hear things that would be impossible if they had not had an out-of-body experience. And the powerful and persuasive historical data that support the supernatural resurrection of Jesus.

We *are* an immaterial soul, and we *have* a physical body. Our spirit will endure after our death before being reunited with our resurrected body at the consummation of history. The same Jesus who proved his divine nature by returning from the dead has told us that our eternal destination hinges on how we respond to him. We can either pay the penalty for our own sins, or we can gratefully receive his payment on the cross on our behalf.

All of which brings us full circle. I began this book by quoting William Peter Blatty about his motivation for writing the classic horror film *The Exorcist*. "I wanted to write about good and evil and the unseen world all around us," he said. "I wanted to make a statement that the grave is not the end, that there is more to life than death." Then he added, "If demons are real, why not angels? If angels are real, why not souls? And if souls are real, what about your own soul?"[10]

That last question has gone unanswered—until now. What does all of this evidence for a supernatural world mean to you personally?

In other words, *what about your own soul?* How can you go beyond *seeing* the supernatural to *seizing* the supernatural?

If you look to the Bible for answers, you may feel intimidated at first. After all, it's more than seven hundred thousand words in length. But the essentials of what you need to know about the destiny of your own soul can be summarized in just twenty-one words. One verse. One message. One hope.

"For the wages of sin is death," Romans 6:23 tells us, "but the gift of God is eternal life in Christ Jesus our Lord."

In other words, *the wages of sin*—what we've earned and deserve because of our disobedience and wrongdoing—*is death*, which means eternal separation from God, because he is perfect and holy, and we are not.

But, the verse continues, *the gift of God*—which we cannot earn, merit, or deserve—*is eternal life*, which means a transformed life in this world and then a glorious existence forever in heaven.

How is this available? Only through *Christ Jesus our Lord.* Jesus paid the penalty we deserved for the sins we've committed so he could offer forgiveness as a gift of his grace. Removing our sin makes it possible for us to be united forever with our perfect God, who becomes our Lord—that is, our leader.

Like any gift, forgiveness and eternal life need to be received with gratitude, as well as with an attitude of repentance and faith. "And everyone who calls on the name of the Lord will be saved," says Acts 2:21.

What does this look like in a prayer? How about this prayer that you could express to God right now:

Jesus, thank you for helping me see the reality of the
supernatural. Right now, as best I can, I do believe you are
the Son of God. You proved it by returning from the dead.
And I admit the obvious. I am a sinner. I confess this and
turn from my wrong beliefs and actions. In an attitude of

*repentance and faith, I receive your free gift of forgiveness
and eternal life. Thank you for paying the penalty I deserved
so that we can be united forever. Please fill me with your
Holy Spirit and help me to live the kind of life you want me
to live, because from this moment on, I am yours.*

Simple enough? *Profound* enough? Frankly, it *is* enough—if it's a sincere expression of your newfound faith in Jesus and his provision for you. This single heartfelt prayer is sufficient to swing open the door to a supernatural world of beauty, wonder, grace, and love.

And it means that someday you will be greeted by Jesus himself, who will kiss you with the kisses of his mouth and welcome you to dwell with him forever.

I'll see you there!

ACKNOWLEDGMENTS

It was Mike Briggs and his team at Zondervan who first envisioned a book about the supernatural and suggested I investigate the topic. Without their creative spark, this book would never have been researched and written.

Then the entire team at Zondervan—especially Webster Younce, Paul Pastor, Dirk Buursma, Alicia Mey Kasen, and others—made invaluable contributions to bringing this project to fruition. Their talent and diligent work are reflective of the excellence I've experienced through dozens of projects with Zondervan over the years.

My literary agent, Don Gates, shepherded this work through the publishing process with care and insight. As usual, Mark Mittelberg, my friend and ministry associate for nearly forty years, offered invaluable guidance. He edits everything I write before I submit it to the publisher. And thanks to my wife, Leslie, for her ongoing encouragement despite the sacrifices that are necessary in wrestling a book to completion.

Most of all, I'm grateful to God for the privilege of sharing his message of hope and grace through books that can be sent around the world. It's my prayer that this book will honor him—and point spiritually curious people toward the redemption only available through Jesus.

MEET LEE STROBEL

Atheist-turned-Christian Lee Strobel, the former award-winning legal editor of *The Chicago Tribune*, is a *New York Times* bestselling author of more than forty books and curricula that have sold millions of copies worldwide. He was described in *The Washington Post* as "one of the evangelical community's most popular apologists."

Lee was educated at the University of Missouri (Bachelor of Journalism degree) and Yale Law School (Master of Studies in Law degree). He was a journalist for fourteen years at *The Chicago Tribune* and other newspapers, winning Illinois' highest honors for both investigative reporting and public service journalism from United Press International.

After probing the evidence for nearly two years, Lee became a Christian in 1981. He subsequently became a teaching pastor at three of America's largest churches and hosted the weekly national network TV program *Faith Under Fire*. In addition, he taught First Amendment law at Roosevelt University and was professor of Christian thought at Houston Christian University.

In 2017, Lee's spiritual journey was depicted in an award-winning motion picture, *The Case for Christ*, which was shown in theaters around the world. Lee won awards for his *books The Case for Christ, The Case for Faith, The Case for a Creator*, and *The Case for Grace.* His latest books are *The Case for Miracles, The Case for Heaven,* and *Is God Real? Exploring the Ultimate Question of Life.* In 2023, he was honored with the Pillar Award for History from the Museum of the Bible.

Lee and Leslie have been married for more than fifty years. Their daughter, Alison, is a novelist and homeschooling expert, and their son, Kyle, earned a doctorate in theology at the University of Aberdeen and teaches spiritual formation at the Talbot School of Theology at Biola University.

NOTES

Introduction

1. Lee Strobel, "Does Science Support Miracles? New Study Documents a Blind Woman's Healing," *The Stream*, May 16, 2020, https://stream.org /does-science-support-miracles-new-study-documents-a-blind-womans -healing. See Clarissa Romez et al., "Case Report of Instantaneous Resolution of Juvenile Macular Degeneration Blindness after Proximal Intercessory Prayer," *Explore* 17, no. 1 (January–February 2021): 79–83, www .sciencedirect.com/science/article/pii/S1550830720300926?via%3Dihub.

2. Billy Hallowell, "Dan Bongino Emotionally Recounts Supernatural Experience the Morning His Mom Died," *Faithwire*, March 21, 2024, www .faithwire.com/2024/03/21/dan-bongino-emotionally-recounts-supernatural -experience-the-morning-his-mom-died-ive-never-believed-more-in-the -power-of-jesus.

3. Suzanne Stratford, "Do You Believe in Angels? Ohio Pastor Talks about What He Believes Was Angelic Encounter," Fox 8 News, February 22, 2016, https://fox8.com/news/do-you-believe-in-angels-ohio-pastor-talks -about-what-he-believes-was-angelic-encounter.

4. Terry Mattingly, "'The Exorcist' at 50—If Demons Are Real, How about Angels? What about an Eternal Soul?," *GetReligion.org*, November 26, 2023, www.getreligion.org/getreligion/2023/11/21/the-exorcist-at-50-if -demons-are-real-how-about-angels-what-about-an-eternal-soul.

5. Yosra Iagha and James Melzer, "15 Scariest Horror Movies of All Time, According to Rotten Tomatoes," *Movieweb.com*, December 28, 2023, https://movieweb.com/scariest-movies-of-all-time-according-to-rotten -tomatoes/#.

6. Deborah Netburn, "'It's a Lot of UFO Stuff and a Lot of Healing': Inside

L.A.'s Wackiest Spiritual Convention," Yahoo, February 19, 2024, www
.yahoo.com/lifestyle/lot-ufo-stuff-lot-healing-110030259.html.

7. See Rick Porter, "'Supernatural' by the Numbers: A 15-Year Ratings History,"
Hollywood Reporter, November 19, 2020, www.hollywoodreporter.com/tv/tv
-news/supernatural-by-the-numbers-a-15-year-ratings-history-4095007.

8. See review at www.amazon.com/True-Tales-Weird-Experiences
-Supernatural/dp/1161395326/ref=sr_1_5?.

9. *Secrets of the Supernatural, Hearst* magazine special edition, July 30, 2024.

10. Becka A. Alper et al., "Spirituality among Americans," Pew Research
Center, December 7, 2023, www.pewresearch.org/religion/2023/12/07
/spirituality-among-americans.

11. Megan Brenan, "Belief in Five Spiritual Entities Edges Down to New
Lows," Gallup, July 20, 2023, https://news.gallup.com/poll/508886/belief
-five-spiritual-entities-edges-down-new-lows.aspx.

12. There are at least two species of what is known as *scientism*. Explained
philosopher J. P. Moreland, "Strong scientism is the view that the only
knowledge we can have about reality are those that have been properly
tested in the hard sciences (especially physics and chemistry). All other
claims—e.g., theological, ethical, political, aesthetic—are mere expressions
of emotion and private opinions. Weak scientism allows that there may be
modestly justified beliefs outside science, but the settled assertions of the
hard sciences are vastly superior to claims outside science." J. P. Moreland,
"The Rise of Scientism," *Talbot Magazine*, June 4, 2019, www.biola.edu
/blogs/talbot-magazine/2019/the-rise-of-scientism.

13. Alex Rosenberg, *The Atheist's Guide to Reality: Enjoying Life without
Illusions* (New York: Norton, 2011), 6, 8.

14. John F. Haught, "The Cosmic Adventure: Science, Religion and the Quest
for Purpose," Religion Online, accessed August 31, 2024, www.religion
-online.org/book-chapter/chapter-2-scientific-materialism.

15. Melissa Cain Travis, "Scientific Materialist Manifesto: The Pursuit of
Meaning in a Godless Universe," *Christian Research Journal* 43, no. 2
(June 2021), www.equip.org/articles/scientific-materialist-manifesto-the
-pursuit-of-meaning-in-a-godless-universe.

16. Jessica Tracy, "You Can Be a Materialist and Find Meaning in the
Universe," *Psyche*, September 25, 2023, https://psyche.co/ideas/you-can-be-a
-materialist-and-find-meaning-in-the-universe.

17. Robert W. Funk, Roy W. Hoover, and The Jesus Seminar, *The Five Gospels:
What Did Jesus Really Say?* (San Francisco: HarperSanFrancisco, 1993), 2.

18. Moreland, "Rise of Scientism."

19. In the survey, 28 percent of respondents somewhat agreed and 18 percent

strongly agreed with the statement "science contradicts Christianity," while 20 percent strongly disagreed and 33 percent somewhat disagreed with the statement. I commissioned the Barna Group to conduct this online survey among 1,500 US adults from July 28 to August 7, 2023. The sample error is +/- 2.0 percentage points at the 95 percent confidence level. Quotas were set to obtain a minimum readable sample by a variety of demographic factors, and samples were weighted by region, ethnicity, education, age, and gender to reflect their natural presence in the American population (using US Census Bureau data for comparison).

20. Richard C. Lewontin, "Billions and Billions of Demons," review of Carl Sagan, *The Demon-Haunted World: Science as a Candle in the Dark* (New York: Ballantine, 1997), *New York Review*, January 9, 1997, www.nybooks.com/articles/1997/01/09/billions-and-billions-of-demons, italics in original.

21. See philosopher Douglas Groothuis's endorsement of J. P. Moreland, *Scientism and Secularism: Learning to Respond to a Dangerous Ideology* (Wheaton, IL: Crossway, 1998), i—a conviction shared by science philosopher Stephen Meyer, who called Moreland "one of the great Christian philosophers of our time" (ii).

22. See Moreland, *Scientism and Secularism*, chapter 4 ("Scientism Is Self-Refuting," pp. 49–54) and chapter 12 ("Five Things Science Cannot In Principle Explain [But Theism Can,]" pp. 135–58); see also Moreland, "Key Insights from *Scientism and Secularism: Learning to Respond to a Dangerous Ideology*," Thinkr, accessed August 31, 2024, https://thinkr.org/newsletter/scientism-and-secularism-learning-to-respond-to-a-dangerous-ideology; Moreland, "5 Things Science Cannot Explain (but Theism Can)," Crossway, May 1, 2024, www.crossway.org/articles/5-things-science-cannot-explain-but-theism-can.

23. See Lee Strobel, *The Case for Miracles* (Grand Rapids: Zondervan, 2018), 30.

24. Michael S. Heiser, *The Unseen Realm* documentary, October 12, 2022, www.youtube.com/watch?v=2QM7anD5vSI.

25. Bridgette Cameron Ridenour, *Overlooked* (Dewey, AZ: Writing Momentum, 2023). The account of the miscarriage and its aftermath are found on pages 85–98.

Chapter 1: The Invisible You: The Existence of Your Soul

1. Quotes excerpted from Ralph Lewis, "Is There Life after Death? The Mind-Body Problem," *Psychology Today*, July 18, 2019, www.psychologytoday.com/us/blog/finding-purpose/201907/is-there-life-after-death-the-mind-body-problem. He tells his story in Ralph Lewis, *Finding Purpose in a Godless World* (Amherst, NY: Prometheus, 2019).

2. Daniel C. Dennett, *Consciousness Explained* (Boston: Little, Brown, 1991), 33, italics in original.

3. Colin Blakemore, *The Mind Machine* (London: BBC Books, 1990), 270.

4. Physicalism, also known as monism (literally, *one-ness*), and dualism are broad terms that have been broken down by philosophers into a dizzying number of subcategories, including substance dualism, naturalistic dualism, holistic dualism, emergent dualism, two-aspect monism, reflexive monism, constitutional materialism, nonreductive physicalism, eliminative materialism, and so forth. For the purposes of my discussion, I will basically deal with the overarching claims of physicalism and dualism.

5. Colin McGinn, *The Mysterious Flame: Conscious Minds in a Material World* (New York: Basic Books, 1999), 13–14.

6. Mark C. Baker and Stewart Goetz, eds., *The Soul Hypothesis: Investigations into the Existence of the Soul* (New York: Bloomsbury, 2013), 1, 2.

7. Daniel Dennett, *Freedom Evolves* (New York: Viking, 2003), 1.

8. Baker and Goetz, *Soul Hypothesis*, 20.

9. Paul Copan, *How Do You Know You're Not Wrong? Responding to Objections That Leave Christians Speechless* (Grand Rapids: Baker, 2005), 95, italics in original.

10. Most Christian philosophers believe animals also have souls. Writes philosopher J. P. Moreland, "The animal soul is not as richly structured as the human soul, it does not bear the image of God, and it is far more dependent on the animal's body and its sense organs than is the human soul" (see *The Soul: How We Know It's Real and Why It Matters* [Chicago: Moody, 2014], 141–45).

11. Arthur C. Custance, *The Mysterious Matter of Mind* (Grand Rapids: Zondervan, 1980), 90.

12. Quoted in Lee Strobel, *The Case for a Creator* (Grand Rapids: Zondervan, 2004), 261, italics in original.

13. Moreland, *The Soul*, 44.

14. Matthew 14:16.

15. See Moreland, *The Soul*, 71.

16. Luke 23:43: "Today you will be with me in paradise."

17. 1 Peter 3:18–20.

18. 2 Corinthians 5:8.

19. See Matthew 22:23–33; Acts 23:6–10.

20. Patricia S. Churchland, *Touching a Nerve: The Self as Brain* (New York: Norton, 2013), 63.

21. All interviews conducted for this book are edited for content, conciseness, and clarity.

Chapter 1: Interview with Sharon Dirckx, PhD

1. Psalm 8:3–4.
2. See Sharon Dirckx, *Am I Just My Brain?* (London: Good Book, 2019), 47–48. She attributes this thought experiment to Frank Jackson.
3. See Gottfried Wilhelm Leibniz, *Philosophical Papers and Letters*, 2nd ed. (Boston: Kluwer Academic, 1976).
4. Adrian Owen, "How Science Found a Way to Help Coma Patients Communicate," *The Guardian*, September 5, 2017, www.theguardian .com/news/2017/sep/05/how-science-found-a-way-to-help-coma-patients -communicate.
5. Wilder Penfield, *The Mystery of the Mind: A Critical Study of Consciousness and the Human Brain* (Princeton, NJ: Princeton University Press, 1975), 77–78.
6. See Dirckx, *Am I Just My Brain?*, 69, 84.
7. Dirckx, *Am I Just My Brain?*, 64.
8. Sam Harris, *Free Will* (New York: Free Press, 2012), 5, italics in original.
9. See Nick Pollard, *Evangelism Made Slightly Less Difficult: How to Interest People Who Aren't Interested* (Downers Grove, IL: InterVarsity, 1997), 47–70.
10. Dirckx also deals with other theories, such as *compatibilism*, or *soft determinism*, and *libertarianism*. See her *Am I Just My Brain?*, 75–90.
11. We also discussed *panpsychism*, the increasingly popular idea that all particles have both physical and conscious dimensions. "In other words," I said, "consciousness was baked into the system from the very beginning. That's clever, but it doesn't explain where it all came from, does it?" Said Dirckx, "It doesn't. And it doesn't explain why humans are unique in their consciousness compared to the rest of the animal kingdom. Also, here's a big problem: It's impossible to confirm this theory. To verify consciousness, you need word-based language to express it, and the natural world doesn't have this ability." She added, "If electrons are conscious and we have trillions of them in us, how can we account for the unity with which we experience the world? We don't have trillions of separate conscious experiences; we have one." To me, panpsychism seems like a big stretch.
12. Quoted in Stewart Goetz and Charles Taliaferro, *A Brief History of the Soul* (Malden, MA: Wiley-Blackwell, 2011), 7.
13. Goetz and Taliaferro, *Brief History*, 6.
14. See Dirckx, *Am I Just My Brain?*, 32–33.
15. For evidence and arguments pointing toward the truth of biblical Christianity, see my interview with philosophy professor Chad Meister in Lee Strobel, *Is God Real? Exploring the Ultimate Question of Life* (Grand Rapids: Zondervan, 2023), 115–36.

16. Genesis 1:27: "So God created mankind in his own image, in the image of God he created them; male and female he created them."

17. There are some Christians who are physicalists. According to philosopher J. P. Moreland, some Christian physicalists take the *extinction/re-creation view*: "When the body dies the person ceases to exist since the person is in some sense the same as his or her body. At the future, final resurrection, persons are re-created [by God] after a period of non-existence." Others take the *immediate resurrection view*: "At death, in some way or another, each individual continues to exist in a physical way." See Moreland, *The Soul*, 71.

18. Dirckx, *Am I Just My Brain?*, 131.

Chapter 2: Astounding Miracles Today

1. The Mayo Clinic confirms there is no cure for gastroparesis (see "Gastroparesis," Mayo Clinic, accessed August 31, 2024, www.mayoclinic .org/diseases-conditions/gastroparesis/symptoms-causes/syc-20355787).

2. Clarissa Romez, David Zaritzky, and Joshua W. Brown, "Case Report of Gastroparesis Healing: 16 Years of a Chronic Syndrome Resolved after Proximal Intercessory Prayer," *Complementary Therapies in Medicine* 43 (April 2019): 289–94, www.sciencedirect.com/science/article/pii /S0965229918313116.

3. Richard L. Purtill, "Defining Miracles," in *In Defense of Miracles: A Comprehensive Case for God's Action in History*, ed. R. Douglas Geivett and Gary R. Habermas (Downers Grove, IL: InterVarsity, 1997), 72.

Chapter 2: Interview with Craig S. Keener, PhD

1. Quoted in Philip Yancey, "Jesus and Miracles," August 20, 2015, *Philip Yancey* blog, www.philipyancey.com/Jesus-and-miracles, emphasis added.

2. Gardner was a Fellow of the Royal College of Obstetricians and Gynecologists and of the Association of Surgeons in East Africa. He served as an examiner to the University of Newcastle-upon-Tyne. He was ordained in the United Free Church of Scotland. See Rex Gardner, *Healing Miracles: A Doctor Investigates* (London: Darton, Longman & Todd, 1986), back cover.

3. Gardner, *Healing Miracles*, 202–5.

4. Gardner, *Healing Miracles*, 206.

5. Gardner, *Healing Miracles*, 165.

6. Harold P. Adolph, *Today's Decisions, Tomorrow's Destiny* (Spooner, WI: White Birch, 2006), 48–49; Scott J. Kolbaba, *Physicians' Untold Stories* (North Charleston, SC: CreateSpace, 2016), 115–22.

7. "I can do all this through him who gives me strength."

8. Interestingly, the visiting minister, Wesley Steelberg Jr., had himself been healed of a heart condition when he had been given just hours to live; see Craig S. Keener, *Miracles: The Credibility of the New Testament Accounts* (Grand Rapids: Baker Academic, 2011), 1:431–32.

9. See Chauncey W. Crandall IV, MD, *Raising the Dead: A Doctor Encounters the Miraculous* (New York: FaithWords, 2010), 1–5.

10. Crandall, *Raising the Dead*, 171–73.

11. Robert A. Larmer, *Dialogues on Miracle* (Eugene, OR: Wipf & Stock, 2015), 117–19.

12. "I would like to use my rudimentary French by talking with her." The French version looks better in print than when I stumbled through it aloud.

13. For example, see Luke 4:40, which reads, "At sunset, the people brought to Jesus all who had various kinds of sickness, and laying his hands on each one, he healed them."

14. James 5:14.

15. See Troy Bedinghaus, "Eye Chart Test: Uses and How to Understand the Results," VeryWell Health, December 29, 2023, www.verywellhealth.com /snellen-eye-chart-3422168#.

Chapter 3: Life-Changing Spiritual Encounters

1. See Lee Strobel and Mark Mittelberg, *The Unexpected Adventure: Taking Everyday Risks to Talk with People about Jesus* (Grand Rapids: Zondervan, 2009), 272–74.

2. See Mark Mittelberg, *Confident Faith: Building a Firm Foundation for Your Beliefs* (Carol Stream, IL: Tyndale, 2013), 155–57.

3. See Luke 14:15–24.

4. Nabeel Qureshi, *Seeking Allah, Finding Jesus: A Devout Muslim Encounters Christianity* (Grand Rapids: Zondervan, 2014); see also Lee Strobel, *The Case for Miracles: A Journalist Investigates Evidence for the Supernatural* (Grand Rapids: Zondervan, 2018), 139–41.

5. Tyler Huckabee, "How M.I.A. Found Jesus," *Relevant*, September 21, 2022, https://relevantmagazine.com/magazine/how-m-i-a-found-jesus, italics in original.

6. Henry Price's friend was the eminent philosopher and theologian John Hick. Price was Hick's doctoral advisor. See Harold Netland, *Religious Experience and the Knowledge of God: The Evidential Force of Divine Encounters* (Grand Rapids: Baker Academic, 2022), 38–39.

7. The story is told in John Hick, *John Hick: An Autobiography* (Oxford: Oneworld, 2002), 74–75.

8. Dallas Willard, *Hearing God: Developing a Conversational Relationship with God* (Downers Grove, IL: InterVarsity, 2012), 21.

9. T. M. Luhrmann, *When God Talks Back: Understanding the American Evangelical Relationship with God* (New York: Vintage, 2012), xi, xv.

10. Luhrmann, *When God Talks Back*, xx. The study found that 23 percent of Americans called themselves charismatic, called themselves Pentecostal, or spoke in tongues at least several times a year ("A Ten Country Survey of Pentecostals" [Washington, DC: Pew Research Center, 2006]).

11. Quoted in Naomi Reese, "The Evidential Value of Religious Experience: An Interview with Harold Netland," *Worldview Bulletin*, March 17, 2022, https://worldviewbulletin.substack.com/p/the-evidential-value-of-religious?utm_source=publication-search.

12. Netland, *Religious Experience*, 3.

13. Randy Alcorn, "Can Cancer Be God's Servant? What I Saw in My Wife's Last Four Years," Eternal Perspective Ministries, December 19, 2022, www.epm.org/blog/2022/Dec/19/cancer-servant, italics in original.

14. Douglas Groothuis, *Christian Apologetics: A Comprehensive Case for Biblical Faith* (Downers Grove, IL: IVP Academic, 2011), 388.

Chapter 3: Interview with Douglas Groothuis, PhD

1. See Strobel, *Case for Miracles*, 235–53.

2. Douglas Groothuis, *Walking through Twilight* (Downers Grove, IL: InterVarsity, 2017).

3. Genesis 1:27: "So God created mankind in his own image, in the image of God he created them; male and female he created them."

4. See Francis A. Schaeffer, *Escape from Reason* (Downers Grove, IL: IVP, 2006), 33–36.

5. See Isaiah 6.

6. John 10:10 ESV: "The thief comes only to steal and kill and destroy. I came that they may have life and have it abundantly."

7. See Galatians 5:22–23 ESV.

8. 1 John 4:1: "Dear friends, do not believe every spirit, but test the spirits to see whether they are from God, because many false prophets have gone out into the world."

9. See Rudolf Otto, *The Idea of the Holy*, 2nd ed. (New York: Oxford University Press, 1958).

10. See Richard Swinburne, *The Existence of God*, 2nd ed. (New York: Oxford University Press, 2004), 303.

11. See Swinburne, *Existence of God*, 322–24.

12. Sigmund Freud, *The Future of an Illusion* (Garden City, NY: Anchor, 1961), 49.

13. Hans Küng, *Does God Exist? An Answer for Today*, trans. Edward Quinn (1980; repr., Eugene, OR: Wipf and Stock, 2006), 301.

14. See Matthew 5:22.

15. See Paul Vitz, *Faith of the Fatherless: The Psychology of Atheism* (Dallas, TX: Spence, 1999).

16. Said C. S. Lewis, "When I was an atheist I had to try to persuade myself that most of the human race have always been wrong about the question that mattered to them most" (*Mere Christianity* [1943; repr., New York: Macmillan, 1960], 43).

Chapter 4: Mystical Dreams and Visions

1. I have changed her name to protect her privacy.

2. John 14:6.

3. Cited in Tom Doyle, *Dreams and Visions: Is Jesus Awakening the Muslim World?* (Nashville: Thomas Nelson, 2012), 127.

Chapter 4: Interview with Tom Doyle, MABS

1. Tom Doyle, *Killing Christians: Living the Faith Where It's Not Safe to Believe* (Nashville: W Publishing, 2015), back cover.

2. Doyle changes the names of the people he talks about in the Middle East to protect their identity and keep them from potential danger. The name Rachel at the end of this chapter is also fictitious to avoid conflict with her Muslim relatives.

3. John 14:27.

4. Doyle tells a more complete story about Noor in his *Dreams and Visions*, 3–12.

5. Genesis 18:25.

Chapter 5: The Encouraging Truth about Angels

1. Cited in "Majority of People Worldwide Believe in Angels, 36% Had Angelic Encounters, Study Finds," PR Newswire, March 12, 2024, https://finance.yahoo.com/news/majority-people-worldwide-believe-angels-150000951.html.

2. Genesis 3:24 NET.

3. Craig S. Keener, *The IVP Bible Background Commentary: New Testament* (Downers Grove, IL: InterVarsity, 1993), 779.

4. Ron Rhodes, *The Secret Life of Angels: Who They Are and How They Help Us* (Eugene, OR: Harvest House, 2008), 10.

5. "Angels," *Newsweek*, December 26, 1993, www.newsweek.com/angels-190644.

6. Cited in Megan Brenan, "Belief in Five Spiritual Entities Edges Down to New Lows," Gallup, July 20, 2023, https://news.gallup.com/poll/508886/belief-five-spiritual-entities-edges-down-new-lows.aspx.

7. Billy Graham, *Angels: God's Secret Agents* (1975; repr., Nashville: Thomas Nelson, 1994), 3–4.

Chapter 5: Interview with Douglas E. Potter, DMin: Part 1

1. Graham A. Cole, "10 Things You Should Know about Angels," Crossway, November 10, 2019, www.crossway.org/articles/10-things-you-should-know-about-angels.
2. Peter R. Schemm Jr., "The Agents of God: Angels," in *A Theology for the Church*, rev. ed., ed. Daniel L. Akin (Nashville: B&H, 2014), 249.
3. Rhodes, *Secret Life*, 16, 163.
4. Graham A. Cole, *Against the Darkness: The Doctrine of Angels, Satan, and Demons* (Wheaton, IL: Crossway, 2019), 47, referencing Psalm 121:1–2, italics in original.
5. Arno Clemens Gaebelein, *The Angels of God* (New York: Our Hope, 1924), 101.
6. Timothy Jones, "Rumors of Angels?," *Christianity Today*, April 5, 1993, www.christianitytoday.com/1993/04/rumors-of-angels.
7. Genesis 1:1.
8. See Job 38:6–7.
9. See Colossians 1:16–17.
10. See John 1:1–3.
11. See Job 38:7; Psalm 148:1–3.
12. Mika Ahuvia, "Gender and the Angels in Late Antique Judaism," *Jewish Studies Quarterly* 29, no. 1 (2022): 1–21.
13. See Genesis 19:1–2.
14. See Matthew 28:2–3.
15. Rhodes, *Secret Life*, 55.
16. Millard J. Erickson, *Christian Theology* (Grand Rapids: Baker, 1987), 440.
17. See Jude 9; Daniel 12:1.
18. See Luke 1:19, 26–28.
19. See Isaiah 40:26.
20. Daniel 10:13.
21. Revelation 4:8.
22. See Romans 8:38; Ephesians 1:21; 3:10; 6:12.
23. See Cole, *Against the Darkness*, 68.
24. T. C. Hammond, *In Understanding Be Men: A Handbook of Christian Doctrine*, 5th ed. (London: Inter-Varsity, 1956), 63. Cole adds, "Seraphim and cherubim do seem to stand in a class apart, given their biblical descriptors" (*Against the Darkness*, 68).
25. Hebrew *mal'ak*; Greek *angelos*.
26. Acts 12:21–23.

27. See Peter Kreeft, *Angels (and Demons): What Do We Really Know about Them?* (San Francisco: Ignatius, 1995), 126.

28. Revelation 19:10.

29. Matthew 26:53.

30. Martin Luther, *Small Catechism*, accessed August 31, 2024, https://catechism.cph.org/en/daily-prayers.html.

31. Michael F. Bird, "Do We Have Guardian Angels?," *Word from the Bird*, June 7, 2024, https://michaelfbird.substack.com/p/do-we-have-guardian-angels?.

32. Cole, *Against the Darkness*, 71.

33. Peter Kreeft, *Angels (and Demons): What Do We Really Know about Them?*, 93, italics in original.

34. See Cole, *Against the Darkness*, 71.

35. Herman Bavinck, *God and Creation*, vol. 2 in *Reformed Dogmatics*, ed. John Bolt (Grand Rapids: Baker Academic, 2004), 467.

36. Cole, *Against the Darkness*, 72. Cole adds, "However, the idea of angels having 'a corporate guardianship' responsibility does have biblical warrant, as Psalm 91:11–12 suggests." He notes that John Calvin and Karl Barth make this point.

37. Cole, *Against the Darkness*, 72.

38. Emphasis added.

39. See Walter C. Kaiser Jr. et al., *Hard Sayings of the Bible*, rev. ed. (Downers Grove, IL: IVP Academic, 2010), 526–27.

Chapter 6: The Sobering Reality of Satan and Demons

1. Richard Gallagher, MD, *Demonic Foes: My Twenty-Five Years as a Psychiatrist Investigating Possessions, Diabolic Attacks, and the Paranormal* (San Francisco: HarperOne, 2022), 43–44.

2. Gallagher, *Demonic Foes*, ix.

3. Gallagher, *Demonic Foes*, 9.

4. John Blake, "When Exorcists Need Help, They Call Him," CNN, August 4, 2017, www.cnn.com/2017/08/04/health/exorcism-doctor/index.html.

5. See Gallagher, *Demonic Foes*, 8.

6. Gallagher, *Demonic Foes*, 53.

7. See Steven Novella, "A Psychiatrist Falls for Exorcism," *Neurologica* blog, July 5, 2016, https://theness.com/neurologicablog/a-psychiatrist-falls-for-exorcism.

8. Gallagher, *Demonic Foes*, 11.

9. "'The Patient Is the Exorcist': Interview with M. Scott Peck," Beliefnet, January 2005, www.beliefnet.com/faiths/2005/01/the-patient-is-the-exorcist-interview-with-m-scott-peck.aspx.

10. "'Patient Is the Exorcist.'"

11. M. Scott Peck, *People of the Lie: The Hope for Healing Human Evil* (New York: Touchstone, 1983), 183.

12. M. Scott Peck, *Glimpses of the Devil: A Psychiatrist's Personal Accounts of Possession, Exorcism, and Redemption* (New York: Free Press, 2009). Though he became a professing Christian, Peck retained some theological quirks. See Robert Velarde, "Tale of Two Exorcisms," *Christian Research Journal* 29, no. 2 (2006), updated October 31, 2023, www.equip.org/articles /glimpses-of-the-devil-a-psychiatrists-personal-accounts-of-possession -exorcism-and-redemption.

13. Billy Hallowell, *Playing with Fire: A Modern Investigation into Demons, Exorcism, and Ghosts* (Nashville: Emanate, 2020), xix.

14. Craig S. Keener, "Spirit Possession as a Cross-Cultural Experience," *Bulletin for Biblical Research* 20, no. 2 (2010): 215, 217–18, https://www.pas .rochester.edu/~tim/study/Keener%20Possession%20.pdf.

15. Megan Brenan, "Belief in Five Spiritual Entities Edges Down to New Lows," Gallup, July 20, 2023, https://news.gallup.com/poll/508886/belief -five-spiritual-entities-edges-down-new-lows.aspx.

16. Ron Rhodes, *The Secret Life of Angels: Who They Are and How They Help Us* (Eugene, OR: Harvest House, 2008), 185.

17. Lyrics by Keith Gordon Green and Melody Green, "No One Believes in Me Anymore (Satan's Boast)," © Sony / ATV Music Publishing LLC.

18. See Rhodes, *Secret Life*, 194–96.

19. Charles H. Kraft, *Defeating Dark Angels: Breaking Demonic Oppression in the Believer's Life*, rev. ed. (Minneapolis: Chosen, 2016), 21.

20. T. Desmond Alexander, *From Eden to the New Jerusalem: An Introduction to Biblical Theology* (Grand Rapids: Kregel, 2008), 100.

21. Walter C. Kaiser Jr., *Tough Questions about God and His Actions in the Old Testament* (Grand Rapids: Kregel, 2015), 103.

22. C. S. Lewis, *The Screwtape Letters* (New York: Macmillan, 1966), 17.

Chapter 6: Interview with Douglas E. Potter, DMin: Part 2

1. Quoted in Matthew Paul Turner, "Why American Christians Love Satan," DailyBeast, February 16, 2014, www.thedailybeast.com/why-american -christians-love-satan.

2. W. Scott Poole, *Satan in America: The Devil We Know* (Lanham, MD: Rowman & Littlefield, 2009), x.

3. Bill Ellis, *Raising the Devil: Satanism, New Religions, and the Media* (Lexington, KY: University Press of Kentucky, 2000), 287.

4. *Harper's Magazine*, August 2024 cover, https://harpers.org/archive/2024 /08; Sam Kestenbaum, "The Demon Slayers: The New Age of American

Exorcisms," *Harper's Magazine* (August 2024), 23, https://harpers.org/archive/2024/08/the-demon-slayers-sam-kestenbaum-exorcisms.

5. See Job 1:8–9; 1 Timothy 3:6; 1 Peter 5:8; Revelation 12:12.

6. See Luke 4:3, 9.

7. For example, see Benjamin Shaw, *Trustworthy: Thirteen Arguments for the Reliability of the New Testament* (Downers Grove, IL: IVP Academic, 2024); Peter J. Williams, *Can We Trust the Gospels?* (Wheaton, IL: Crossway, 2018).

8. See Matthew 4:1–11.

9. See Luke 8:29–30.

10. See 1 Timothy 4:1–2.

11. See Matthew 25:41; Revelation 12:7.

12. Isaiah 14:13–14.

13. Matthew 4:10.

14. See Revelation 12:9; cf. Isaiah 14:12.

15. See 1 John 5:18; cf. Ezekiel 28:15.

16. See Ephesians 2:2; cf. Isaiah 14:12.

17. Revelation 12:4 suggests that one-third of the angels followed Lucifer in rebellion.

18. Barth denies that God created Satan or demons, saying that their "origin and nature lie in nothingness" (*Church Dogmatics* III/3, trans. R. J. Ehrlich [Edinburgh: T&T Clark, 1960], 521–22). British Baptist theologian Nigel Wright criticized Barth for playing "mental gymnastics" (*The Satan Syndrome* [Grand Rapids: Zondervan, 1990], 40). For a further discussion of Barth's view, see James K. Beilby and Paul Rhodes Eddy, eds., *Understanding Spiritual Warfare: Four Views* (Grand Rapids: Baker Academic, 2012), 24–26.

19. See Graham A. Cole, *Against the Darkness: The Doctrine of Angels, Satan, and Demons* (Wheaton, IL: Crossway, 2019), 101–2.

20. See Job 1:16, 19.

21. See Norman L. Geisler and Douglas E. Potter, *The Doctrine of Angels and Demons* (Indian Trail, NC: NGIM, 2016), 45–46.

22. See Matthew 12:24.

23. See 2 Corinthians 12:7–9.

24. See Geisler and Potter, *Doctrine of Angels*, 49–52.

25. See John 12:31; 14:30; 16:11.

26. Gary Habermas, "Academic Surprise: Jesus's Healings, Exorcisms Virtually Undisputable," *Christian Post*, March 25, 2024, www.christianpost.com/voices/surprise-jesuss-healings-exorcisms-virtually-undisputable.html.

27. Quoted in Habermas, "Academic Surprise."

28. See Mark 5:5–20.

29. John 10:20.

30. Acts 16:16–18.

31. Cole, *Against the Darkness*, 132.

32. See Cole, *Against the Darkness*, 132.

33. See Ephesians 1:1–3; 1 Thessalonians 3:5; 1 Corinthians 7:5; Revelation 12:10; 2:10; Genesis 3:1–5; James 3:13–16; 1 Timothy 3:6. See Rhodes, *Secret Life*, 204–5.

34. Mark 8:31–33.

35. See Acts 5:3.

36. See Acts 2:28.

37. See Psalm 41:9; John 17:12; Acts 1:16.

38. Beilby and Eddy, *Understanding Spiritual Warfare*.

39. See Cole, *Against the Darkness*, 163–201.

40. See Cole, *Against the Darkness*, 163.

41. Cole, *Against the Darkness*, 163.

42. Cole, *Against the Darkness*, 164.

43. Billy Graham, *Angels: God's Secret Agents* (1975; repr., Nashville: Thomas Nelson, 1994), 104.

44. See Ephesians 6:16.

45. Ephesians 6:11.

46. Clinton E. Arnold, *Ephesians*, Zondervan Exegetical Commentary on the New Testament (Grand Rapids: Zondervan, 2010), 474.

47. See Revelation 20:14.

48. See Lewis, *Screwtape Letters*, 17.

49. Romans 8:37.

50. Romans 8:38–39, emphasis added.

51. 1 John 4:4.

Chapter 7: Deathbed Visions: Glimpses of the Afterlife?

1. Trudy Harris, *Glimpses of Heaven: True Stories of Hope and Peace at the End of Life's Journey*, rev. ed. (Grand Rapids: Revell, 2017), 158–61.

2. Quoted in David Jeremiah, *Angels: Who They Are and How They Help . . . What the Bible Reveals* (Eugene, OR: Multnomah, 2006), 19.

3. Lee Strobel, *Is God Real? Exploring the Ultimate Question of Life* (Grand Rapids: Zondervan, 2023), 161.

4. Harris, *Glimpses of Heaven*, 19.

5. In the foreword to Harris, *Glimpses of Heaven*, 12.

Chapter 7: Interview with J. Steve Miller, PhD

1. H. Sidgwick et al., "Report on the Census of Hallucinations," *Proceedings of the Society for Psychical Research* 10 (1894): 25–422, https://archive

.org/details/proceedingssoci03britgoog/page/n86/mode/1up; see also "Eleanor Sidgwick," *PSI Encyclopedia*, accessed August 31, 2024, https://psi -encyclopedia.spr.ac.uk/articles/eleanor-sidgwick.

2. See Phoebe Zerwick, "Readers Share Stories of Their Loved Ones' Deathbed Visions," *New York Times* magazine, April 10, 2024, www .nytimes.com/2024/04/10/magazine/readers-share-stories-of-their-loved -ones-deathbed-visions.html.

3. See Charles Neider, ed., *The Autobiography of Mark Twain* (New York: Harper and Brothers, 1959), 99–102.

4. See Karlis Osis and Erlendur Haraldsson, *At the Hour of Death: A New Look at Evidence for Life after Death*, 3rd ed. (Norwalk, CT: Hastings, 1997).

5. Bill Guggenheim and Judy Guggenheim, *Hello from Heaven! A New Field of Research—After-Death Communication—Confirms That Life and Love Are Eternal* (New York: Bantam, 1955), 243.

6. See Sir William Barrett, *Death-Bed Visions: The Otherworldly Experiences of the Dying* (1926; repr., Philadelphia: Greenpoint, 2023), 10–15.

7. Barrett, *Death-Bed Visions*, 1.

8. Section 804 (b)(2) of the *Federal Rules of Evidence*, Cornell Law School, accessed August 31, 2024, www.law.cornell.edu/rules/fre/rule_804.

9. Komp wrote several books about her experiences with dying children, including her memoir, *A Window to Heaven: When Children See Life in Death* (Grand Rapids: Zondervan, 1992). This anecdote is told on page 28.

10. See Angela M. Ethier, "Exploring Parents' Memories of Their Child's Death Related Sensory Experiences as a Dimension of Grieving," *Texas Medical Center Dissertations*, January 2007, https://digitalcommons.library .tmc.edu/dissertations/AAI3281710.

11. See Penny Sartori, *The Near-Death Experiences of Hospitalized Intensive Care Patients: A Five-Year Clinical Study* (Lampeter, Wales: Mellen, 2008).

12. See Romans 2:4.

13. Raymond Moody, *Glimpses of Eternity: Sharing a Loved One's Passage from This Life to the Next* (New York: Guideposts, 2010), 14.

14. Barrett, *Death-Bed Visions*, 108.

15. See Jenny Streit-Horn, "A Systematic Review of Research on After-Death Communication," diss., University of North Texas, August 2011, www.sgha .net/library/dissertation.pdf.

16. Guggenheim, *Hello from Heaven!*, 330–31.

17. See Guggenheim, *Hello from Heaven!*, 328–29.

18. See Guggenheim, *Hello from Heaven!*, 276.

19. See Guggenheim, *Hello from Heaven!*, 89–90.

20. Matthew 16:26.

Chapter 8: Extraordinary Near-Death Experiences

1. The story is told in John Burke, *What's after Life? Evidence from the* New York Times *Bestselling Book* Imagine Heaven (Grand Rapids: Baker, 2019), 5–7; see also "Mary NDE," Near-Death Experience Research Foundation, accessed August 31, 2024, www.nderf.org/_borders/mary's_NDE.htm. Note: Mary is a pseudonym.

2. See Raymond Moody, *Life after Life*, rev. ed. (New York: HarperOne, 2015).

3. From the foreword in Janice Miner Holden, Bruce Greyson, and Debbie James, eds., *The Handbook of Near-Death Experiences: Thirty Years of Investigation* (Santa Barbara, CA: Praeger, 2009), vii, italics in original; Philippians 4:7: "And the peace of God, which transcends all understanding, will guard your hearts and your minds in Christ Jesus."

4. Holden, Greyson, and James, *Handbook of Near Death*, vii.

5. Cited in Sarah Knapton, "Near Death Experiences Are Felt by One in 10 People, Study Finds," *The Telegraph*, June 28, 2019, www.telegraph.co.uk /science/2019/06/28/one-10-people-has-had-near-death-experience-study -finds.

6. See Kyle Swenson, "'The Boy Who Came Back from Heaven' Now Wants His Day in Court," *Washington Post*, April 13, 2018, www.washingtonpost .com/news/morning-mix/wp/2018/04/11/the-boy-who-came-back-from -heaven-now-wants-his-day-in-court.

Chapter 8: Interview with John Burke

1. See R. C. Sproul, *Now, That's a Good Question* (Wheaton: Tyndale, 1996), 300.

2. See J. P. Moreland and Gary R. Habermas, *Immortality: The Other Side of Death* (Nashville: Thomas Nelson, 1992).

3. John Burke, *Imagine Heaven: Near-Death Experiences, God's Promises, and the Exhilarating Future That Awaits You* (Grand Rapids: Baker, 2015), 51.

4. See Bonnie Malkin, "Girl Survives Sting by World's Deadliest Jellyfish," *The Telegraph*, April 26, 2010, www.telegraph.co.uk/news/7638189/Girl -survives-sting-by-worlds-deadliest-jellyfish.html.

5. For a full report on Ian McCormack's experience, see Burke, *Imagine Heaven*, 139–41.

6. See Jeffrey Long, *Evidence of the Afterlife: The Science of Near-Death Experiences* (San Francisco: HarperOne, 2010), 169.

7. See Burke, *Imagine Heaven*, 239.

8. See J. Steve Miller, *Near-Death Experiences as Evidence for the Existence of God and Heaven: A Brief Introduction in Plain Language* (Acworth, GA: Wisdom Creek, 2012), 83–85.

9. Matthew 10:26.

10. Matthew 12:37.

11. Hebrews 9:27, emphasis added.

12. See Revelation 11:15–18.

13. Cited in Holden, Greyson, and James, *Handbook of Near-Death*, 70.

14. Cited in "One in 10 Had NDEs according to Study," IANDS, June 28, 2019, https://iands.org/1361-european-study-says-one-in-10-have-ndes.html.

15. Storm's story is told in Burke, *Imagine Heaven*, 215–21.

16. Kevin and Alex Malarkey, *The Boy Who Came Back from Heaven: A Remarkable Account of Miracles, Angels, and Life beyond This World* (Carol Stream, IL: Tyndale, 2010).

17. "'The Boy Who Came Back from Heaven' Recants Story, Rebukes Christian Retailers," *Pulpit & Pen*, January 13, 2015, http://pulpitandpen .org/2015/01/13/the-boy-who-came-back-from-heaven-recants-story-rebukes -christian-retailers.

18. Burke, *Imagine Heaven*, 326.

19. See Penny Sartori, *The Near-Death Experiences of Hospitalized Intensive Care Patients: A Five Year Clinical Study* (Lewiston, NY: Mellen, 2008), 212–15.

20. Cited in Long, *Evidence of the Afterlife*, 72–73.

21. Cited in Janice Miner Holden, "Veridical Perception in Near-Death Experiences," in Holden, Greyson, and James, *Handbook of Near-Death*, 185–211.

22. Quoted in Raymond Moody, *The Light Beyond: Explorations into the Afterlife* (New York: Bantam, 1988), 108.

23. Kenneth Ring and Sharon Cooper, *Mindsight: Near-Death and Out-of-Body Experiences in the Blind* (Palo Alto, CA: William James Center for Consciousness Studies, 1999), 136.

24. For these and other cases, see Moreland and Habermas, *Immortality*, 74–80.

25. See Burke, *Imagine Heaven*, 47–48.

26. Long, *Evidence of the Afterlife*, 44.

27. Burke, *Imagine Heaven*, 102–3.

Chapter 9: What Can We Know about Heaven?

1. Psalm 19:1.

2. Cited in James Bishop, "An Atheist Astrophysicist's Conversion to Christian Theism," Bishop's Encyclopedia of Religion, Society and Philosophy, May 23, 2015, https://jamesbishopblog.com/2015/05/23/former-atheist -astrophysicist-sarah-salviander-explains-her-journey-to-christianity; see also Gerald L. Schroeder, *The Science of God: The Convergence of Scientific and Biblical Wisdom* (New York: Free Press, 2009).

3. Quoted in Walter Isaacson, "Einstein & Faith," *Time*, April 5, 2007, http://ymlibrary.com/download/Topics/God/Faith-Hope-Trust/Faith-Hope-Trust-Stories-Inspiration/Einstein%20and%20Faith.pdf.

4. Quotes taken from personal email correspondence dated September 18, 2020; see also Sarah's testimony: "My Testimony," SixDay Science, May 11, 2015, https://sixdayscience.com/2015/05/11/my-testimony.

5. 1 Corinthians 2:9 NLT.

6. Martin Luther, *D. Martin Luthers Werke: Kritische Gesamtausgabe*, 3:276.26–27 (no. 3339); quoted in J. Todd Billings, *The End of the Christian Life: How Embracing Our Mortality Frees Us to Truly Live* (Grand Rapids: Brazos, 2020), 182.

7. Billings, *End of the Christian Life*, 182, italics in original.

8. John Eldredge, *The Journey of Desire: Searching for the Life You've Always Dreamed Of*, rev. ed. (Nashville: Nelson, 2016), 115, italics in original.

Chapter 9: Interview with Scot McKnight, PhD

1. John 6:40.

2. 2 Peter 1:11.

3. 1 John 2:25.

4. 2 Corinthians 5:1.

5. N. T. Wright, *Simply Good News: Why the Gospel Is News and What Makes It Good* (San Francisco: HarperOne, 2015), 99, italics in original.

6. See Bart D. Ehrman, *Heaven and Hell: A History of the Afterlife* (New York: Simon & Schuster, 2020), xxi.

7. See Isaiah 25:6–10; 26:19; Hosea 6:1–2; Ezekiel 37; Daniel 12:2–3. Scot McKnight said to me, "In God's providence and in the unfolding of revelation and redemption, we only learn about a new life beyond death in the final sections of the Old Testament—the Prophets."

8. See Rodney Stark, *What Americans Really Believe: New Findings from the Baylor Study of Religion* (Waco, TX: Baylor University Press, 2008), 69–74.

9. Billings, *End of the Christian Life*, 151; see Maggie Fox, "Fewer Americans Believe in God—Yet They Still Believe in Afterlife," *Today*, March 21, 2016, www.nbcnews.com/better/wellness/Fewer-americans-believe-god-yet-they-still-believe-afterlife-n542966.

10. See Fox, "Fewer Americans Believe in God."

11. Ecclesiastes 3:11.

12. C. S. Lewis, *The Weight of Glory* (1949; repr., San Francisco: HarperSanFrancisco, 2001), 29, 32.

13. C. S. Lewis, *Mere Christianity* (1943; repr., New York: Macmillan, 1960), 120.

14. Jerry Walls, *Heaven: The Logic of Eternal Joy* (New York: Oxford University Press, 2002), 31.

15. Luke 23:43.

16. See Acts 7:55.

17. John 11:11.

18. Revelation 21:1–2.

19. Revelation 21:22.

20. See John 14:2–3.

21. 1 Corinthians 15:28.

22. See 1 Corinthians 15:20–28.

23. 1 Corinthians 15:44.

24. Arthur O. Roberts, *Exploring Heaven: What Great Christian Thinkers Tell Us about Our Afterlife with God* (San Francisco: HarperSanFrancisco, 2003), 114.

25. For a discussion of this issue, see C. S. Lewis, *The Great Divorce* (San Francisco: HarperOne, revised edition, 2015).

26. See John 14:2–3.

27. See Nigel Dixon, *Villages without Walls: An Exploration of the Necessity of Building Christian Community in a Post-Christian World* (Palmerston North, NZ: Vox Humana, 2010), 54–62.

28. See Revelation 21–22.

29. Hans Boersma, *Seeing God: The Beatific Vision in Christian Tradition* (Grand Rapids: Eerdmans, 2018), 11.

30. Quoted in Boersma, *Seeing God*, xiii.

31. Psalm 27:4.

32. 1 Corinthians 13:12.

33. Matthew 5:8.

34. Exodus 33:20.

35. Revelation 22:4.

36. John 14:9.

37. Matthew 17:2.

38. Kieran Kavanaugh, ed., *John of the Cross: Selected Writings* (New York: Paulist, 1987), 285.

39. Jonathan Edwards, "Sermon on Revelation 21:18," *WJE Online* 42, Jonathan Edwards Center, http://is.gd/WSuP77.

40. Quoted in Ed Romine, "Spurgeon on the Hope of Heaven," Spurgeon Center for Biblical Preaching at Midwestern Seminary, May 3, 2018, www.spurgeon.org/resource-library/blog-entries/charles-spurgeon-on-heavens-hope.

41. Michael Reeves, *Delighting in the Trinity: An Introduction to the Christian Faith* (Downers Grove, IL: IVP Academic, 2012), 75.

42. John Eldredge, *All Things New: Heaven, Earth, and the Restoration of Everything You Love* (Nashville: Nelson, 2017), 25.

43. N. T. Wright, *Surprised by Hope: Rethinking Heaven, the Resurrection, and the Mission of the Church* (San Francisco: HarperOne, 2008), 93.

Chapter 10: The Logic of Damnation

1. David Bentley Hart, *That All Shall Be Saved: Heaven, Hell, and Universal Salvation* (New Haven, CT: Yale University Press, 2019), 208.
2. Quoted in Robert Short, *Short Meditations on the Bible and Peanuts* (Louisville, KY: Westminster John Knox, 1990), 127.
3. Steve Gregg, *Why Hell? Three Christian Views Critically Examined* (Grand Rapids: Zondervan, 2024), 17.
4. Cited in Mark Strauss, "The Campaign to Eliminate Hell," *National Geographic*, May 13, 2016, www.nationalgeographic.com/culture/article/160513-theology-hell-history-christianity.
5. See Tracy Munsil, "AWVI 2020 Survey: 1 in 3 US Adults Embrace Salvation through Jesus; More Believe It Can Be 'Earned,'" August 4, 2020, www.arizonachristian.edu/2020/08/04/1-in-3-us-adults-embrace-salvation-through-jesus-more-believe-it-can-be-earned.
6. Matthew 7:13.
7. For example, "I will show you whom you should fear: Fear the one who, after he kills, has authority to throw you into hell [*geenna*]. Yes, I tell you, fear this one!" (Luke 12:5 MOUNCE).
8. Mark Jones, *Living for God* (Wheaton, IL: Crossway, 2020), 223.
9. John Gerstner, *Repent or Perish* (Morgan, PA: Soli Deo Gloria, 1990), 31.
10. Preston Sprinkle, gen. ed., *Four Views on Hell* (Grand Rapids: Zondervan, 2016), 12.
11. Quoted in Gerry Beauchemin, *Hope beyond Hell* (Olmito, TX: Malista, 2007), 4.
12. Clark Pinnock, "The Destruction of the Finally Impenitent," *Criswell Theological Review* 4, no. 2 (Spring 1990): 253, https://davidlarkin.files.wordpress.com/2012/05/pinnock-the-destruction-of-the-finally-impenitent-original-paper.pdf.
13. Francis Chan and Preston Sprinkle, *Erasing Hell: What God Said about Eternity, and the Things We've Made Up* (Colorado Springs: Cook, 2011), 14–15.

Chapter 10: Interview with Paul Copan, PhD

1. See Paul Copan, *Is God a Moral Monster? Making Sense of the Old Testament God* (Grand Rapids: Baker, 2011); Paul Copan and Matthew Flannagan, *Did God Really Command Genocide? Coming to Terms with the Justice of God* (Grand Rapids: Baker, 2014).
2. See Paul Copan, *Loving Wisdom: A Guide to Philosophy and Christian Faith*, 2nd ed. (Grand Rapids: Eerdmans, 2020), 246–57.
3. C. S. Lewis, *The Problem of Pain* (1940; repr., New York: Macmillan, 1962), 118.

4. See Genesis 18:25.

5. See Robert Bellah et al., *Habits of the Heart: Individualism and Commitment in American Life* (Berkeley: University of California Press, 2007); Allan Bloom, *The Closing of the American Mind*, rev. ed. (New York: Simon & Schuster, 2012).

6. See Greg Lukianoff and Jonathan Haidt, *The Coddling of the American Mind: How Good Intentions and Bad Ideas Are Setting Up a Generation for Failure* (New York: Penguin, 2018).

7. Jesus in Luke 13:3: "Unless you repent, you too will all perish."

8. Other well-known figures and respected scholars who interpret the flames nonliterally include Billy Graham, C. S. Lewis, D. A. Carson, J. I. Packer, Sinclair Ferguson, Charles Hodge, Carl Henry, F. F. Bruce, Roger Nicole, Leon Morris, Robert Peterson, and J. P. Moreland. "These scholars note that fire imagery is used in many other places in the Bible—not just in passages relating to hell—in obviously nonliteral ways," said Francis Chan and Preston Sprinkle (*Erasing Hell* [Colorado Springs: Cook, 2011], 154).

9. See 2 Thessalonians 1:9. Writes Copan, "God, of course, will be aware of those separated from him; they will still be 'tormented . . . in the presence of the holy angels and in the presence of the Lamb' (Revelation 14:10). The point here is that Christ/God is obviously aware of those who experience this separation ('in the presence of the Lamb'). Nevertheless, the emphasis in 2 Thessalonians 1:9 is that unbelievers are cut off from his blessing as the source of hope and joy ('away from the presence of the Lord')" (*Loving Wisdom: A Guide to Philosophy and Christian Faith*, 247–48).

10. See Revelation 14:13.

11. See Acts 7:54.

12. Dallas Willard, *The Allure of Gentleness: Defending the Faith in the Manner of Jesus* (San Francisco: HarperOne, 2016), 67.

13. Michael Card, "Who Can Abide?," from the album *The Word: Recapturing the Imagination*, https://genius.com/Michael-card-who-can-abide-lyrics.

14. Willard, *Allure of Gentleness*, 67, 69.

15. Rob Bell, *Love Wins: A Book about Heaven, Hell, and the Fate of Every Person Who Ever Lived* (San Francisco: HarperOne, 2011), 102; cf. 175.

16. Thomas Aquinas, *Effects of Sin, Stain, and Guilt*, vol. 27 of *Summa Theologiae* (Cambridge: Cambridge University Press, 2006), 25.

17. D. A. Carson, *How Long, O Lord? Reflections on Suffering and Evil*, 2nd ed. (Grand Rapids: Baker Academic, 2006), 91.

18. See Lee Strobel, *The Case for Faith* (Grand Rapids: Zondervan, 2000), 169–194.

19. Craig Blomberg, *Interpreting the Parables*, 2nd ed. (Downers Grove, IL: IVP Academic, 2012), 236.

20. Augustine, *The City of God*, trans. Marcus Dods (Moscow, ID: Roman Roads, 2015), 743.
21. See Matthew 12:31. Theologians generally consider blasphemy against the Holy Spirit to be a lifetime of turning a deaf ear to God's initiating grace.
22. See John 19:11.
23. Genesis 18:25.
24. See Revelation 16:9–11, 21.
25. N. T. Wright, *Following Jesus* (Grand Rapids: Eerdmans, 1995), 100.
26. See Lewis, *Problem of Pain*, 125.
27. See Romans 6:23.
28. Quoted in Strauss, "Campaign to Eliminate Hell."
29. Christopher M. Date, Gregory G. Stump, and Joshua W. Anderson, eds., *Rethinking Hell: Readings in Evangelical Conditionalism* (Eugene, OR: Wipf & Stock, 2014), xvi.
30. For example, see Matthew 3:12; 7:19; John 15:6.
31. See Hebrews 10:26–29.
32. See Genesis 19.
33. See Jude 7.
34. Bart D. Ehrman, *Heaven and Hell: A History of the Afterlife* (New York: Simon & Schuster, 2020), 155.
35. See *Jewish Wars* 2.8.14; *Antiquities* 18.1.3.
36. See Matthew 8:12; 13:42, 50; 22:13; 24:51; 25:30.
37. Robert A. Morey, *Death and the Afterlife* (Minneapolis: Bethany House, 1984), 117–18.
38. G. K. Beale, *The Book of Revelation*, New International Greek Testament Commentary (Grand Rapids: Eerdmans, 1999), 762–63.
39. See Matthew 7:13.
40. See Ephesians 2:1.
41. Quoted in "#103: Polycarp's Martyrdom," Christian History Institute, accessed August 31, 2024, https://christianhistoryinstitute.org/study/module/polycarp.
42. Hart, *That All Shall Be Saved*, 208.
43. See Michael McClymond, "David Bentley Hart's Lonely, Last Stand for Christian Universalism," Gospel Coalition, October 2, 2019, www.thegospelcoalition.org/reviews/shall-saved-universal-christian-universalism-david-bentley-hart. McClymond responds in this article to the three main arguments for universalism that Hart posits in his book.
44. Bell, *Love Wins*, 107. Francis Chan and Preston Sprinkle write, "Bell never actually comes out and says this is what he believes . . . But he presents this position in such favorable terms that it would be hard to say that he is not advocating it" (*Erasing Hell*, 40).

45. Hart, *That All Shall Be Saved*, 84.

46. See 1 John 2:2, John 1:12.

47. 1 Timothy 4:10: "This is why we labor and strive, because we have put our hope in the living God, who is the Savior of all people, and especially of those who believe."

48. Colossians 1:22–23, emphasis added.

49. See 2 Thessalonians 1:9.

50. See Galatians 1:8–9.

51. See Mark 1:5.

52. See Luke 19:10.

53. See John 17:12.

54. John 19:30.

55. See Isaiah 53:11.

56. William Barclay, *William Barclay: A Spiritual Autobiography* (Grand Rapids: Eerdmans, 1977), 67.

57. See Zephaniah 2:11.

58. See Psalm 66:3.

59. Michael McClymond, *The Devil's Redemption* (Grand Rapids: Baker Academic, 2018).

60. Quoted in Paul Copan, "How Universalism, 'The Opiate of the Theologians,' Went Mainstream," *Christianity Today*, March 11, 2019, www.christianitytoday.com/ct/2019/march-web-only/michael-mcclymond-devils-redemption-universalism.html.

61. See Romans 6:23.

62. Augustine, *City of God*, 749.

Chapter 11: Life after Death: Evidence for the Resurrection

1. See Richard Whitehead, "Forensic Statement Analysis: Deception Detection," Law Enforcement Learning, accessed August 31, 2024, www.lawenforcementlearning.com/course/forensic-statement-analysis.

Chapter 11: Interview with J. Warner Wallace, MTS

1. This is a paraphrase of the C. S. Lewis quote, "One must keep pointing out that Christianity is a statement which, if false, is of *no* importance, and, if true, of infinite importance" (*God in the Dock: Essays on Theology and Ethics* [1970; repr., Grand Rapids: Eerdmans, 2014], 102, italics in original).

2. See Lee Strobel, *The Case for Miracles* (Grand Rapids: Zondervan, 2018), 57–61.

3. See Luke 1:1–3.

4. See 1 Peter 5:1; 2 Peter 1:16–17.

5. See 1 John 1:1.

6. Acts 4:20.

7. Acts 10:39.

8. See 1 Corinthians 15.

9. Simon Greenleaf, *The Testimony of the Evangelists: The Gospels Examined by the Rules of Evidence* (Grand Rapids: Baker, 1984), 34.

10. Michael R. Licona, *Why Are There Differences in the Gospels? What We Can Learn from Ancient Biography* (New York: Oxford University Press, 2017).

11. See John 20:2. "The other disciple, the one Jesus loved" is the way the apostle John refers to himself.

12. Luke 24:24: "Then some of our companions went to the tomb and found it just as the women had said, but they did not see Jesus."

13. Licona quotes are taken from Jonathan Petersen, "Why Are There Differences in the Gospels? An Interview with Michael R. Licona," Bible Gateway, June 27, 2017, www.biblegateway.com/blog/2017/06/why-are-there -differences-in-the-gospels-an-interview-with-michael-r-licona (emphasis added).

14. See J. J. Blunt, *Undesigned Coincidences in the Writings Both of the Old and New Testament: An Argument of Their Veracity* (1847; repr., London: Forgotten Books, 2017); Lydia McGrew, *Hidden in Plain View: Undesigned Coincidences in the Gospels and Acts* (Chillicothe, OH: DeWard, 2017).

15. See Matthew 4:18–22.

16. See Luke 5:1–11.

17. See Matthew 26:67–68.

18. See 1 Corinthians 15:17.

19. Surah 4:157–158 in the Qur'an: "That they said (in boast) 'We killed Christ Jesus, the son of Mary, the Messenger of Allah'—but they killed him not, nor crucified him, but so it was made to appear to them, and those who differ therein are full of doubts, with no (certain) knowledge, but only conjecture to follow, for of a surety they killed him not—Nay, Allah raised him up unto Himself; and Allah is exalted in Power, Wise . . ."

20. Josephus, Tacitus, Mara bar Serapion, Lucian, and the Talmud.

21. See Gary R. Habermas and Michael R. Licona, *The Case for the Resurrection of Jesus* (Grand Rapids: Kregel, 2004).

22. Bart Ehrman, *How Jesus Became God: The Exaltation of a Jewish Preacher from Galilee* (San Francisco: HarperOne, 2014), 7, 157, italics in original.

23. Craig A. Evans, "Getting the Burial Traditions and Evidences Right," in *How God Became Jesus: The Real Origins of Belief in Jesus' Divine Nature*, ed. Michael F. Bird et al. (Grand Rapids: Zondervan, 2014), 73.

24. Evans, "Getting the Burial Traditions," 76.

25. Evans, "Getting the Burial Traditions," 89.

26. Evans, "Getting the Burial Traditions," 93.

27. See 1 Corinthians 15:4. Wallace also noted that a 2007 documentary, *The Lost Tomb of Jesus,* claimed to have found the family tomb of Jesus, including an ossuary labeled in Aramaic "Jesus, Son of Joseph." Subsequently, scholars have undermined the film's credibility. However, said Wallace, embrace of the movie by skeptics at the time shows their inconsistency. "Often skeptics deny the fact Jesus would be buried in a grave—until, of course, it serves their purpose to claim there is a grave of Jesus. You can't have it both ways."

28. Jodi Magness, "Jesus' Tomb: What Did It Look Like?," in *Where Christianity Was Born,* ed. Hershel Shanks (Washington, DC: Biblical Archaeology Society, 2006), 224.

29. Acts, Clement of Rome, Polycarp, Ignatius, Dionysius of Corinth (quoted by Eusebius), Tertullian, and Origen.

30. See Sean McDowell, *The Fate of the Apostles: Examining the Martyrdom Accounts of the Closest Followers of Jesus* (New York: Routledge, 2016).

31. 2 Corinthians 5:17.

Chapter 12: Ghost Stories, Psychics, and the Paranormal

1. "Real Ghost Stories," Your Ghost Stories, accessed August 31, 2024, www.yourghoststories.com.

2. See Benjamin C. F. Shaw, *Trustworthy: Thirteen Arguments for the Reliability of the New Testament* (Downers Grove, IL: IVP Academic, 2024).

3. Quoted in "Insider Report: Jimmy Carter's Psychic Connection," NewsMax, January 1, 2006, www.newsmax.com/pre-2008/insider-reportjimmy-carter-s/2006/01/01/id/683874. The original interview with Carter was published in *GQ* magazine and excerpted in *The Weekly Standard.*

4. Cited in David W. Moore, "Three in Four Americans Believe in Paranormal," Gallup, June 16, 2005, https://news.gallup.com/poll/16915/Three-in-Four-Americans-Believe-Paranormal.aspx.

5. Cited in Michael Lipka, "18 Percent of Americans Say They've Seen a Ghost," Pew Research, October 30, 2015, www.pewresearch.org/short-reads/2015/10/30/18-of-americans-say-they've-seen-a-ghost.

6. Cited in Claire Gecewicz, "'New Age' Beliefs Common among Both Religious and Nonreligious Americans," Pew Research, October 1, 2018, www.pewresearch.org/short-reads/2018/10/01/new-age-beliefs-common-among-both-religious-and-nonreligious-americans.

Chapter 12: Interview with Ron Rhodes, ThD

1. 2 Corinthians 4:4.

2. See Kathryn Hulick, "The Science of Ghosts," Science News Explores, October 31, 2019, www.snexplores.org/article/science-ghosts.

3. See Philippians 1:21–23.

4. See 2 Corinthians 11:14.

5. See 1 Samuel 28:3–24.

6. See Matthew 17:1–11; Mark 9:2–12; Luke 9:28–34.

7. For a discussion of why the medium of Endor was not the cause of Samuel's spirit to appear, see Ron Rhodes, *The Truth Behind Ghosts, Mediums and Psychic Phenomena* (Eugene, OR: Harvest House, 2006), 131–33. His view is that God "sovereignly and miraculously allowed Samuel's spirit to appear in order to rebuke Saul for his sin. Samuel's spirit did not appear as a result of the medium's powers (for indeed, no human has the power to summon dead humans—Luke 16:24–27; Hebrews 9:27), but only because God sovereignly brought it about. This view is supported by the fact that Samuel actually returned from the dead (1 Samuel 28:14), and this caused the medium to shriek with fear (see verse 12). The medium's cry of astonishment indicates that this appearance of Samuel was not the result of her usual tricks" (p. 132).

8. See "Psychic Medium Salary in California," Zip Recruiter, July 12, 2024, www.ziprecruiter.com/Salaries/Psychic-Salary--in-California#.

9. See Michael Shermer, "Talking Twaddle with the Dead," *Skeptic*, February 3, 2011, www.skeptic.com/reading_room/talking-twaddle-with -the-dead.

10. See also Acts 19:19.

11. Leviticus 19:31; 20:6.

12. See Acts 16:16–19.

13. Proverbs 18:17 ESV.

14. John 14:6.

15. See 1 Timothy 4:1.

16. See Matthew 24:4–8, 23–26.

17. See 2 Corinthians 11:3.

18. See 2 Corinthians 2:11.

19. John 8:12.

Conclusion

1. See 2 Kings 6:8–22. The king of Syria was also known as the king of Aram.

2. See Revelation 20:1–3, 10.

3. 2 Corinthians 4:18.

4. See "Abduction," *Stanford Encyclopedia of Philosophy*, March 9, 2011, substantially revised May 18, 2021, https://plato.stanford.edu/entries /abduction.

5. See Ephesians 6:10–18.

6. James 4:7.

7. Melvin Morse, writing in Raymond Moody, *The Light Beyond* (New York: Bantam, 1988), 108.

8. See Ed Romine, "Spurgeon on the Hope of Heaven," The Spurgeon Center, March 3, 2018, www.spurgeon.org/resource-library/blog-entries /charles-spurgeon-on-heavens-hope.

9. 1 John 4:1.

10. Quoted in Terry Mattingly, "'The Exorcist' at 50: If Demons Are Real, How About Angels? What About an Eternal Soul?," Get Religion, November 26, 2023, www.getreligion.org/getreligion/2023/11/21/the-exorcist-at-50-if -demons-are-real-how-about-angels-what-about-an-eternal-soul.